St. Helens Pals

[St. Helens Library and Archives]

St. Helens Pals

11th (Service) Battalion South Lancashire Regiment
(St. Helens Pioneers)

David Risley
&
Richard Waring

St. Helens Townships Family History Society

First published in the United Kingdom in 2014 by

St. Helens Townships Family History Society

ISBN 978-0-9929745-0-3

Printed and bound by Bell & Bain Ltd, Glasgow

Contents

Foreword

Pioneer battalions of the Great War have been regularly confused with the later Labour Corps, and also with the Pioneer Corps of the Second World War. Although this is an understandable misconception, the three organizations were very disparate. Created to assist the Royal Engineers in coping with the additional work required by the trench stalemate at the end of 1914, pioneer battalions were either specially raised or were existing infantry battalions converted to the role. The units selected were originally comprised of a mixture of skilled men and those who were used to wielding a pick and shovel in civilian life. Although few of the battalions later produced unit histories, and divisional accounts often make only cursory mention of their work, the role of pioneer units in providing skilled labour for the enormous range of engineering work required by the unexpected conditions was vital in easing the burden of both RE and infantry.

The 11th (Service) Battalion South Lancashire Regiment, the St. Helens Pioneers, was one of the forty-six New Army battalions raised as, or converted to, pioneers. The battalion began its life as a conventional infantry unit before becoming a pioneer unit in early 1915. It then joined 30th Division, a formation which, on 1 July 1916, was to become one of that fateful day's most successful divisions. In May 1918, the battalion was reduced to cadre but was later reconstituted and was to serve with a further two divisions before the war ended. Although by that time few of the original September 1914 members remained with the battalion, during its three years overseas the unit had retained links with the town of its origin. In the same way as the borough's Territorial Force battalion, the cadre, together with the unit's winner of the Victoria Cross, was awarded a civic welcome. Like all other war-raised formations, the battalion was then disbanded and thus removed from the Active Service List. The survivors, as well as the widows and children of the fallen, were left with their memories and tried as best as they could to get on with their lives in a town which in the post-war years experienced unemployment and poverty. It was hardly the 'Land fit for heroes' they had been promised.

This volume of the battalion's history offers a significant contribution to the historiography of the Great War and, more importantly, to the development of St. Helens as a town and as a community. It has clearly been a successful labour of love for the Family History Society and its members are to be congratulated for having produced a thoroughly researched, very readable, well illustrated and easily accessible source. Set within the context of how the conflict affected the town as a whole, the story of the pioneers' activities in France and Belgium, as well as the genealogically important nominal roles of officers and men, will be welcomed by those of the present generation seeking to learn more of their grandparents and great-grandparents' involvement in the Great War.

Bill Mitchinson MA PhD FRHistS
King's College, London at the Joint Services Command and Staff College
May 2014

Acknowledgements

The authors gratefully acknowledge the assistance of the following in gathering research material, granting permission to use copyright material, and providing invaluable assistance in various ways:

Mark Abbott, Heather Appleton, Bryan Ball, Jonathan Ball, Merrick Baker Bates, Michael Blackburn, Chris Bluck, Sue Brooks, Winifred Castle, Graeme Clarke, Sheenagh Collins, John Cowell, Nick Cross, Jane Davies, Susan Davies, Simon Eley, Alfred Fairhurst, Carol Farrar, Sue Flynn, Alfred Gasser, Paul Hartley, Kevin Helsby, Derek Hewitt, Tony Hignett, Eileen Hill, Richard Houghton, Ann-Veronica Howitt, Imperial War Museum, Bryan Jones, Harry Jones, Jeff Keenan, Dave Kelly, Lancashire Infantry Museum, Dennis Martland, Norette Moore, Ste Murgatroyd, Stephen Nulty, David Ian Pendlebury, Guy Percival, Tony Redcliffe, Judith Risley, Susan Risley, David N. Robinson, Pat Sawyer, Mike Scott, Sue Shields, Steve Spencer, Stewart Squires, St. Helens Local History & Archives Library, Leslie Staniland, Maureen Travers, Ronald Tucker, University of Manchester Faculty of Humanities, Stephen Wainwright, Norma Waring, Janice Webb, Kate Wills, Elaine Wilde, Daphne Wilson, Val Wilson, Brenda Winstanley.

In particular the authors want to thank Peter Harvey for managing the project, Major (retd) Douglas Farrington for his help with regimental archives, Charles Fair for his great help throughout, Jill Woodhouse for giving permission to use photographs from the C. C. Champion collection, Peter and Maggi Paylor for editing this book, and the Heritage Lottery Fund without which this book would not have been possible. It goes without saying that we are delighted and grateful that Bill Mitchinson, author of the only comprehensive overview of pioneer battalions in the Great War, very kindly took the time to read this and write the foreword.

Finally, I must acknowledge my wife Judith's patience and support over the last couple of years, during which time 'the Pals' came to dominate our lives.

David Risley
6 May 2014

Abbreviations

A.S.C.	Army Service Corps	Lt.	Lieutenant
Attd.	Attached	Lt.-Col.	Lieutenant-Colonel
A/	Acting	Maj.	Major
Bde.	Brigade	Man R	Manchester Regiment
B.E.F.	British Expeditionary Force	M.C.	Military Cross
Bn.	Battalion	M.G.C.	Machine Gun Corps
C.R.E.	Corps of Royal Engineers	M.M.	Military Medal
Capt.	Captain	M.M.B.	Medium Mortar Battery
C.O.	Commanding Officer	N.C.O.	Non-Commissioned
Col.	Colonel		Officer
Coy.	Company	Off(s)	Officer(s)
Cpl.	Corporal	ORs	Other Ranks
C.S.M.	Company Sergeant Major	Pl.	Platoon
d.	Died	Pte.	Private
d.o.w.	Died of wounds	P.W.V.	Prince of Wales's
dem.	Demobilized		Volunteers
des.	Deserted	Q.M.	Quartermaster
dis.	Discharged	R.A.M.C.	Royal Army Medical Corps
D/	Depot	R.E.	Royal Engineers
D.C.M.	Distinguished Conduct	Regt.	Regiment
	Medal	rel.	Relinquished Commission
D.L.I.	Durham Light Infantry	R.F.A.	Royal Field Artillery
D.S.O.	Distinguished Service	Rfn.	Rifleman
	Order	R.S.F.	Royal Scots Fusiliers
F.A.	Field Ambulance	R.S.M.	Regimental Sergeant Major
G/	Garrison Battalion	Sgt.	Sergeant
Glouc R	Gloucester Regiment	S.L.R.	South Lancashire Regiment
G.O.C.	General Officer	S.W.B.	South Wales Borderers
	Commanding	T.C.	Tank Corps
How.	Howitzer	T.F.	Territorial Force
H.Q.	Headquarters	T.M.B.	Trench Mortar Battery
k.i.a.	Killed in action	V.A.D.	Voluntary Aid Detachment
King's	King's (Liverpool)	Wilts.	Wiltshire Regiment
	Regiment	W.O.	Warrant Officer
L/Cpl.	Lance Corporal	Worcs.	Worcester Regiment
L/Sgt.	Lance Sergeant	Yorks	Yorkshire Regiment
Lan. Fus.	Lancashire Fusiliers		
Lce.	Lance		
L.F.	Lancashire Fusiliers		
Lieut.	Lieutenant		

Army Structure in 1914

The following is a simplified structure of the British Army at the start of the Great War, showing the rank of the officer commanding and the approximate number of men at each level. In late 1917 the structure changed with brigades reducing to three battalions and battalions reducing to three companies. Note that the British Army was comprised of more than one 'Army'. Also, whilst an Army had nominally two Corps and a Corps nominally two Divisions, both of these units would be expanded and contracted depending on the situation. When expanded, an Army might have as many as 200,000 men.

Army	General or Field Marshall H.Q. + 2 or more Corps + Army Troops	85,000
Corps	Lt-General H.Q. + 2 or more Divisions + Corps Troops	38,500
Division	Major-General H.Q. + 3 Brigades + Divisional Troops (the latter would include Pioneers, R.E., R.A.M.C., A.S.C. and Artillery)	18,179
Brigade	Brigadier-General H.Q. + 4 Battalions	4,055
Battalion	Lieutenant-Colonel H.Q. + 4 Companies	1,007
Company	Major or Captain 4 Platoons	210
Platoon	Lieutenant or 2nd Lieutenant 4 Sections	52
Section	Corporal or Lance Corporal 12 Privates	13

30th Division Order of Battle

Infantry Brigades

Grantham	89th Brigade	90th Brigade	91st Brigade
	17th King's	16th Man R	20th Man R
	18th King's	17th Man R	21st Man R
	19th King's	18th Man R	22nd Man R
	20th King's	19th Man R	24th Man R

Dec 1915	89th Brigade	90th Brigade	21st Brigade
	17th King's	16th Man R	18th King's
	19th King's	17th Man R	19th Man R
	20th King's	18th Man R	2nd Yorks
	2nd Beds	2nd R.S.F.	2nd Wilts

Feb 1918	89th Brigade	90th Brigade	21st Brigade
	17th King's	16th Man R	17th Man R
	18th King's	2nd R.S.F.	2nd Yorks
	19th King's	2nd Beds	2nd Wilts

Divisional Troops

Artillery	148th Bde R.F.A.	149th Bde R.F.A.	150th Bde. R.F.A.
	151st (How) Bde.		
	V.30 T.M.B.		
	X.30 M.M.B.	Y.30 M.M.B.	Z.30 M.M.B.

Royal Engineers	200th Field Coy.	201st Field Coy.	202nd Field Coy.

R.A.M.C.	96th F.A.	97th F.A.	98th F.A.

Pioneers	11th S.L.R.	(until June 1918)
	6th S.W.B.	(from July 1918)

25th Division Order of Battle

Infantry Brigades

Oct 1918	74th Brigade	75th Brigade	7th Brigade
	9th Yorks	1/8 R. War	9th Devons
	11th Shwd F.	1/8 Worc. R	20th Man R
	13th D.L.I.	1/5 Glouc. R	21st Man R

Divisional Troops

Artillery	110th Bde R.F.A.	112nd Bde. R.F.A.	
	X.25 M.M.B.	Y.25 M.M.B.	
Machine Guns	25th M.G.C.		
Royal Engineers	105th Field Coy.	106th Field Coy.	130th Field Coy.
R.A.M.C.	75th F.A.	76th F.A.	77th F.A.
Pioneers	11th S.L.R.		

List of Maps

The maps that accompany some of the chapters are intended to give the reader an indication of the places mentioned in the narrative. They are not intended to be strictly accurate or to an exact scale.

An Eventful Journey

War was declared on 4 August, 1914. Like the rest of the country, St. Helens only noticed the impending hostilities towards the end of July. Curiously the first resident of the town to be affected wasn't actually in the town as the events unfolded. The Rev. R. D. Lord, curate of St. Thomas' in Westfield Street, was on a motorcycling holiday in Switzerland and Germany. He crossed into Germany from Basel on 28 July, intending to be home in England by the 31st. Rev. Lord would have been completely unaware that the 28th was the day Austria-Hungary declared war on Serbia and set the ball rolling. However, sight-seeing through South-West Germany, he noticed much military activity as Germany mobilized so he decided to cut short his trip.

He was first arrested by soldiers in Ludwigshafen, a major rail junction along the Rhine. They searched him and on finding his camera marked him down as a spy. Fortunately, a local English-speaking "gentleman" managed to persuade the troops that Rev. Lord was an innocent tourist and, after asking directions for Rotterdam, he was released and headed north for Cologne and then the Dutch frontier. All was not plain sailing. Just short of Bingen am Rhein he took a wrong turning and damaged his back tyre. Stopping in a village he consulted his map and took out his tool kit to repair the tyre. Seeing a stranger using a map and waving a pair of pliers about, the village burgomaster decided he was a dangerous saboteur intent on cutting the local telegraph wires. The village policeman was summoned. He agreed with the Burgomaster and decided to take Rev. Lord into Bingen Prison. Curate and bobby pushed the damaged bike to the local railway station to catch the train to Bingen and Rev. Lord ended up spending the night on a straw mattress in the jail.

After breakfast a statement had to be given to an English-speaking female clerk who told him that Germany was at war with France and Russia but not yet with Britain. The more cheering news was that the local chief of police believed Rev. Lord to be innocent but he would have to appear before a magistrate before he could be sent on his way. This was duly done and he set off for Cologne by train with his damaged motorcycle. On Cologne station his luggage went astray and while that was being found he was arrested and searched yet again. Prison didn't ensue this time and he was allowed to leave for Rotterdam. Even then his troubles were not quite over as he had missed the boat-train and had to travel to Ostend and thence to England, eventually arriving in St. Helens a wiser, more experienced curate than when he left. His adventures may have influenced his sermon a week or two later when he told his congregation, including a good number of recruits, that it was important that we British should not lose our Christian ideals during the war, even if the Germans already had!

A Company of Pals

The South Lancashire Regiment (Prince of Wales's Volunteers) had been formed in 1881 and consisted of two battalions; the 1st formed from the former 40th Regiment of Foot, and the 2nd from the former 82nd of Foot. Recruiting occurred mainly in South Lancashire centred on Warrington and St. Helens, with the Regimental Depot at Peninsula Barracks in Warrington. The regiment's nickname was the 'Fighting Fortieth' after the original 40th of Foot. It was also known as 'The Excellers', taken from the roman numerals for 40, 'XL'. The 40th of Foot fought in the 1801 campaign against the French in Egypt and for its part was awarded the distinction of carrying a Sphinx, inscribed with the word 'Egypt', on its Colours and badges. The 82nd's first Colonel was part of the household of the Prince of Wales, and so the Regiment became known as the Prince of Wales's Volunteers and took the Prince's three-feathered Plume as its badge. A plume of ostrich feathers, and the motto 'Ich Dien', were found on the helmet of the blind King of Bohemia after he was killed at the battle of Crecy in 1346. The victor, Edward the Black Prince, adopted the plume and motto for his crest, and as such they have ever since been borne by Princes of Wales. The plume, the sphinx and the motto all became parts of the badge of The South Lancashire Regiment.

In 1914 there were about 2,000 St. Helens men in the Territorial Force. There were three units of Territorials in the town; the two field companies (Engineers) of the West Lancashire Division, the 3rd West Lancashire Field Ambulance, and the 5th Battalion of the South Lancashire Regiment. The two field companies of the Engineers were based at Engineer Hall on Croppers Hill and were commanded by Colonel G. E. Sayce, with each company having a Major in charge, although at the outbreak of war one did not have a Major in post. The Field Ambulance, part of the Royal Army Medical Corps, was also based at Croppers Hill and commanded by Colonel G. Gullan. By far the largest group was the 5th South Lancs, an infantry rifle battalion based at the Drill Hall in Mill Street and commanded by Colonel L. E. Pilkington. All of these units had just arrived at Hornby, between Lancaster and Kirkby Lonsdale, for their annual camp when war was declared and they were recalled after only being there for a few hours. These units were immediately mobilized, and those men amongst them who were in the Special Reserve quickly went to the front. These were men who had enlisted for part-time soldiering but to a greater degree than the Territorials. They enlisted for 6 years, which began with 6 months full-time training, and accepted the possibility of being called up when needed. They also had 3 or 4 weeks training each year.

There were about 600 reservists in the town, a mix of ex-soldiers in the Army Reserve and those in the Special Reserve, and on 3 August crowds of them had built up in Church Street until 8 p.m. when their recall notices went up in the General Post Office. Streams of men then entered the Post Office to hand over their vouchers for the 3 shillings (15p) 'subsistence money' they were to draw to get them to their depots. No doubt a proportion of the reservists' shillings ended up in Church Street pubs as friends had a last glass before heading off to their various military destinations. These farewell drinks may have influenced the local Licensing Magistrates a couple of days later to order the closure of pubs from 9 p.m. to 8 a.m. With public and press opinion solidly behind them, the publicans simply ignored the injunction, and the police don't seem to have enforced it enthusiastically, possibly because a substantial number of constables had already disappeared into army uniform. The following day, the magistrates backed down and "postponed" the order, much to the disgust of the town's leading Free Churchman and Temperance supporter, the Rev. J. Gwilym Jones of Ormskirk Street Congregational church. Obviously, certain social habits and attitudes were not to be changed by war just yet. Also to be seen in the town centre that evening were armed and uniformed Territorials making for their assembly points in town.

On 5 August, Lord Kitchener issued orders for the expansion of the army. Unlike the popular press, he didn't think it would be "over by Christmas". He expected a long and costly campaign, and believed that overwhelming manpower would win the war. The following day Parliament approved an increase of 500,000 men. On 11 August the local press published Kitchener's appeal for the first 100,000; the famous "Your Country needs you" poster. The appeal was for recruits to the Regular Army, for three years or the duration of the war whichever was longer, and was limited to men aged between 19 and 30. The plan was for each of the county infantry regiments to raise a battalion. These would be numbered in sequence after the Territorial battalions. The first 100,000 was raised in just two weeks, and became known as K1, with 'K' standing for Kitchener. They were also to be known as the New Army to distinguish them from the Regular Army and the Territorial Force. The new battalions would be known as Service Battalions, and would have '(Service)' after their battalion number to indicate that the men had signed up for war service, that is, the duration of the war only.

On 10 August the War Office offered the 5th South Lancs the choice of garrison duty at home or active service overseas. There was reported to be a unanimous response for active service. Three days later, commanded by Major W. N. Pilkington, they left for Edinburgh after being bivouacked in the Town Hall and the Gamble Institute waiting for orders. In October they were moved to Tunbridge Wells and in February 1915, to France. Arriving on the 13th they were attached to 4th Division. In the November they were attached to 36th Division, and in the following January they were transferred to 55th (West Lancashire) Division. The 3rd West Lancashire Field Ambulance also served with 55th Division as did the two field companies of Engineers. Units of engineers that were raised in St. Helens after the start of the war served with 57th (2nd West Lancashire) Division. The West Lancashire Division was formed of Territorials, being one of 14 peacetime Territorial Divisions. When war broke out its infantry units left the Division as they were sent to France as reinforcements for the B.E.F., being attached to whichever Division needed them. In November 1915 the War Office reformed the West Lancashire Division and renamed it the 55th Division. Once it had been reformed, 55th Division relieved the French 88th Division south of Arras before it was moved into the Battle of the Somme later in the year.

By the end of the first week of August, over 8,000 men had enlisted, more than a quarter of the army's annual intake in a single week. In the second week, the week of Kitchener's appeal, more than 43,000 followed them. Very nearly 50,000 signed up in the third week; while the first reports of British troops in action at Mons and Le Cateau in the last week of the month coincided with 63,000 taking the King's shilling. Kitchener's appeal was so successful that on 28 August he appealed for a 'Second Hundred Thousand'. This was one day after Lord Derby announced his intention of raising a battalion of comrades in Liverpool. Locally, recruits came forward in good numbers, but the ball was soon rolling towards a specific battalion for St. Helens within the South Lancashire Regiment – the "Pals".

The first week of the war had also seen up to a hundred 'aliens' report for registration in St. Helens. The Weights and Measures section in the police headquarters at the Town Hall was serving as an Aliens' Office. Half a dozen were said to be Germans, who were presumably interned or repatriated.

At the same time as the first four Armies were being raised (K1-K4), another group of Service Battalions was also being raised by committees from cities, towns, organisations and individuals. The expense of raising, clothing, housing and feeding these battalions was met by the committees until they were taken over by the War Office in 1915. The War Office then refunded the committees their expenses. These Battalions were officially known as Locally Raised Battalions, and went on to supply most of the Infantry for the new 4th Army. They used the Divisional numbers (30th-35th) from the old 4th Army (K4) when the latter was broken up. A 5th New Army was raised (36th-40th Divisions) also made up from Locally Raised Battalions. The Locally Raised Battalions had an additional title in brackets, often including the word 'Pals', showing their connection with the area, town or organisation which raised them. The War Office imposed conditions on the forming of these locally raised units. They had to be raised by a private individual or committee; have £50,000 financial backing; be able to provide uniforms, equipment and accommodation. The War Office wouldn't support these units financially, but would reimburse if they were accepted. These conditions also meant that Territorial Force battalions were not officially 'Pals' even though that term was widely used at the time.

The new Divisions were each made up of three Brigades which were numbered so that the middle brigade number was three times the Division number. The St. Helens Pals would eventually join 30th Division, the first of the Pals Divisions, sometimes referred to as Derby's Division. It comprised 89th, 90th, and 91st Brigades. Each Brigade comprised 4 infantry battalions. The Division also had other units such as artillery, engineers, and medical services. Although the St. Helens Pals were raised as an infantry battalion, in 1915 they became 30th Division's pioneers. The 30th Division's crest was a version of Lord Derby's, similar to the cap badge of the Liverpool Pals, but without the family motto, and with the eagle looking down on a cap rather than a swaddled child.

Lord Derby (1865-1948), 17th Earl, formerly Edward George Villiers Stanley, served as British Minister of War from 1916 to 1918. Prior to this he was notably involved with recruiting. General Sir Henry Rawlinson had suggested on 19 August 1914 that men might be more willing to enlist if they could serve with people they knew. This was the idea of the 'Pals Battalions'. On Lord Kitchener's orders Rawlinson raised the 10th (Service) Battalion of the Royal Fusiliers, which was unofficially known as "The Stockbrokers' Battalion." It was made up of men who worked in the offices of the City of London, many of them clerks, and was effectively the first Pals battalion. One of these original 'Stockbrokers', Stanley Bacon, a clerk at the Stock Exchange, would eventually become an officer in the St. Helens Pals. Lord Derby then tested this idea further when he announced he would try to raise a battalion in Liverpool, comprised only of local men. Enough men enlisted in response to his speech at the Territorial drill hall in Liverpool to form four battalions, the 17th, 18th, 19th and 20th Service Battalions of the King's (Liverpool) Regiment. These were also known as the 1st, 2nd, 3rd and 4th City Battalions. At the same time, the Mayor of Manchester called on the men of his city to volunteer. They came forward in such numbers as to fill eight battalions, the 16th to 23rd Battalions of the Manchester Regiment.

On 1 September, Lord Derby, with the Mayor, Sir David Gamble, held a meeting at the Theatre Royal to raise a St. Helens battalion of the South Lancashire Regiment. Earlier in the day a local newspaper had published a letter from a retired Colour-Sergeant, William Milligan, suggesting that if the town couldn't raise a battalion it could certainly raise a "Pals Company for St. Helens". He also suggested using Lord Derby's influence to get this company attached to the South Lancashire Regiment. Milligan was already instructing both men and women in handling a rifle at the St. Helens Civilian Rifle Club.

This was part of the National Rifle Association's scheme to provide a corps of "crack shots" to act as musketry instructors to the units then being formed around the country.

Long before the start of the meeting masses of people were in the streets nearby. The theatre was packed and an overflow meeting had to be held in the Assembly Room at the Town Hall. Thousands more stood in the square unable to get into either meeting. At the theatre, those on stage included Lady Derby, Lady Gerrard, E. H. Cozens-Hardy (a Pilkington Bros. director), H. A. C. Goodwin, some Stapleton-Brethertons (local gentry), Mr. Rigby-Swift (local Conservative M.P.), Mr. James Sexton (Labour candidate for the town), some of the Pilkington family, officers of the Territorials, sundry councillors of all parties, Anglican and Nonconformist clergymen, and prominent Catholic laymen.

Sir David Gamble opened the meeting at the theatre, saying it was not a time for speech making but for action. He asked all men between the ages of 19 and 35 to join, and asked all ladies to make sure they did. The implication is that women should make use of the white feather. In August, Admiral Charles Fitzgerald had founded the Order of the White Feather with support from the prominent author Mrs. Humphrey Ward. The organization aimed to shame men into enlisting by getting women to give white feathers to men not wearing uniform. The white feather referred to the white feather in a game bird's tail being widely regarded as a mark of inferior breeding. In popular parlance to show a white feather was to display signs of cowardice, as a properly bred fighting cock would demonstrate aggression in the ring. The main speech came from Lord Derby who said:

> "There is not a man in this country who is not absolutely determined, come what may, if we lose every life and spend every penny, we are going to see it through to the bitter end. We are fighting for England and England's honour"

He appealed for volunteers, again asking for:

> "... unmarried men between the ages of 19 and 35 with no responsibilities, with a country to fight for abroad."

He promised potential recruits that their families would be taken care of, encouraging families to approach the Soldiers' and Sailors' Families' Association (S.S.F.A.) and not regard it as a charity. He also promised proper support for those disabled in the fighting. The audience cheered repeatedly throughout his speech. In conclusion Lord Derby said

> "I have spoken of the South Lancashire Regiment, and if you have read the papers you will have read words which must stir your blood,

of the gallant fight made by your own regiment in the late battle. Every man that lies dead of that regiment wants one of you to come forward and avenge his death."

Lord Derby was referring to the 2nd Battalion of the South Lancs who had been in action at Mons and Le Cateau which were the first two major battles of the war. The meeting continued with patriotic songs being sung, before Mr. Rigby Swift, K.C., the M.P. for St. Helens, spoke:

"We are fighting the great cause of democracy against military autocracy; we are fighting the great battle of liberty, the great fight of liberty and justice and truth ... We are also fighting for our very existence."

He hoped the war would be over soon, but said he knew that the end was still some months away.

Mr. J. Sexton, the Labour candidate, addressed the meeting. He said that he was anti-military and that he belonged to a party that questioned the wisdom of having a large Navy. But he questioned it no longer. He went on to say:

"We all have our place to keep the industrial peace of the world while the young men of the country are fighting the battles of England abroad ... If this is no time for political quarrels, it is still less time for industrial quarrels."

Volunteers were asked to stand and cross the square to the Gamble Institute where they could give in their names and addresses. As they did the audience started to sing "Soldiers of the King," followed by the band's rendering of a contemporary, and appropriate, favourite, "All Pals".

At the Town Hall the meeting was chaired by Alderman Bishop, accompanied by councillors, clergymen and more of the Pilkington family. Between the speeches and while waiting for Lord Derby there was singing led by Dr. Siddall's male voice choir. The National Anthem, the "Marseillaise", the Russian National Hymn and "The Pals" a piece specially composed for the evening by Dr. Siddall, were sung. The Mayor and Lord and Lady Derby made their appearance having come from the theatre. Lord Derby repeated his appeal:

"Married men of course will be taken, but it is not to the married men to-day that I am making my earnest appeal. It is to unmarried men between 19 and 35. I make to him my appeal to come and do his duty, and I make my appeal as public and as strong as I can to his employer to give him back his place when he comes back from the war."

He continued:

"Those who come back wounded may feel for the rest of their lives the effect of their patriotism, and I venture to say there is not a single living man who dare, here or in Parliament, to say anything but that the nation shall give them adequate recompense for their services."

After the meeting the choir appeared on the Town Hall steps and led the crowds in further singing, including "Rule Britannia" and the National Anthem again.

More than 700 volunteered at the meetings and there was a stream of men going to the Gamble Institute where a large number of clerks were waiting. Earlier in the day 300 men had already volunteered and that night Lord Derby was able to contact Lord Kitchener and inform him that a complete battalion had been raised.

Not all of the volunteers actually enlisted, and not all of those that came forward were accepted. This was mainly due to either being under age or in poor health. Some were too old and were debilitated after working 20 or 30 years in the mines. Even men of 19 or 20 were in poor health, with some already showing early signs of tuberculosis. The lower age limit was 18 to enlist but 19 before a man could be sent overseas. The upper age limit was 38; raised to 40 in May 1915. Men at both ends of the age band lied in order to enlist.

John Knowles, of Raglan Street, a labourer at Beecham's, enlisted as a bugler, giving his age as 14 years and 9 months. He was discharged the first week of December after the battalion received a letter from the War Office. James Appleton, a glass cutter of Russell Street, enlisted as a side drummer, giving his real age of 16. He was discharged on Christmas Eve. Six days later he enlisted again at Sutton Barracks, giving his age as 19 and changing his next of kin from his mother to his father. He was discharged again for being under age in October 1915 before the battalion left for France. He eventually enlisted again as by 1918 he was serving as a private in the 1/5th South Lancs. Arthur Shacklady, a Grocer's Assistant of Duke Street, enlisted as a bugler, giving his real age of 16. He was to be discharged on Christmas Eve. Undaunted, he went to Prescot and enlisted with the King's (Liverpool) Regiment. He went to France with the King's, winning the Military Medal in 1917 and dying of wounds a month after the Armistice.

John Lawrenson, a miner of York Street, had previous service with the 1st and 2nd battalions of the South Lancs. He had first enlisted in 1889 and served in Malta, Egypt, India and the Boer War. He was 42 when he re-enlisted with the Pals but didn't go to France, being transferred to agricultural work until 1919. William Hudson, a labourer of Atherton Street, was one of the first to enlist, giving his age as 36. He was discharged as medically unfit after 66 days. Not surprising really, considering he was actually 53 years of age.

There were also several cases of father and son enlisting together. Thomas and Thomas Whalley, of Oldfield Street were discharged after 25 and 51 days respectively. The father was older than he had claimed and suffered from palpitations. The son was found to be under age and of poor physique. Richard Sanford, a miner of Volunteer Street, enlisted at the age of 45. Two of his sons also enlisted with the Pals. A third son was killed with the 5th South Lancs. Even more common were brothers enlisting together. George Carney of Sandon Street was one of three brothers to join the Pals; the others being Thomas and William. George was discharged in February 1915 as medically unfit because he was under the minimum height and chest sizes of 5' 3" and 34" respectively. He enlisted with 2/5th South Lancs a month later and served until 1919 including a spell in India with the 1st battalion. All three brothers survived the war.

The embryo Pals were first photographed in Higher Grade schoolyard, College Street, on 8 September. At that time there were no officers and no uniforms or equipment. The only man in uniform was William Milligan, the letter writer, who was what was commonly known as a 'dug out'; an ex-soldier, usually an N.C.O., who came forward to help train the new recruits. He had served as Colour-Sergeant with the 5th Battalion South Lancashire Regiment, the local territorials, living in Kiln Lane, and working as the town's Chief Nuisance Inspector; what we would now call an Environmental Health Officer. He drilled the men on the Civilian Rifle Club field and also sent each company on recruiting marches around the town and surrounding areas. Local newspapers commented on the distinction between the companies, comparing the "smart clothes" of the clerks with the colliers' "humbler attire". This original idea of having Clerks, Glassworkers, Miners, and Tradesmen's Companies doesn't seem to have lasted, as later on occupations were spread pretty evenly across the companies. In later years Millington recalled the day he "lost his battalion" when approaching Prescot from the Warrington side. Calling the battalion to a halt he addressed them:

> "Now, me lads, there are Liverpool troops billeted in the old Watch Factory, and I want you to show 'em what St. Helens can do in smartness and march discipline."

The men marched to attention and gave the correct "Eyes right" to the saluting guard of the Liverpool men. It then began to rain and by the time they got to the King's Arms it was pelting down. Milligan carried on undaunted, then:

> "I noticed that everybody seemed to have gone quiet. I looked around, and found I had lost my battalion! They were prepared to face German bullets when the time came, but they would not face the rain when scarcely one of them possessed a mackintosh or overcoat.

They had bolted to the pubs, and I joined 'em until the clouds rolled by."

Officially the acting Commanding Officer was Lt-Col. Robert William Hughes Thomas, a retired Colonel of the 5th South Lancs, who like Milligan had stepped forward as a temporary measure. As he had not been officially gazetted, that is his appointment had not appeared in the *London Gazette*, he could not draw any pay. Because Lord Derby had raised the battalion he was authorised by the War Office to give temporary commissions. He believed he had appointed a Major Quilter as Commanding Officer and in fact Quilter's appointment, backdated to 1 September, had appeared in the London Gazette on 13 October. However, he never turned up and Lord Derby complained to General Robb, the Military Secretary. Robb replied to Lord Derby:

"Quilter was unaware of the appointment and had joined naval brigade so is not available. Would you like to recommend someone or shall I make an appointment."

In another letter, Lord Derby told Robb that it "really is most disheartening and does not encourage one to try and raise fresh forces". Lt-Col. Thomas had to remain in command for a while longer even though he didn't want to.

The Y.M.C.A. Gymnasium became the recruiting office for the new battalion. A good number of clerks had volunteered, or were lent by offices in the town, to complete the paperwork; while several local doctors carried out the medical examinations. The Y.M.C.A. also made all of its rooms, such as the reading room and billiards room, available for use by the new battalion and it became the temporary headquarters. Within less than a week recruiting stopped as the battalion was complete. In addition to Colonel Thomas, Mr. Cozens-Hardy and Colour-Sergeant Milligan, Dr. Cates the Medical Officer of Health was assisting, including making arrangements for free dental treatment for the recruits.

The first NCOs were more 'dug outs', all men with long military service who had returned to the colours to help train the new recruits. These men included Sergeant Roberts, who was appointed orderly room sergeant; C.S.M. Francis Evans who had served for 21 years with the "Fighting Fortieth"; Sergeant Spencer, known as "Long Tom", who had served 21 years in the Devon Regiment and was drill instructor; C.S.M. Raven, formerly of the South Lancashire Regiment who had served in South Africa; Staff Sergeant W. Matthews who had served 13 years in the Royal Field Artillery, including the 1st and 2nd Chitral Expeditions to the North West Frontier in1895 and the China campaign, was orderly room clerk; Q.M.S. A. Marsh, late of the King's Royal Rifle Corps and Leicester Regiment, who had served in the Boer War; R.S.M. H.

J. Evans, who had served for 22 years with the Hampshire Regiment; C.S.M. P. Harrison, who had served in the Boer War; and C.S.M. Thomas, formerly of the 5th South Lancashire Regiment. The arrival of these men allowed Colour-Sergeant Milligan to leave the Pals and re-enlist with the 2/5th South Lancs despite being 48 years of age. He was later transferred to the Royal Army Medical Corps and discharged in 1919 after 4 and a half years of service, including going overseas to Italy and France.

The last week of September saw the arrival of some officers. Captain Earle and Captain Bonnyman joined the battalion; Lieut. Potter was appointed adjutant, and Lieut. Goodwin the orderly officer. They were followed by Charles Champion (known as Carl) who had come from Haileybury College in Hertfordshire, where he was science master, to join his uncle Major Frederick Evans. Evans was a retired Territorial from Cheshire whose sister lived in St. Helens. The day after his arrival, Carl Champion took drill and a route march. His brother Alan motored up from Wolverhampton, with Alton Smith, a couple of days later in his Singer to see Colonel Thomas. On their way home they stopped off at Smith's in Chester to order their uniforms. Both joined the battalion in the first week of October. A third Champion brother, Eric, was to join the battalion a little later. Apart from some, like Alan Champion, who had been in the Officers Training Corps at public school, many of the early junior officers had little or no experience. They were simply appointed after an interview and were expected to learn on the job. It was not until 1915 that any formal training began, and that would only last about a month at a 'school of instruction'. The system of Officer Cadet Battalions did not come about until 1916. Initially the Pals' officers lived at the Fleece Hotel, but soon moved to the Raven. Later some of them were put up at Windle Hall, home of the Pilkington family.

Training began in Sherdley Park. According to Richard Hesketh, possibly the last survivor of the battalion, they lacked uniforms and weapons and trained with broom handles. At the time, Sherdley Park was the estate of Captain Michael Hughes of Sherdley Hall. After being educated at Eton and Oxford, he had spent 12 years in the Life Guards. In 1893 he commanded a squadron in front of Queen Victoria at the Trooping of the Colour. Hughes later retired to Sherdley Hall, but this didn't last long as he chose to serve in the Boer War commanding various units. He received a hero's welcome when he got off the train on his return to St. Helens. Too old to fight in the Great War the now Lt-Col. took command of the 7th Battalion Royal Inniskilling Fusiliers, training recruits at Tipperary. His wife, Edith, was instrumental in forming a branch of the British Red Cross in St. Helens; and during the Great War she was involved, with Lady Gamble, in the Tobacco Fund, that sent pipes and tobacco to soldiers on the front line under the 'Smokes for Tommy Campaign'. She was also involved with sending motor ambulances to the Front. Shortly after the Second World War the park was sold to St. Helens Corporation.

The Pals' uniforms were originally grey, a temporary measure paid for by the Town Council. Richard Hesketh recalled that he went to a mill in Atherton to see his 'best girl' wearing his new grey uniform and was arrested for looking like a German spy, being kept in the police cells overnight. He was then on a charge for missing parade the next day. Being under arrest was no excuse!

Catering was in the hands of Messrs. Cooper, of Liverpool, who had been appointed by the Council.

The contract to supply the Pals with boots was placed with Edwin Hulme, at the "K" Boot Depot in Ormskirk Street. The company placed an advert in the *St. Helens Reporter* in January, 1915, with glowing testimonials for the boots that had "triumphed" in the Boer War.

> "We learn on good authority that at the recent inspection in London, of the Yeomanry by the Prince of Wales (afterwards King Edward VII), H.R.H. commended the Commanding Officer on the appearance of the men, and especially remarked upon their boots, which were the noteworthy "K's"

The boots didn't arrive soon enough for Private Thomas Wilson, a 38 year old collier from Sutton, who committed suicide in mid-September. He had enlisted on 5 September despite a history of poor health. Both he and his wife, Jane, thought the army would "make a man of him". On Monday, 14 September, he had been to drill and had come home in the early afternoon saying he had been dismissed because his boots weren't fit for marching. The recruits were still wearing their work boots as army boots had not yet been issued. He was under the totally wrong impression that he was in disgrace with his superiors. That night he went to an outbuilding and slit his throat with his razor. Wilson's widow and three children were none too well off. The men of the battalion clubbed together and raised £10 15s. This was passed to Mrs. Wilson in weekly installments of 15s (75p).

LORD KITCHENER'S ARMY.

NEW ST. HELENS BATTALION

OF THE SOUTH LANCS. REGIMENT

as announced by LORD DERBY, September 1st.

Applications to join THE NEW ST. HELENS BATTALION should be made AT THE RECRUITING OFFICE, Y.M.C.A., NORTH ROAD, where Medical Examination, etc., is now in progress.

As far as possible, those joining will be GROUPED IN COMPANIES ACCORDING TO OCCUPATIONS.

The names already received appear to justify separate Companies for:--

Collieries.   *Tradesmen.*
Sheet Glass Works.   *Clerks.*
Plate Glass Works.   *Labourers.*

As soon as the Officers and Depot for this New St. Helens Battalion have been appointed, it will be sworn in and sent to quarters.

In the meantime those who have been examined should return to their usual occupations until notice is sent them through the post in the course of a few days.

DAVID GAMBLE, Mayor.

Town Hall, St. Helens,
September 3rd, 1914.

The "St. Helens Reporter" Ltd. Printers, 78, Church Street, St. Helens

[St. Helens Library and Archives]

The Founders of the Pals
Sir David Gamble, Lt.-Col. R. W. H. Thomas, Hon. E. H. Cozens-Hardy
[St. Helens Reporter]

Higher Grade schoolyard, 8 September 1914
[St. Helens Library and Archives]

The first Officers and " Dug Outs", October 1914
[St. Helens Newspaper & Advertiser]

Early Days

➔

Pilkington Bros. donated one of their glassworks sites at Sutton for use as barracks. The site had been built in 1836 and Pilkington Bros. had acquired it in 1905 but had never used it for production. In the middle of September the tradesmen's and clerks companies were paraded at the Y.M.C.A., and marched to Sutton, where they began renovating the works, making it ready as accommodation. About a week later it was ready and the men went into barracks on 23 September. Kitchens had been erected and the old warehouse turned into a dining hall. The casting hall was used for sleeping with long rows of straw beds. 150 tons of straw bales had been laid out and covered with canvas bags containing loose straw. These were then covered with blankets. It was reported they were "scrupulously tidy". The works offices were used by the officers as battalion headquarters. The upper floor had been fitted out by the Y.M.C.A. for "amusement, entertainment, reading and light recreation". The latter seems to have comprised boxing, a piano and board games. The Y.M.C.A. also provided stamps and some 10,000 letters were written in the time that the battalion was billeted there. Edith Hughes, of Sherdley Hall, provided 60 books as the beginnings of a library and appealed for the public to donate more. Although local newspapers described the barracks in glowing terms, at the end of the war pension claims concerning rheumatism often ascribed its onset as due to the wet conditions at Sutton barracks.

Reveille was sounded at 6 a.m. and was followed by 'ablutions' before one and a quarter hours 'Swedish' drill started at 6.30. Swedish drill was the aerobics of the early 1900s and the foundation for modern gymnastics. The principles were detailed in a 1910 book "The Swedish Drill Teacher" by M. H. Spalding. Breakfast at 8 a.m. was the 1914 equivalent of the 'full English,' but each morning the meal was built around something different. Eggs on Sunday were followed by corned beef on Monday, sausages on Tuesday, brawn on Wednesday, liver and bacon on Thursday, fish on Friday and potted meat on Saturday. Oddly, in a nation then addicted to tea, coffee was the only drink served on 4 days of the week. On weekdays, breakfast preceded morning parade at 9 a.m. to be followed by two and a half hours morning drill. This took place in Sherdley Park and on fields behind St. Helens Hospital. Midday brought dinner. The Pals' menu alternated. Half the battalion got roast beef or mutton with vegetables, half got a meat and vegetable stew and then switched the next day. Afters comprised plum or jam pudding and obviously a British army couldn't have existed without tea. One reporter thought:

"cooking arrangements ... excellent ... considering the circumstances.
... Not a man can complain about the food. Many of them are living

now better than they ever did in their lives and they are showing the beneficial effects of the improved diet."

The British Army aimed to put over 4,000 calories a day into the stomach of a front line soldier and those in initial training would have received very little less. During the war, the army had a good reputation for getting the food to the troops.

By 2.30 p.m. they were ready for more drill or perhaps a 7 or 8 mile route march which happened 3 or 4 times a week. Selecting a local target like Carr Mill and marching there and back didn't just exercise the men; it was also a good recruiting advertisement. 5 o'clock brought tea-time. A pint mug of tea, plus bread and butter were invariable, but were accompanied on Sunday by jam, on Monday by cake, on Tuesday by cheese and salad, on Wednesday by marmalade, on Thursday by potted meat, on Friday by salmon and on Saturday by jam. After tea if there was to be no night route march, the men were dismissed until 9.45 p.m. when they had to be back in quarters preparatory to 'Lights Out' at 10 p.m. The only change to this routine came at weekends. On Saturday the morning drill before dinner was followed by a kit inspection, after which the men were dismissed until 9.45 p.m. On Sunday there was a morning Church parade and in that more religious age about 600 men attended the various services, and then again all were dismissed until 9.45 p.m.

In case this gives the impression of a problem-free time it should be noted that on 11 December there was an explosion from within the ranks of the St. Helens Hairdressers' Association. It had expelled one of its members as a 'knobstick', an archaic term for a blackleg. He had gained the position of barber to the Pals by offering to cut and shave for a mere penny a time and by offering to work on Sundays, thus undercutting established rates. Had he been willing to work for free as his contribution to the war effort, then the Association would have accepted that, but knobstick rates and hours were not on. In the words of the Secretary of the Association, this one-sided breaking of an agreement between barbers smacked of "the cult of Kaiserism". However, it seems that several members of the Hairdressers' Association had been asked some weeks previously to come to the assistance of the "regimental barber" who found the work too much for him. On being told that the price to be charged must not exceed 1d (0.4p) per shave and 1½d per haircut, the union barbers promptly declined to take on the job, the terms being considerably under the Hairdressers Association rates of 1½d per shave and 3d per haircut.

The battalion had also appointed a police unit to patrol the town and make sure Pals, supposedly identifiable by a white armlet on the left arm, didn't get into too much trouble. One local newspaper was quite tongue-in-cheek in its report that the guard-room was seldom empty, "The lads will get into mischief somehow". It suggested that transgressions were due to an understandable unfamiliarity with the myriad regulations of army life and what it coyly referred to as an over-indulgence in "the milk".

Although barracked at Lancots Lane, the Pals training continued to take place at Sherdley Park and Garswood Park. They also dug practice trenches at the 'Old Bonk' nearby; the area of waste land with chemical tips, colliery slag heaps, and pools of water that local children called the Green and White Oceans. This area ran from Fleet Lane, behind Morris Street, and along Watery Lane up to Berry's Lane. A. T. Champion recalled that they were very short of rifles at this time, with each company only having 25.

On 8 October there was a presentation to Staff Sergeant Matthews at Sutton Barracks. On behalf of the battalion, Colonel Thomas presented him with a gold guard and locket for his watch as an appreciation of his services during the formation of the battalion. Colonel Thomas mentioned the great help that Staff Sergeant Matthews had been to him. At the presentation, Captain Michael Hughes was thanked for his generosity in lending his park (Sherdley Park) as a drill ground. Hughes said he had seen three years with the White Dragoons at Berlin many years ago and he knew that the war had been brewing since 1870. The same month saw No. 1 Platoon of 'A' Company stealing a march on the rest of the battalion by holding a dinner and musical evening at the Wheatsheaf Hotel, St. Helens Junction. C.S.M. Thomas was presented with a pipe, pouch, and cigarette holder, gifts from the N.C.O.'s and men of the platoon, as appreciations of the regard for his services, and with regrets at his transfer from 'A' Company to 'C' Company.

Later in October one of the local 'aliens' turned out to be Father Fisher, a Jesuit who had been on his way to the foreign missions in Bombay when caught out by the war. Unable to travel to his post he was acting as an assistant to the Jesuits at Lowe House and Holy Cross. Apparently he was popular with the congregations and would have been surprised one evening, when returning from visiting some parishioners, to be arrested in Holy Cross presbytery by two police officers. They helped him pack then took him to the police station. On his pointing out that he hadn't eaten and it was past his dinner time, the officers took him back to Holy Cross for his evening meal before returning him to custody. He was then sent off to Ellesmere Port and the beginning of the internment process. As with the Reverend Lord, the war made no exceptions for the clerical collar, although it was still possible to observe the common courtesies.

While the men of St. Helens were being patriotic or thinking of adventure, their families were wondering how they would manage without the men's wages. On 5 August, repeating what had been done 15 years previously on the outbreak of the South African War, the Council set up a St. Helens War Committee. This comprised councillors and council officials and was chaired by the mayor, Sir

David Gamble. The committee's purpose was to establish a Mayor's Relief Fund to collect voluntary contributions to be distributed as payments for soldiers' wives and families in hardship. It was also decided to help the families of those thrown out of work as a result of the crisis. The payments to soldiers' dependants were meant to supplement existing army separation allowances. These had a maximum rate of 11s (55p) per week for a wife but in fact this seems to have been the rate for the wives of N.C.O.s; the vast majority received only 7s 7d (37½p) per week plus 1s 2d per week per child. As a rough rule of thumb the St. Helens War Committee decided that a wife should receive an income of 14s (70p) per week for herself, i.e. 7s 7d separation allowance, plus a contribution of 6s 5d from the Fund, and receive 2s for each child under 14, 1s 2d from the army and 10d from the Fund. As for the families of those recently made unemployed because of the decline in glass exports due to the crisis, then if jobs could not be found for the breadwinner then their "... necessities shall receive consideration."

The original idea was for the bulk of the contributions to go to the Prince's Fund in London from where it would be distributed as needed. St. Helens sent off nearly £4,500 in August and that's when the trouble started. The Prince's Fund had no mechanism to administer the money so it made use of the Soldiers and Sailors Families Association (S.S.F.A.). This was a long established Victorian charity that assisted service families who had fallen on hard times. The problem was that the S.S.F.A. was used to dealing with the groups that largely made up the old regular army; the urban unemployed, the unskilled and rural labourers, all of whom had low incomes in civilian life and were generally too young to have large families. Its relief scale, topping up the separation allowances to 14s for a wife and 2s per child up to a maximum of three, looked quite generous. However, for many of the men now joining the army it was anything but, and for two reasons. Firstly, St. Helens was a town with many miners and Catholics, and both groups tended to have large families. Secondly, some of the jobs they left behind were amongst the best paid industrial jobs in the country. A miner could expect a weekly wage packet of £2, but on enlisting he would receive 7s (35p) per week. The Army would give his wife 12s 3d (61p) for herself and her children. If the man sent her half his pay each week, the S.S.F.A. would step in with 4s 3d (21p) to give the woman a total of £1. Her standard of living and that of her children would have dropped by half. When it became clear this would cause hardship in the town, the Council dispatched Mayor Gamble and Alderman Foster to London to plead with the S.S.F.A. that exceptions be made. This was met with a flat refusal, as was the request to return the money St. Helens had already given to the fund.

The War Committee viewed higher scales as a matter of honour; a promise made to men on enlistment that their families would not suffer because of their patriotic action. Existing rates would be maintained and no more money would be sent to London. Resentment of the S.S.F.A. lasted and regular, scathing editorials appeared in the local newspapers. Nor was it just the press that talked of obligations to soldiers' families. On 13 September in a sermon preached at the Parish Church packed with Territorials and new recruits, the Vicar of St. Helens, the Reverend Albert Baines, said the Empire had three lines of defence: the character of the Empire's men, the response of the Empire's sons, and the homes of the people. He emphasized that the breadwinner should have no anxiety while he was away that there should be any scarcity of bread in his home.

Ward committees were established; where the ward councillors would recruit prominent local residents to help process claims and submit them to the central fund. Roughly £3,000 was already available from existing charitable funds such as the one left over from the South Africa War, held by the Corporation. The new contributions got off to a flying start with over £3,300 pledged at the first meeting including £1,000 from Sir Joseph Beecham and £1,000 from Greenall Whitley. Widowed mothers counted as wives, mothers-in-law living with daughters-in-law, and fathers too old to work but living with the son's family all received allowances. Interestingly, in a time supposedly far more strait-laced than now, illegitimate children counted for relief like any other child, as did partners who had never bothered to marry. Grants were given in 6d and 1s coupons that were accepted as rent and in shops. Landlords and shopkeepers took them to the Town Clerk for reimbursement. Additionally, some local companies paid a percentage of a man's wage to his family while he was away. Beecham's for instance paid 10 percent each week, and this was not restricted to married men. One of the Pals, Albert Milligan, of Ormskirk Street, was unmarried but his family still received 10 percent of his previous wage for the 234 weeks he was away.

Lt-Col. Thomas relinquished his commission in mid-November due to illness. He was replaced by Lt-Col. Pawle, a retired solicitor living in London, who until 1910 had served with 10th County of London Battalion; Territorials of the London Regiment. Pawle took over on Monday 16 November, having seen Lord Derby the week before. Lord Derby wrote to the War Office asking them to gazette Colonel Thomas so that he could draw the pay he was entitled to.

December saw a Whist Drive and Dance held by the battalion at the Town Hall that raised £36 10s for the Soldiers Fund that provided winter comforts for the troops at the front. This was followed by a presentation at the Town Hall where the Mayor, David Gamble, the Hon. Cozens-Hardy, and Colonel Thomas were each given a framed copy of a commissioned photograph of themselves. The ceremony took place in the Mayor's Parlour, the photos being presented by a group of N.C.O.s. Colonel Thomas was also given an inscribed gold ring as a token of the battalion's appreciation.

At the end of the month, Private Fitzpatrick became a local hero. He was a passenger on a bus leaving Clock Face for St. Helens when he saw a runaway horse and trap, belonging to a Sutton butcher, Mr. Whalley, tearing along. He jumped from the bus and stopped the animal, preventing a serious accident.

In January local newspapers carried a recruiting advert for another company of 250 men to be trained at Garswood Park. Men could apply at either Sutton Barracks or the Y.M.C.A. The newspaper put a remarkably optimistic spin on life as a soldier declaring that the men in the Sutton barracks:

> "… revel in the new order of things that gives them fine healthy physiques and leaves them with scarcely a care in the world. They are in very truth in an enviable position, and if more of the young men of St. Helens realised this it would not take them long to discard the attire associated with tedious labour for the uniform of the St. Helens Battalion. He can do your duty to-day and live the free and happy life more fitting to youth, and then if the supreme test comes on the great wide battlefields of Europe, what more noble sacrifice could be made than that which overtakes him while his face is towards the enemy."

This was to be 'E' Company, commanded by Alan Champion with Walker, Rowley and Manning as his subalterns. Archibald Manning had returned from Argentina, where he lived and worked in Buenos Aries, to enlist as a private in the 28th Battalion London Regiment, the Artists Rifles, before being granted a commission. The battalion was now being inspected fairly often, sometimes by Lord Derby himself.

The end of the month saw the death from pneumonia of Private John Edwards at his home in Gladstone Street. A tram driver, he had enlisted at Sutton Barracks on 15 December 1914 and had been with the battalion for only 44 days. While he was lying ill at home, his mother-in-law, Jane Elizabeth Brown, who lived with him and his wife, caught cold and died on the same day from the same cause. 'A' Company under the command of 2nd Lieut. Thompson lined the street near Private Edwards' house and afterwards followed the cortege to the Cemetery. The coffin of the dead soldier was wrapped in a Union Jack with his military cap and belt on it. Private Edwards' comrades acted as bearers. The 'Last Post' was played at the graveside and a firing party fired three volleys. He had died aged 28 without going to war, leaving a wife, Annie Isabel, and two children.

On 3 February Private Cornelius Carter committed suicide after only 17 days in the battalion. Allowed home a few days earlier due to illness, he was found by his relatives hanging from a clothes-line in the kitchen. As Carter was in 'E' Company, its commander, Lieut. Alan Champion, had to attend the inquest. The reason for Carter's suicide is unknown as the Coroner prevented the details of the case from being printed in the local newspapers.

By this time, Sherdley Park and Garswood Park weren't the Pals only training ground. They were marching from their Sutton Barracks to Liverpool to train in Sefton Park, reaching there about mid-day. They would then march through the centre of the city before marching back to Sutton again. The total distance would have been about twenty-eight miles, taking over five hours marching. Pecks Hill was another destination where they made practice attacks on a farmhouse there.

Also in early February, Tom Forester, the Warwickshire and Derbyshire cricketer, was given a commission in the battalion; and around this time Lieut. Alan Champion was keeping two monkeys and three bantams as pets in the duty room, but soon had to get rid of them as they were making such a mess.

Before the battalion left St. Helens, the C.O., Colonel Pawle, was taken ill, with pneumonia and appendicitis while at Windle Hall. Pawle relinquished his commission on 7 February and Sir John Harrington, K.C.M.G., K.C.V.O., C.B., took over the following day. Harrington was a retired Indian Army officer who had recently been serving with the 9th Essex Regiment. His service embraced the Nile Expedition of 1898, including the Battle of Khartoum; the South African War, for which he was awarded the Queen's and the King's Medals with six clasps; the 1904 campaign in Somaliland; and the operations at Nandi in 1905-6.

Officers of the Pals, October 1914
[St. Helens Newspaper & Advertiser]

Marching from Sutton Barracks to Church Parade, 21 February 1915.
[St. Helens Library and Archives]

Church Parade, 21 February 1915.
[St. Helens Library and Archives]

Church Parade at St. Mary's, Lowe House, 21 February 1915
[Brenda Winstanley]

Bangor

The battalion moved to Bangor on 22 February, leaving St. Helens in two trains. The previous day had seen a farewell church parade that attracted a crowded congregation to the Parish Church. The Reverend Baines preached the sermon, based on the first chapter of Joshua saying "Be strong and of good courage". He also said that St. Helens was proud of its battalion. About 350 of the Catholic members of the battalion, under the command of Major Bonnyman, attended a service at Lowe House, where Mass was celebrated by the Rev. Father Sandiford. The Rev. Father Shapter preached a sermon on the need for prayer and fasting and pointed out that the Royal Irish Regiment, then in training, had attended a three-day spiritual retreat.

The following morning, led by the regimental band, they marched along whistling and singing or shouting to friends among the spectators. As they approached the station, excitement ran high, and the crowds were kept in check by mounted and foot police officers, under the command of Superintendent Dunn. At the station they were given final words of encouragement from the Mayor, Sir David Gamble, who was accompanied by the Rev. A. Baines, the Hon. T. Cozens-Hardy, Captain Sparrow (the recruiting officer for St. Helens), and the Chief Constable, Mr. A. R. Ellerington. It was about half-past ten when the trains loaded with the troops set off on the journey to North Wales to the accompaniment of cheers, singing and laughter, and the explosion of the fog signals that had been put on the track.

The battalion of about 1,250 men was under the command of Sir John Harrington, with Major Bonnyman in command of 'A' Company, Captain Barrington-Ward in command of 'B' Company, Major Evans, the Champion brothers' uncle, in command of 'C' Company, Captain Potter in command of 'D' Company, Lieut. Alan Champion in command of 'E' Company, and Lieut. Carl Champion as adjutant. The other officers on parade were Captain Huggins, Lieuts. Fletcher, Burn, Ratcliffe, Langford, Pethick, Parr, Thompson, Forrester, Eric Champion, Douglas, Rowley, Woods, Brook, Walker, and Dixon. Thirty men under the command of Lieut. Dixon remained at Sutton for a week to clear up the barracks before rejoining the battalion at Bangor.

By the time the battalion left St. Helens, more than 10,000 men of the town and the surrounding district had joined the Army. Of the Pals battalion more than 150 had been discharged so far, mainly as medically unfit but also some for being under age. Many of these went on to enlist again with one of the town's territorial units. Francis Crilly, of Glover Street, was discharged on 6 February as being under height and chest measurements. That same day he went to Warrington and enlisted again into the South Lancs. In 1917 he was awarded the Military Medal, and in 1918 was reported as missing during the German offensive in March. He was later reported to have been buried at Mons. Samuel Critchley enlisted three times, with different units, despite being deaf since childhood. Joseph Heslip enlisted four times!

The Lancots Lane site that had been used as the barracks became a munitions factory which had the official name 'Ministry of Munitions Inspection Bond 1201'. In Charles Forman's 'Industrial Town', published in 1978, an unnamed munitions worker described how she'd organised a trades union because of the poor working conditions for women. These included working outside in the rain and stacking 24" steel shells. The women played football against different departments as well as against teams such as Rainhill Munitioneers. Eventually the female works team was re-formed as St. Helens Ladies A.F.C.

At Bangor, the battalion consisted of one Lieutenant Colonel, one Major, four Captains, seven Lieutenants, and twelve 2nd Lieutenants, for a total of 25 officers, or one over its establishment. The battalion's arrival provided a boost for the town's tradesmen with butchers, grocers and provision dealers busy supplying the needs of the men. The men were lodged in boarding houses around the town; 'A' company at the top in Upper Bangor; 'B' company near the station; 'C' company all down the main street; 'D' company near the pier; and 'E' company down by the shore. The officers stayed at the Castle Hotel and the British Hotel near the railway station. The N.C.O.s established their Mess at the Queen's Head Café in the high street.

The day after their arrival in Bangor the men were paraded at nine o'clock and the whole battalion, under Lieut. Pethick, went for a route march of about 12 miles in Anglesey. A snowstorm started and on the men's return it was so bad they had to stay in their billets for the rest of the day. The battalion was putting in hard work, day and night. Each night about 9 o'clock the men, armed with picks and shovels, went to Penrhyn Park for trench-digging and other training, carried out under cover of darkness. Penrhyn Park was owned by Lord Penrhyn who had served in the Life Guards. The battalion was still in grey uniforms but their equipment was now up to date and some of the officers had been provided with horses. Tools, however, were still in short supply. Soon after their arrival in Bangor the companies, and individual sections, were photographed outside the Pritchard-Jones Hall at the University of Bangor. The photographs were taken by the celebrated photographer John Wickens, famous for his photographs of Lloyd George.

At the end of February, County Carriers Ltd., based at the Queen's Garage, Boundary Road, advertised a char-a-banc trip to Bangor. The company had been bought by a Mr. Murray in 1912 and is now well known as Ellisons Travel. The trip, "circumstance and weather permitting", was aimed at the families and friends of the Pals. It would leave the Town Hall at 8 a.m. on 4 March and cost 11 shillings (55p), which was a tidy sum then. The advert went on:

"Provided one is well wrapped up there is nothing more invigorating than a motor trip at this season of the year".

According to Alan Champion there was a "distinct unpleasantness" between Sir John Harrington and Major Bonnyman at Bangor and the latter left to take over some Fusiliers of the Public Schools Brigade. The company commanders were reorganised again. Alan Champion got 'A', Barrington-Ward kept 'B', Carl Champion got 'C' and Potter kept 'D'. Harry Brooke became Adjutant.

By early April there were rumours that the battalion was to leave Bangor about the middle of the month, and there was an influx of wives and sweethearts from St. Helens to see their men in training. That month Private George Ollerton, a miner from Parr, was discharged after 238 days as medically unfit due to dyspepsia. On his discharge papers his character was described as "Fair". A week later he enlisted with 3rd/5th South Lancs going to France before the Pals did. In June 1917, at Ypres, he murdered one of his comrades and was sentenced to death. The sentence was eventually commuted to two years hard labour in No. 1 Military Prison at Rouen. In August 1918 he was released and rejoined his battalion; serving with them until he was demobilized in 1919. He did not return to St. Helens but went to live in Atherton.

Meanwhile in St. Helens a further company was recruited by Captain Sparrow. Later to be 'F' company, the advertisement referred to it as the 'Lusitania' company; playing to the emotions of the time over the ship's sinking by a German U-Boat on 7 May. The advert wanted 350 "handy men" for "Fighting and Engineering". Some of the recruits for the new company were photographed by the bandstand in Queen's Recreation Ground. Also advertising for recruits was the 7th Battalion Inniskillings who were commanded at Tipperary by Captain Hughes, of Sherdley Park. It was not the only regiment appealing to the many Irish people who lived in St. Helens. The Connaught Rangers also had a recruiting presence at the Town Hall.

In April, 250 men of the Pals became lost in the fog when searching Snowdonia for escaped German officers. Two companies had been sent out one Saturday morning about six o'clock to search the section of the Snowdon Range that lies between the Conway River and Bethesda and Capel Curig, in search of the fugitives. 'D' Company marched the five miles from Bangor to Bethesda, and then the eight miles towards Capel Curig, where they began an ascent of the mountain. Assembled on the summit, they were lined out with 40 yards between each man. When the lines were formed, the order was given to march straight ahead, each man keeping a sharp look out on all sides. Because of the rough terrain, the line was soon broken and sections of the men had to make detours, but the principle of the orders was carried out, and the whole mountain top within the range of the line was searched. The search continued until late in the evening and by this time 'D' Company was scattered on the uplands, and very tired from its 14 hours trek.

The return march began at dusk. With the help of some local policemen and the use of whistles and shouting, the officers succeeded in getting most of the company across the mountains, and down onto the main road. They then marched back to Bangor, having covered nearly 48 miles during the search. A considerable number of the men, however, were lost and sensibly decided to stay on the mountain at night, rather than risk death in the darkness. On Sunday the mountains were covered with mist all day, and some anxiety was felt about the men who were still missing, so search parties were sent out for them. Most of the missing men belonged to 'D' Company, with others from 'B' Company. Fortunately, they all returned safely on Monday, none the worse for their adventure.

While they were at Bangor the battalion was converted from an infantry battalion to a Pioneer battalion. These came into being as a result of an Army Order of December 1914 in response to the huge demand for labour to support the infantry. Building and maintaining a vast network of trenches, roads, light railways, camps, and dumps needed enormous effort. Men, horses and mules were also needed to move the massive quantities of stores and ammunition. The Pioneers were to solve this problem. Each Division was allocated a Pioneer Battalion that would be used for these various types of labouring work. The Pioneers were still trained as infantry and capable of fighting, but they would also be trained for work alongside the Royal Engineers, and would normally be used for this sort of work. They were a mixture of men, such as miners, who were experienced with picks and shovels, and others who were skilled in various trades. In theory each Pioneer battalion was to have 16 carpenters and joiners, 16 blacksmiths, 16 masons and bricklayers, 8 tinsmiths, and 4 engine drivers and fitters. Whilst some battalions were unhappy at becoming Pioneers, others were pleased as they saw it as being specially selected for their skills. Also, there was the matter of an extra 2d per day pay!

It was not all training at Bangor; rugby matches were played against the students of Normal College (a teacher training college) and the London Welsh at Llandudno. They were victorious in both and entertained the visitors to tea in the N.C.O.s' mess at the Queen's Head Café. The football team went over to Beaumaris where they beat the Royal Anglesey Royal Engineers by three goals to one.

Sgt. John Henry Sharratt and 19th Section 'B' Coy, Bangor, 1915
[Maureen Travers]

L/Cpl. Bert Allender (rightmost), Boarding Houses, Bangor, 1915
[Daphne Wilson]

'A' Company, Bangor, 1915
[Lancashire Infantry Museum]

'C' Company, Bangor, 1915
[Bernard Smith]

'F' Company recruits at Queen's Recreation Ground, St. Helens, May 1915
[Janice Herbert]

Orderlies at the Prescot Watchworks, 1915
[Nick Cross]

Church Parade in grey uniforms, Bangor, 1915
[C. C. Champion Collection]

Church Parade in khaki, Bangor, 1915
[C. C. Champion Collection]

Grantham

The four battalions of the Liverpool Pals left Prescot for Grantham on 29 April. They had been stationed at the Watch Factory and in Knowsley Park. The next day, Friday afternoon, the St. Helens Pals, to be known in future as the St. Helens Pioneers, were inspected at Penrhyn Park by Colonel Thomas and the Hon. M. Cozens-Hardy. A rumour had got about that Lord Derby was to inspect the battalion; however he did not attend, to the disappointment of those there. On 4 May, 11th South Lancs left Bangor for Grantham in two trains. A third train took 'E' Company back to St. Helens under the command of 2nd Lieut. Clarence Smith, accompanied by 2nd Lieut. Hubert Edwardes. Major Frederick Evans also returned and was put in charge of the Depot.

The battalion moved to Belton Camp at Grantham, Lincolnshire, and was attached to 30th Division. The camp was in the grounds of Belton House, now owned by the National Trust, but then the family seat of Lord and Lady Brownlow. The Division was completed not only by the arrival of the Pals but also of the Manchester battalions. The 20th, 21st and 22nd Manchesters ("Manchester Pals") came from Morecambe, with the 24th ("Oldham Pals") coming from Llanfairfechan. From midday onwards, half battalions of the Manchesters marched from the station to the camp at half-hourly intervals. Each half battalion was played into the park by bands from the infantry brigades already there. The exception was the Oldham Pals who brought their own band. The St. Helens Pals went into the camp as a complete battalion just in time for tea.

The camp could hold 12,000 men and it was the first time they had lived in huts. The barracks were very basic and bathing parades took place in the River Witham which flows to the South of Grantham. The entire water supply for everything came in through a single one inch pipe so the supply was terribly inadequate. Brigadier Stanley, commanding 89th Brigade, was quoted as saying:

"Ours not to reason why, ours but to wash - or try."

The St. Helens Pals' barracks were in the most unattractive part of the camp, next to the 24th Manchesters, so they transformed it; building plots either side of the doors and at each end of the barrack rooms. The designs were picked out in stone or grass, and stood out very vividly on the sand foundations. Inscriptions amongst them included "Avenge Scarborough", "Down with the Kaiser", "Good Luck to our Allies", and "Remember Belgium". Two plots in particular had cleverly worked designs of the ill-fated Lusitania.

Training was to be a mix of work with the Royal Engineers, trench work, Brigade work, route marches and battalion schemes. Although their khaki arrived along with 400 new rifles, there was still a severe shortage of arms, ammunition and equipment. They had courses in erecting fencing and light railway construction. The railway was to be used to carry stores from the Army Service Corps Depot to the upper camp and Carl Champion referred to it as "our first railway". It was not all pioneer work though. There was still physical exercise with platoons being examined by the Inspector of Gymnasia Northern Command, bayonet practice, and also musketry on the nearby Peascliffe range; now part of a golf course.

During June, the battalion was engaged in attack operations in Willoughby Park and Harlaxton Park, which were private estates a few miles away. They were also taught how to construct bridges, one of which was inspected by Major-General Dickson who expressed his satisfaction both with the bridge and the obstructions works erected in the adjoining field. During his inspection the General picked out one man from 'C' Company and asked him to lay out his kit. This was done, and well enough to get high praise. The battalion was apparently still looking for suitable candidates to become officers. An advert was placed in the Liverpool Echo on the 18th:

"Wanted ... Lancashire Men, with engineering qualifications; handy, practical men, desirous of commissions."

Applications could be made to either Colonel Thomas in St. Helens or Sir John Harrington at Grantham.

The month also saw the death of Private Thomas Beesley. He had been taken ill suddenly on the Sunday and was operated on for appendicitis. Although the operation was successful, pneumonia set in and on the Thursday he died, aged 19. He was buried in St. Helens. Private Stephen Allen was discharged as unfit for service due to early signs of tuberculosis. He had lied about his age in order to enlist, saying he was 19 when he was actually only 16. A happier event was the marriage of Private Joseph Waring to Elizabeth Flynn at Bangor, and Sir John Harrington was advertising for a battalion tailor who would be paid 4s (20p) per day and all found. Shortly after, James Walsh was specially enlisted at Grantham as the tailor. He came from Liverpool and was immediately made a sergeant. After only three months he discharged on medical grounds.

On 5 July, Private John Martin was sent to prison by the St. Helens magistrates; sentenced to two months hard labour for assaulting a policeman, Constable Glover, on the previous Saturday evening. Lieut. Gardner attended the trial and told the court that Martin was a very bad character and that "they could do nothing with him". After completing his sentence he returned to the battalion and served with them in France. By mid-July the Division still had only one gun carriage, and that was for funerals. Also in the middle of the month there was a cricket match against the 16th Battalion of the Manchesters.

Unfortunately the Pals could only manage 31 runs all out against the Manchesters' 139. During the time at Grantham, a number of officers came and went, and 400 new rifles arrived.

In St. Helens, a committee for the making of munitions was formed under the chairmanship of Cozens-Hardy. The old side of the Cowley Hill works was turned into a munitions shop, starting off with about 10 men and boys. It was quickly extended and women began to be employed. By the end of the war there were about 1,300 women and 500 men. It produced a total of 650,000 shells and 400,000 shell noses which had already been partly manufactured by other local firms. The profits were used to establish and maintain the Pilkington Special Hospital.

On 24 July, 90th Infantry Brigade carried out a practice attack on the 11th South Lancs at Denton Park. Major-General W. Fry (G.O.C. 30th Division) was present. By this time the route marches were often covering more than twenty miles at a time, with regular bayonet practice and musketry in between.

The end of July saw Isaac Myers in court in St. Helens, charged with desertion from the Pals. He said "I made a mistake when I joined the army", to which the Chief Constable replied "The Army made a bigger mistake in taking you". Myers continued "I have a conscientious objection to serving" and "There is a great difference between military discipline and Christ's discipline" to which the Chief Constable again replied "I suppose they've made you work".

The battalion was adopted by the War Office on 15 August when it was taken from 30th Division and temporarily placed under War Office control. That same weekend a recruiting meeting in Fisher Street, near Peckers Hill Road, turned into what the local newspapers called "a sensation". A councillor acted as chairman and appealed for recruits as usual. The meeting then took an unexpected turn when someone in the audience asked the councillor why he was asking other men's sons to go to war when his own two sons had not enlisted. The councillor's answer didn't please the crowd and police were called to restore order.

On 20 August the Bishop of Liverpool, Dr. Chavasse, the father of Captain Noel Chavasse who was to win the Victoria Cross twice, visited Belton Camp during his holidays to see the 89th Infantry Brigade; the 1st, 2nd, 3rd and 4th City Battalions of the King's Liverpool Regiment. He went first to the Church of England Men's Society Pavilion where a reception was held. On the Sunday he held three church parades, one for the 1st and 2nd battalions, one for the 3rd and 4th battalions and one for the 11th South Lancs and the Army Service Corps.

On a less spiritual note August had also seen the appointment of the first woman police officer with powers of arrest. Edith Smith was sworn in at

Grantham Town Hall. She had been brought in mainly to deal with the problem of prostitution in the town. The large number of troops in the camps at Belton Park and Harrowby had resulted in 'women of ill-repute' being attracted to the town. Edith was described as "a woman of outstanding personality - fearless, motherly and adaptable". By 1917, there were more than 2,000 Ediths patrolling in the country.

During their time at Grantham, C.S.M. Christopher Coates and Sgt. Frederick Collier both left 'A' Company for the Inns Of Court Officer Training Corps, and were granted commissions in the Manchester Regiment. Sergeant Prescott took over as C.S.M. of 'A' Company. In 1917 Collier died of wounds in St. Omer General Hospital. His father, a St. Helens Councillor, travelled to France and was with him when he died.

The next move for the Division was to Larkhill on Salisbury Plain for final training before going to France. The move began towards the end of August with battalions of the King's, and continued until nearly the middle of September with 91st Brigade and the St. Helens Pals moving around the 12th. As the Division started to leave Belton Park for Larkhill, the pioneers were still working on the camp, completing the light railways and the road to the camp hospital. Only a couple of days before leaving the officers and sergeants took part in a tactical scheme in the neighbourhood of Londonthorpe. The 11th South Lancs, as divisional troops, had to prepare the parish for defence, and to hold the same until relieved.

At the last church parade over £40 was collected and given to the vicar for the erection of a memorial marking the association of the 30th Division with the town. The Vicar of Grantham was to decide what form the memorial should take for the Parish Church, St. Wulfram's. He chose a paten and chalice. The chalice is sometimes referred to as the "Tanners Chalice" as the soldiers were reputed to have given a "tanner", sixpence (2½p), each towards the cost. It was made of silver and gold and represents New Jerusalem in Chapter 21 of the Book of Revelations:

> "And God shall wipe away all tears from their eyes, and there shall be no more death, neither sorrow, nor crying, neither shall there be any more pain: for the former things are passed away. And I John saw the holy city, new Jerusalem, coming down from God out of heaven, prepared as a bride adorned for her husband."

The paten was much plainer and was engraved with the names of all of the units in the Division. They were to be used for the first time on Easter Day 1916. Although they are now normally kept locked in a safe, they are still used at Christmas to this day. After 30th Division had left, the camp at Belton Park became the training ground for the Machine Gun Corps.

Belton Camp, Grantham
[David N. Robinson]

Y.M.C.A. Hut at Belton Camp, Grantham
[David N. Robinson]

Grantham, 1915
[St. Helens Library and Archives]

Sgt. (later C.S.M.) Matthew Carroll (leftmost)
with some of his men and their Boer War rifles
[Denise Dewsnip]

Belton Camp, Grantham, and 'our first railway'
[Stewart Squires]

Sergeants' Mess, Grantham, 1915
[Maureen Travers]

'D' Company bathing parade in the River Witham, Grantham, 1915
[Janette Micallef]

'C' Company digging trenches, Grantham, 1915
[C. C. Champion Collection]

'C' Company on Peascliffe Range, Grantham, 1915
[C. C. Champion Collection]

Lt. Williams on Peascliffe Range, Grantham, 1915
[C. C.Champion Collection]

Officers' staff car driven by Lt. & Q.M. A. H. Rice, Grantham, 1915
[C. C.Champion Collection]

Battalion Band, Grantham, August 1915
[Lancashire Infantry Museum]

Battalion Band, Grantham, 1915
[C. C.Champion Collection]

Off to football passing sacks used for bayonet practice, Grantham, 1915
[C. C. Champion collection]

Larkhill

The battalion moved to Camp No. 25 at Larkhill where a little less than two months final training was carried out before embarking for France. Larkhill was only about a mile or so from Stonehenge and had been an army camp before the war. Originally it was a tented camp, with permanent huts first being built there in 1914. During the war, 34 battalion-size garrisons were built and it could accommodate 50,000 men. It was often the last training camp for troops before they went to France as it was big enough for divisional training. Altogether, around 750,000 men were in training on Salisbury Plain.

It was only now that the artillery was able to start firing practice. The men were granted a week's leave at the end of the month. When the first batch was due to return to Larkhill there was a mix up over the train and a number of men missed it. These men found themselves in St. Helens Magistrates Court the next day, on charges of being absent without leave. The leave for the second batch was held up while this was sorted out. During the time the battalion was at Larkhill, the C.O. Lt-Col. Harrington lived at Durrington Manor.

Around this time the selection started of who was and who wasn't to go to France with the battalion. Those who were not required were posted to the 13th South Lancs at the Depot in Prescot. Training comprised a lot of R.E. work, building bridges, barbed wire entanglements, and tunnelling. It was also time to complete their musketry training. On one occasion 'A' Company started firing at a 500 yards target while a man was behind the 300 yards elevated firing point. He lay flat and refused to move until they had finished.

On 10 October, Private Lawrence Holland died in hospital at Netheravon in Wiltshire. He had been admitted on the 5th, very ill with pneumonia. He was aged 32 and left a wife, Ellen, and five children. No. 4 District Infantry Records at Shrewsbury had refused to supply a Railway Warrant to enable a relative to visit him in hospital.

It wasn't long before sports began again. In the middle of the month there was an inter-regimental contest between the St. Helens Pals and the 17th (1st City) King's. Unfortunately the King's won all of the running and boxing. The Pals had to be satisfied with the regimental and the sergeants tug-of-war contests. The day finished with a rugby match which the Pals comfortably won by 16 points to 3. Not surprising considering who was in the team; Sergeant Jimmy Flanagan, the Saints player; several junior league players including C.S.M. "Butcher" Prescott and Teddy McLoughlin; Major Potter, who had played for Harlequins and Middlesex; and Lieut. Craig who was a London Scottish threequarter.

During October it seems that the final decisions were being taken on who would be going to France with the battalion and who would be promoted among the N.C.O.s. Length of service didn't come into this. Some of the men who went had only been in training for a relatively short time, and some who stayed behind were amongst the first volunteers in 1914. Clearly the battalion was looking to men's abilities. As before, those who were not chosen to go were sent back to Prescot and transferred to the 13th South Lancs which had been formed at Oswestry in September 1914 and subsequently moved to the Prescot watchworks. In 1916 it would move again, this time to Altcar. Although 20 men of the 13th battalion were later sent to the 11th as reinforcements, a good number of the remaining men were transferred to Garrison Battalions of the Manchester Regiment and ended up going to Mesopotamia or India to replace regular soldiers destined for the Western Front. Others were discharged to work in industry, often for making munitions. During the middle of 1915 it became confusing as to whether a man enlisting at Prescot was joining the 11th or the 13th battalion.

Between leaving St. Helens and going to France 3 men had died from pneumonia and 88 had been discharged, nearly all due to being medically unfit. Others had been discharged for being under age, and unfortunately 9 had deserted. By now more than 250 had been and gone in the battalion.

Building a Trestle Bridge, Larkhill, 1915
[C. C. Champion Collection]

N.C.O.s, Larkhill, 8 September 1915
[Michael Blackburn]

Entrenching, Larkhill, 1915
[C. C. Champion collection]

'C' Company Orderly Room, Larkhill, 1915
[C. C. Champion collection]

To France

On 31 October, 1915, at 1 a.m., orders were received at Larkhill that 30th Division, less the Divisional Artillery, was to be held in readiness to embark week ending November 6th. Advance parties were to proceed to France on November 1st and 2nd. Ten officers went via Southampton on the 1st, and a billeting party went via Folkestone on the 2nd. Normally the King would inspect a New Army Division before it went out to France but he had had a bad fall from a horse while inspecting troops in France at the end of October. His place was taken by Lord Derby on the 4th, with the St. Helens Pals having a mobilization parade the same day. This was attended by the Mayor, Sir David Gamble, the Hon. E. H. Cozens-Hardy, and Colonel Thomas. They had gone to convey the good wishes of the town to those leaving for foreign service. The Mayor, wearing his chain of office, addressed the battalion, expressing the town's confidence in "such a splendid force". Lord Derby wrote to Cozens-Hardy that he had seen the St. Helens Battalion and "they were splendid in every way".

The battalion was to move at 2 a.m., leaving by train for Southampton where they remained all day, waiting to embark on the *S.S. Mona's Queen*, an Isle of Man paddle steamer. This they did at 5 p.m. with the transport and the C.O. embarking on the *S.S. Invicta*, an old cross-channel steamer. They had a good crossing, accompanied by only one destroyer, arriving at Le Havre around midnight. They disembarked at 8 a.m., 29 officers and 1,007 other ranks, and marched two miles to a rest camp just outside Le Havre. That evening they entrained at the Gare des Merchandises for Pont Remy, a journey that took all night travelling in wagons labelled '8 horses or 40 men'. From there they marched to an area of concentration at Ailly Le Haut Clocher near Amiens and on the 8th were billeted at Bussus Bussuel. Over the next few days the other units of 30th Division arrived in France.

89th Brigade, comprised of King's (Liverpool) battalions, arrived in France on 9 November and was placed in billets around the countryside; the 17th at Bellancourt, the 18th at Vauchelles Les Quesney, the 19th at Buigny and the 20th at Pont Remy.

90th Brigade, comprised of Manchester battalions, arrived on 6 November; the 16th being billeted at St. Riquer, the 17th at Domqueur, the 18th at Coulon Villers, and the 19th at Beaumetz.

91st Brigade, also comprised of Manchester battalions, arrived on 10 November; the 20th being billeted at Mouflers Bouchon, the 21st at Surcamp and Vauchelle Les Domart, the 22nd at Brucamps after a very bad Channel crossing that took 11 hours; and the 24th (Oldham Comrades) at Ergnies.

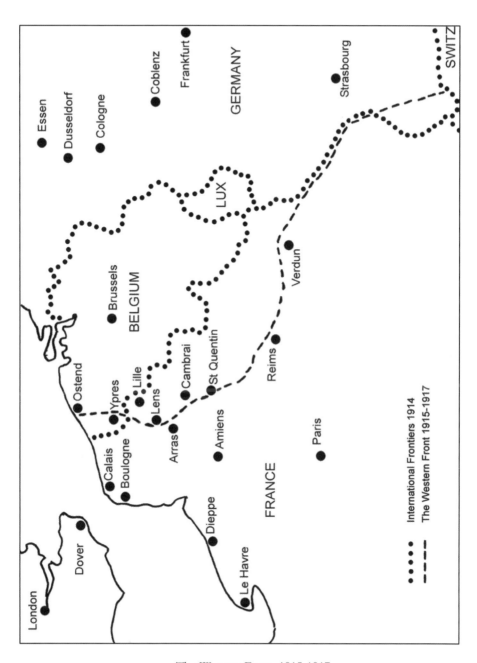

The Western Front, 1915-1917

The three infantry brigades were accompanied by 148th, 149th and 150th Brigades, Royal Field Artillery; 151st Howitzer Brigade, Royal Field Artillery, 11th (Hull) Heavy Battery, Royal Garrison Artillery; 125th Heavy Battery Royal Garrison Artillery; 'D' Squadron of the Lancashire Hussars; 96th, 97th and 98th Field Ambulances; 200th, 201st and 202nd (County Palatine) Field Companies of the Royal Engineers; and of course the Pioneer battalion, 11th South Lancs, the St. Helens Pals. Additionally there were Cyclists and Signals Companies.

By 12 November much of the Division was complete and it was moved to Bethencourt arriving on the 16th, and from there to Flesselles in the Albert-Somme area, coming under 13th Corps. On the way they were billeted about three miles from the 5th South Lancs and so arranged to meet. On a snow-covered morning the Pals formed up in line to give the "Fighting Fifth" three rousing cheers. The battalions were then allowed to fall out for half an hour to have a chat. At Flesselles they practiced bombing and went through a gas test, although by the time 'A' Company got to the room, the gas was nearly all used up and they could go in without their helmets on. Gas was commonplace by this time. More than 124,000 tons were used during the war, half of it by Germany. By 1918 the technology employed about 75,000 civilians, in the warring countries, in its production. During the war, Britain was to launch over 760 gas attacks.

Back in St. Helens a Comforts Fund was organised, promoted by Lord Derby. Colonel Thomas was appointed treasurer and Mrs. Cozens-Hardy as secretary. The fund would work in conjunction with the war parcels depot in Bridge Street which was already sending out parcels from the men's' families. The object of the fund was to supplement the family parcels by supplying things that Sir John Harrington, the commanding officer, suggested for the comfort of his battalion. Donations of money were requested from the public. The fund was started off with donations of £25 from Lord Derby, £50 from Pilkington Bros. Ltd., and £5 from Mrs. G. H. Pilkington. Amongst the early comforts sent were a dozen oilskin coats and sou'westers for the battalion cooks whose work with the travelling kitchen had to be done outside in all weathers. Thousands of articles would eventually be sent including socks, towels, mittens and, of course, cigarettes.

The Pals now had to receive "instruction in trenches" and on the 26th 'A' and 'B' Companies left for Mailly-Maillet where they were attached to 7th Corps for two weeks. Headquarters and 'C' and 'D' Companies had their instruction with the same brigade over the following two weeks. While they were there a German aircraft flew over Mailly-Maillet and dropped two bombs. One didn't explode but the other did near the company billets, fortunately without injuring anyone. The same period saw the battalion's first casualties with two men being wounded by enemy snipers. The men of the battalion now learned that trenches and geographical features had all been given names. The naming of the trenches became general practice during the winter of 1914-15 and these names soon appeared on the embryonic trench maps which were produced in ever growing numbers during the later stages of the war; the British producing some 20 million large-scale maps in all. It was inevitable that British soldiers would familiarize the area they were in with names from back home or ones related to their regiment. In other cases a name in French would be changed and given a witty makeover. The most famous example is probably that of the town of Ypres being known as "Wipers". Another example was the Somme village of Auchonvillers which was known as "Ocean Villas".

They would also be learning the names given to the different types of German shell. A bombardment was known as a 'Hate', which derived from the 'Hymn of Hate against England'. This had been composed in 1914 and distributed throughout the German Army. It was also taught to schoolchildren and performed at concerts. British propaganda used it as evidence of German cruelty and bullying. The bombardment might consist of 'Jack Johnsons' or 'Whizzbangs' or 'Sausages'. Jack Johnsons were large caliber shells that exploded with a distinctive puff of black smoke. The name came from the American heavyweight boxing champion at the time, whose nickname was 'The Big Smoke'. Whizzbangs usually referred to 77mm field gun shells. These travelled faster than sound and troops would hear the whizzing sound of one travelling through the air before they heard the bang of the gun. They gave virtually no warning of incoming fire. Sausages were rounds fired by small German trench mortars. Because they flew slowly through the air they could easily be spotted.

On 6 December 'B' Company had a close shave when coming out of the trenches. They were having an inspection in the open by 'Waterloo Bridge' when they were spotted and shelled pretty badly one shell very nearly hitting Lieutenants Garton and Dixon. It hit the side of the trench but luckily the ground was so soft it only splashed them with mud. A bit of shell went through Sergeant John Henry Sharratt's pack and broke his mess tin.

Ten days later, Private Joseph Beard of 'C' Company became the battalion's first man to be killed when he died in No. 4 Casualty Clearing Station, of wounds he had suffered two days earlier. His wife received a letter from the chaplain telling her of his operation, saying he was "magnificently brave" and that he sent his love to her. She received another chaplain's letter a couple of days later. This time it was to tell her of his death, having been badly wounded in the stomach, and never really being conscious. Private Beard was another who had lied about his age on enlistment, saying he was 33 when he was actually 41. He left a wife and family in Bruce Street.

Three days later and Private Harry Taylor was shot and killed by an enemy sniper. He was aged just 21. Two other men were wounded. The battalion had been sending out night parties to repair trenches and to dig communication trenches between the first line and the support trenches. After several nights of this they received orders to occupy a portion of the line. The dug-outs they found themselves in were four feet by eight, and each held a dozen men. The trench was 140 yards from the Germans, and the noise of the shells, whizzbangs, grenades, and rifle shots must have been a shock as it was their first experience of trench fighting.

19 December saw 'C' Company and part of 'D' Company go into the trenches for 3 days and 3 nights supplying working parties. Private William Groves of 'D' Company was admitted to 96 Field Ambulance with a gunshot wound. A single man aged 33, of Peter Street; he died of his wounds there on Christmas Eve. Before the war he had worked at Greenall Whitley's. The following day Private Frederick Cartwright of 'D' Company was killed by an enemy sniper. The day after that Private Louis Lambert and Private John Stanley both died of wounds and Private Peter Critchley died of alcohol poisoning while on guard duty at Mailly-Maillet. Lance-Corporal Smith, who was in charge of the guard, was remanded for a Field General Court Martial at Bernaville.

On Christmas Day the battalion left Mailly-Maillet and was split up for various works, mainly improving billets. Headquarters and 'B' Company were at Pernois, with 'A' Company at the artillery area near Berneuil, 'C' Company in Outrebois, and 'D' Company at Hem and Hardinval. Some good news was that their old R.S.M., John Thomas Payne, had been commissioned in the 2nd Bedfordshire Regiment. Eventually he would become Lt-Col., and be awarded a Military Cross.

A major change to the Division occurred in December when 91st Brigade was transferred to 7th Division in exchange for 21st Brigade which was made up of Regular Army infantrymen. Additionally, within 30th Division, 19th Manchesters were swapped for 2nd Royal Scots Fusiliers and 18th King's were swapped with 2nd Bedfords. The idea was that all the Division's Brigades now had Regular Army 'stiffeners'. The Division was still mostly a Pals Division though as 21st Brigade now comprised 18th King's Liverpool (2nd Pals), 19th Manchesters (4th Pals), 2nd Wiltshires and 2nd Green Howards. 89th Brigade now comprised 17th King's Liverpool (1st Pals), 19th King's Liverpool (3rd Pals), 20th King's Liverpool (4th Pals) and 2nd Bedfords. 90th Brigade now comprised 2nd Royal Scots Fusiliers, 16th Manchesters (1st Pals), 17th Manchesters (2nd Pals) and 18th Manchesters (3rd Pals). Out of the 12 infantry battalions, 8 were still Pals, along with the pioneers, 11th South Lancs.

In Britain during 1915 the number of volunteers had been falling. Before introducing conscription the government tried another scheme. On 15 July it passed the National Registration Act. This forced all men between 15 and 65 who were not already in the military to register. As well as providing sheer numbers it also showed how many were engaged in each trade. The results were available by mid-September. Almost 5 million men of military age were not in the forces. Of these 1.6 million were in protected or "starred" jobs. In October the Derby Scheme was begun. Men who had not yet volunteered could "attest" then go home to await their turn for call up. The public were warned that voluntary enlistment would soon stop and conscription would likely then begin. While over 2 million men attested, it was discovered that 38% of single men and 54% of married men not in "starred" jobs had still avoided recruitment. This hastened conscription and the Military Service Act came into force on 2 March 1916.

At the start of 1916 the fighting strength of 30th Division was 529 officers and 18,304 other ranks. The St. Helens Pals were still split up in various villages improving billets. 'A' Company was at Puchevillers for railway work under the command of R.C.E. 112th Railway Company R.E. Battalion Headquarters along with 'B' and 'C' Companies were at Froissy. 'D' Company was at Suzanne, where the Machine Gun Section was under the orders of G.O.C. 90th Brigade. One day, when the men had to get down in their dug-outs, it was found there wasn't enough accommodation for all of them. Some of the men, carrying sheets of corrugated iron to protect them from flying splinters, searched for holes in which to make themselves comfortable. One of the men came to a cemetery, and by chance found a newly-dug, empty grave. So in it he went and placed his corrugated iron over the top, and was soon asleep. A little time later some men from a Scottish regiment came along and one of the men lifted the corrugated iron out of curiosity. Seeing a man in the grave he said to his comrades, "Poor chap, he's waiting for somebody to fill in the grave for him," but just at that moment the Pal woke up, and the Scotties got a bit of a shock when they heard the "corpse" shout "Here, 'alf a mo', I'm very much alive." Around the same time 'D' Company's officers' cook had a lucky escape when a shell struck the dugout, passing through the cooking pot but leaving the cook uninjured.

The battalion was divided up most of the time with the companies doing different work at different places, and for a month or two there had probably never been more than two companies together at once. At one time they had twenty-one different working parties out, each doing different kinds of work. The middle of January saw two platoons repairing the Bray to Corbie road, and two repairing and clearing Carnoy Avenue. During the month the battalion also started work on a light railway from Bronfay Farm to a point on the Peronne road. Towards the end of the month work took place on improving and clearing Sheffield Avenue and starting a communication trench that was intended to provide covered communication between Suzanne and Bray.

Friday, 28 January, at Froissy became known as "Black Friday". During the previous week there had been thirty or forty shells a day, but on the 28th 685 shells were fired at the battalion from about a quarter past seven in the morning to four in the afternoon, averaging one per minute. They were working within seventy yards of the German line. At one point Major Potter was with a sick party in a street where there were 300 men when a shell fell practically in the centre of them. To everyone's amazement, only one man was slightly wounded. In a separate incident, Private John Mason was killed and the battalion had to move out of the area. The Germans were attempting to break through. The battalion was detailed for urgent work at Cappy making machine gun emplacements and redoubts, and to place the houses in a state of defence.

In St. Helens, the previous week had seen about 500 people at the Town Hall for a whist drive and dance organized by the sergeants' mess of the 13th battalion. The proceeds went towards the comforts fund for the Pals.

At the end of January the *St. Helens Reporter* received a letter from Corporal Claughton of 'C' Company describing their time in France so far. He said that they had reached their destination after marching with full equipment for five or six weeks. They were in a village of about five hundred people, some two or three miles from the German lines, and were billeted in empty houses. He and a number of others were living on the top storey of a derelict house whose roof was in bad condition, causing the rain to come through onto their beds, but he said "we struggled along cheerfully". Their work was at night, repairing trenches. The first time they went out was to make a communications trench between the first line and the support trenches. This was when they first realised the dangers as two men were wounded. This continued for five nights when they received orders to occupy a portion of the line. He recalled they marched to their new position in the evening finding the way rough and slushy, sometimes above the knees. They also found themselves in the sights of German snipers and machine gunners at times. They were now living in dugouts, each about four feet by eight and the trench was only 140 yards from the Germans. Claughton also said a great amount of caution was needed when on fatigues due to the German star shells that lit up the sky. He ended his letter by saying that the men would be more cheerful if they had more musical instruments; "the artistes are many, but the instruments are very rare". The newspaper asked the readers to send some.

In early February the battalion Headquarters and 'B' and 'C' Companies left their billets in Bray and moved to dugouts near Albert. 'A' Company relieved 'D' Company at Suzanne and 'D' moved to Etinehem. Much of February was taken up with enlarging the dugouts at battalion Headquarters to take the whole of the battalion, and continuing the defensive work at Cappy. During the month a local newspaper gave much space to the 1/5th and 2/5th battalions of the South Lancs. This resulted in Privates Lawson, Potter and

Marsh writing to the editor to remind him that the 11th were now in France, and in action, so could he give the 5th a bit of a rest and publish more on the 11th. It didn't go unanswered. An 'Old Sweat' of the 5th wrote to the newspaper saying:

> "They speak of leaving good situations and homes, and volunteering in time of trouble. Had they enlisted in times of peace they would have left their homes to do their little bit eight or nine months earlier ... as for working with the pick and spade, our boys do that during their leisure moments between patrols and keeping sentry."

On a lighter note, the transport officer, Lieut. Horace Woolcock, wrote to the paper on behalf of his sergeant, Henry Hill, asking for a pair of boxing gloves to be sent out. He also asked for an accordion or a couple of mouth organs so that his section could get some music.

Towards the end of February Lt-Col. Harrington went to England on leave. While there he visited St. Helens on some business with the C.O. at the Depot. When he returned he told Alan Champion that people in the town seemed to have the wind up. The town was "dark as pitch" as there were no lights on in churches and public buildings after 7 o'clock, and the clocks on the church and Beecham's tower were not allowed to strike.

In France, fair progress on the railway had been made by the end of February though the work had been delayed by bad weather and enemy fire. Much of the battalion's work had to be done at night due to the enemy artillery. The end of the month also saw all leave stopped for the men of 13th Corps but fortunately this was only a temporary measure. The weather had included frost and snow and had caused delays in getting supplies up to their lines. Canteen funds were used to purchase 1200 lbs. of cocoa for the men in the trenches.

The beginning of March brought the Division's first gallantry awards when two Military Crosses were awarded to the 18th Manchesters. Also in the first week, the Pals played a football match at Grovetown Camp against the 2nd Bedfordshire Regiment, losing 3-0. Leave was back on the agenda and on 8 April the allocation was increased to 30 men per day. This was none too generous considering there were more than 12,000 men in the Division. Ten days later all leave was cancelled again and men ordered to return to their units. Around the same time a census of religious denominations was taken for the Division. For the Pals this showed there were 643 Church of England, 297 Roman Catholic, 21 Wesleyan, 1 Presbyterian, 20 Congregationalist, 6 Methodist, 6 Baptist and 2 Salvationist.

April, began with digging new fire trenches for 21st Manchesters. On the 16th, Major Gwynn-Williams was invalided to England and Carl Champion replaced him as second in command. In the second half of the month the battalion moved to Vaux-en-Amienois for rest. While there they were inspected by the Divisional Commander, Major General Fry. On parade were 25 officers and 856 other ranks. Although trench work was taking place, the Division was considered to be resting during April and few events were recorded. The end of the month saw the start of courses of instruction for the officers at Divisional School.

Around this time the new steel helmets were being made in enough quantity for them to be issued generally. The 'shrapnel helmet' had been designed in 1915 by an Englishman, John Brodie, and trialed towards the end of that year. It was based on the medieval infantry 'kettle hat'. At first there was nowhere near enough to equip every man so they had been kept in the front line and used by whichever unit was there at the time. Now, more than a million had been made. Initially they were disliked due to their weight but once soldiers saw they were saving lives they soon changed their minds.

In May the *St. Helens Reporter* told of the court case over the film 'Five Nights', shown at the Hippodrome. Based on a novel it had been given an 'A' certificate by the British Board of Film Censors, meaning it could be seen by adults. The film was shown without any problems in places such as Liverpool and Cardiff, but in other places the police opposed its screening, saying it was pornographic. In St. Helens the local justices got involved and the case rumbled on for months with appeals on both sides. The National Film Company took the case to court to fight the local justices on the grounds that they couldn't establish local censorship. The company lost the case and both the film industry and local authorities began, for different reasons, to favour the idea of centralized official censorship.

That month, the Division's Royal Engineer Headquarters were at Etinehem from where a great deal of work was directed preparing the Division's front for the operations to come. This included the construction of additional communication trenches, assembly places, and battle headquarters. On the evening of the 11th, 77 NCOs and men of 'C' Company were engaged on rescue work in trench Y3. This continued in hourly reliefs until the 13th. Also in May, a detachment of 17 men went to the assistance of a Manchester battalion to help them drive out the enemy from a trench they had entered. Several of the enemy were killed and others taken prisoners. The detachment, led by 2nd Lieut. Struthers, a former Bolton and Everton footballer, was complimented by both the Headquarters staff and also the Manchesters.

During the middle of the month Lt-Col. Harrington went to England on sick leave. While there he was appointed Commandant at Audruicq, a large Base Camp near Calais, and was replaced as C.O. by Lt-Col. Herbert Francis Fenn, late of the 21st (Service) Battalion (4th Public Schools) Royal Fusiliers, also known as the City of London Regiment. Fenn was about 34 years old and had originally been a career officer with the Royal Artillery. He had been commissioned as a 2nd Lieut. in 1901 but was "removed from the Army" in 1905 for being absent without leave. When the idea of a University and Public Schools Brigade (U.P.S.) was discussed at a meeting in Claridge's Hotel, London, in August 1914, he had been elected as a committee member. He subsequently joined the U.P.S. 4th Battalion and was appointed as a temporary Major. The battalion had been formed at Epsom in September 1914, and disbanded in April 1916, with many of the men being commissioned as officers. On Fenn's arrival, Captain Carl Champion was appointed temporary Major and made second in command.

For the Sutton bobbies who weren't called up, it was business as usual. They continued their own law enforcement war, rigidly enforcing all statutes and making no concessions for the hostilities taking place in France and the worries of the combatants' families and friends back in England. For example, when Sergeant Adams was doing his rounds in Junction Lane on May 20th, at 10.37 p.m., he found the Sutton Empire still showing a film. They were only licensed under the 1909 Cinematograph Act to exhibit films until 10.30 p.m. and the manager's explanation that the cinema had experienced a technical breakdown fell on deaf ears. The 'Sutton Bug' operator was moving the film by hand attempting to conclude their Saturday evening's entertainment and keep their patrons satisfied. Sergeant Adams was unmoved and on June 9th the *St. Helens Newspaper* reported that the Sutton Picture Company had been fined £1 by magistrates "to warn others that the law must be carried out". The gambling laws were similarly enforced by the St. Helens police with great rigour, even the simple pursuit of pitch and toss. Although played with different variations, it usually involved two coins being tossed with one member of the group or 'school' choosing 'heads' and another 'tails'. There was a winner if the coins both come down heads or tails, otherwise stakes were 'rolled over' to the next toss. The game was especially popular with the Sutton mining community where it had been played since the 18th century.

British Summer Time first came into being on 21 May after a campaign by a Surrey builder William Willett. In 1907 Willett produced a pamphlet "The Waste of Daylight" encouraging people to get out of bed earlier in summer so as not to waste "useful daylight". This was to be achieved by changing the clocks. Although it had been the subject of debate for some years, it was the outbreak of the war and the subsequent need to save coal that made the issue more important.

In late May many men were sent to 30th Division School for two weeks instruction prior to the 'Big Push'. Work during June was mainly on trenches in preparation for the British advance scheduled for the 25th but postponed to 1 July. At the start of the month, 11 platoons of 'A', 'C' and 'D' Companies were in Trigger Valley, 4 platoons of 'B' Company were in F Ravine. 1 platoon of 'D' Company was in the Divisional dugouts near Bray. The battalion headquarters were at Trigger Valley, with the Stores and Transport at Bray. Sergeant McGowan of 'C' Company was court martialled for drunkenness and reduced to the ranks.

Also in June, Private William Pounceby became the first man in the battalion to be decorated when he was awarded the Military Medal. In the previous January he had helped to carry two wounded men, one a French soldier, the other a man of his company, to a dressing station whilst under shell fire. His officer, Lieut. Walker, wrote to Pounceby's mother saying she had every reason to be proud of him.

On the 17th, Private Joseph Fildes was sent back to the base at Etaples then back to England after it had been discovered he was only 16 years of age. He had been in France with the battalion for just three days.

A couple of days later Mr. Foreman, of Speakman Road, received a telegram saying his son Stanley was dangerously ill in a hospital in Rouen. He was told that if he contacted the Records Office at Shrewsbury he would receive a pass so that he could visit his son. Travelling via Liverpool and London he embarked at Southampton for Le Havre where he was met by a young lady of the Y.M.C.A. who took him to the railway station for the train to Rouen. At Rouen he was driven to a hotel and told he would shortly be driven to the hospital. Sadly, on arriving at the hospital he was informed that his son had been buried an hour earlier. The chaplain who had conducted the service spoke to him and told him the boy was buried in the beautiful cemetery of St. Sever. The next day he visited the cemetery seeing rows and rows of graves, strewn with flowers which were tended daily by the ladies of Rouen. That same evening Mr. Foreman began his journey home. It was not until September that his sad story became known through the local newspapers.

Towards the end of June the battalion moved again, this time to Bray. The month had seen a great deal of work preparing for the coming battle. By the 23rd the Division's Battle Front was complete. During the final week the preliminary bombardment of the Germans took place. In the days before the coming offensive, the battalion built a prisoner of war cage at Grovetown Camp. The approaching Battles of the Somme were to last from 1 July until 18 November.

S.S. Mona's Queen
[Frances Coakley]

S.S. Invicta
[David Risley]

The Somme

The French had been pressing for a joint British-French offensive since the beginning of 1916. General Joffre, the French Commander in Chief, had met with General Sir Douglas Haig, Commander-in-Chief of the British Armies, the previous December and urged him to relieve the French 10th Army and participate in a 60 mile wide offensive across the Somme. Haig agreed to take over from the 10th Army in the Lens area. In January Joffre requested that Haig attack north of the Somme with a minimum seven mile wide front about 20 April. Haig could not agree. He said his forces would not be ready and it would be politically unacceptable in Britain. In further discussions in February, Haig agreed to a combined offensive on the Somme about 1 July 1916. In the same month the Germans had struck a heavy blow against the French at Verdun. Joffre requested Haig did all he could to prevent German reserves reinforcing the Verdun front. In April the War Committee approved British participation in the offensive. In May, Haig warned the Government not to expect too much from the offensive due to the small number of British and French Divisions available. All agreed that something must be done to relieve the pressure on the French at Verdun. Joffre wrote to Haig in June saying that the attack must begin on 1 July.

The objective of 30th Division in the Battle of Albert, part of the Somme Offensive, was in three phases. The first was to capture the German reserve line, Pommiers Trench through to Dublin Trench. Then they would capture the village of Montauban which had been taken by the Germans in September 1914 and was a good defensive position, being on a high ridge. Once they had the village and the ridge, the left flank was to take Montauban Alley and on to the downward slope of Caterpillar Valley. The second and third phases depended on the success of the first. They involved taking Bernafay and Trones Woods before moving on the Guillemont. The Division was rightmost in the British attacking line with 18th Division on its left and the French 39th Division on its right. The boundary between 18th and 30th Divisions was the Talus Boise tram line and then the road that ran due north to Montauban. Between 30th Division and the French was the road that ran from Maricourt to the Briqueterie (brickyards) to the southeast of Montauban. 21st Brigade was to take the eastern side of Train Alley, then moving forwards, take and hold Glatz Redoubt. 89th Brigade was to advance through Germans Wood and take Casement Trench, which ran westwards from Dublin Redoubt and hold it until the French had taken Dublin Redoubt. The advance could then continue up the slope towards Montauban. 90th Brigade was to leap-frog this newly taken position and take Montauban.

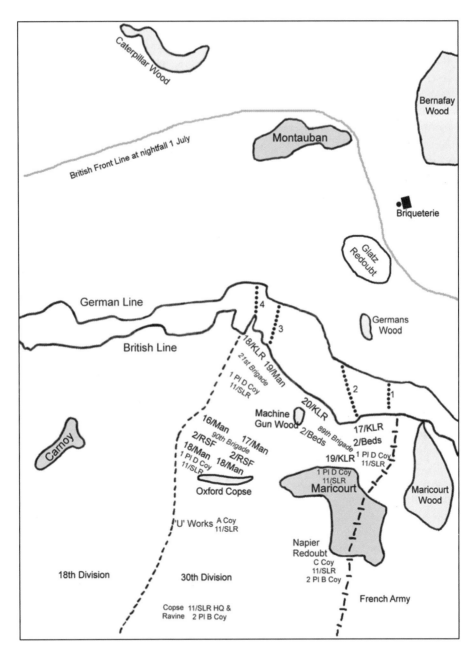

30th Divison position, 30 June 1916
Infantry positions and the four saps dug by 11th South Lancs on 1 July.

By 7.30 p.m. on the 30th the battalion was assembled in trenches at various fixed points. In the evening battalion headquarters was changed to Copse Ravine. 'A' Company was assembled in 'U' Works North of the Peronne Road, ready work on Saps, trenches that are dug towards the enemy. It was split into two parties; No. 3 under the command of Captain Champion to open up Sap 6, and No. 4 under the command of Lieut. Walker was to open up Sap 5. 'B' Company had 2 platoons in trenches near Maricourt at the East face of Napier Keep, and 2 platoons in Copse Ravine as Divisional Reserve. 'C' Company was in trenches at the East face of Napier Keep. 'D' Company had one platoon in trenches near Maricourt at the East face and part of the South face of Chateau Keep, one platoon in Dixons Ditch trench, one platoon in Stanley and Maricourt Avenues, and one platoon in Support and West Avenues. The latter two platoons were maintenance parties. The Lewis Gun Section was assembled in 'U' Works and did not move during the operation. Just before the battalion had moved up to these positions, one man of 'D' Company shot himself through the finger. Although he was supposed to have faced a court martial, it seems he didn't; he was transferred to a Garrison Battalion of the Manchester Regiment for a while and then sent to work in a colliery.

The 11th South Lancs were south of Montauban which was defended by the 6th Bavarian Reserve Infantry Regiment and the 3rd Upper Silesian Infantry Regiment No. 62 who were near the brickyards. To the East of Montauban was Bernafay Wood, and to the East of that was Trones Wood. The battalion's task was to open up four communications trenches; from Sap 6 to the enemy's trenches and onwards (Support Avenue), from Sap 5 to the enemy's trenches and onwards (West Avenue), from Sap 3 to German Wood (Stanley Avenue) and from Sap 4 to the enemy trenches and onwards (Maricourt Avenue). They were also to prepare strong points with 21st and 89th Brigades, and establish dumps of materials in Napier Keep and "U" Works. The new trenches across the former No Man's **Land** would allow men and supplies to be brought up in the event of the expected German counter-attack. As well as his rifle, 170 rounds of ammunition and 2 grenades, each man had to carry a pick or a shovel, 6 empty sandbags and his rations.

The parties for Saps 3 and 4 were to move up to the front line trench via Stanley Avenue as soon as the supporting battalion of 89th Infantry Brigade had left the assembly trenches. The leading man was to wheel to the left on arrival at the front line so that both parties would be opposite the sap they were to deal with. The parties for Saps 5 and 6 were to move up to the front line via Support Avenue as soon as the Supporting Battalion of 21st Infantry Brigade has left its assembly trenches, again with the leading man wheeling to the left on arrival at the front line. All of the parties were to move out to their objectives as soon as the supporting battalions had crossed the enemy's Support Line trench. Work on the communications trenches was to be commenced at both ends. On completion of the trenches each party was to extend its trench into the enemy's lines. The officer in charge of each party had to reconnoitre the enemy's trench that they had to deal with.

A party of 6 men under the command of Lieut. Culshaw was tasked with working water trucks forward from Carnoy and Talus Boise. Culshaw had come home from Canada to enlist and had several years' experience laying railways. His party was to take over 4 water trucks each carrying a 400 gallon tank from 202nd Field Company R.E. and arrange to fill them at Talus Boise during the night before the attack.

At 5.30 a.m. on 1 July the men were eating their breakfast rations and wishing each other the best of luck. For some it was to be their last meal. Private Sowerbutts recalled afterwards that later in the day he saw the chum he'd shared breakfast with shot through the temple. At 7:30 a.m. the battle opened and the Pals began to move to the front line trenches by way of a Sap. One platoon was attached to 200th Field Company R.E. Strong Point Party and one to 202nd Field Company R.E. Strong Point Party. The battalion followed the attacking brigades across the brickstacks at Montauban and began consolidating. No Man's Land was wider here than in many other places. Many of the casualties were caused by the Division on the left being held up, and by the heavy machine gun fire from the enemy.

By 2.45 p.m. the continuations of Maricourt and West Avenues by Nos. 2 and 4 parties had been dug through to the German line with a depth of four feet. Three-quarters of an hour later the continuation of Stanley Avenue by No. 1 party had been completed to a depth of 5 feet through to the German line. The continuation of Support Avenue by No. 3 party was not completed until later in the day due to heavy casualties from German shellfire.

At 6.18 p.m. No. 1 party reported their trench completed up to Strong Point 1/89 and that they were starting work on the Casement Trench. At 9.22 p.m. No. 4 party had practically finished their trench, and a few minutes later a similar report was received from No. 2 party. Meanwhile at 8.45 p.m. the C.O. had been instructed to send one of the platoons in Divisional Reserve to assist with work on the Maricourt to Montauban road. Later on, the other platoon in reserve was sent to open Saps continuing West and Support Avenues. Work continued until 11.20 p.m. when the battalion's parties were withdrawn for rest before continuing work the next day.

The Pals had successfully dug the four communications trenches and worked on the Strong Points and roads. On their left the 8th East Surrey's had attacked, famously kicking footballs into No Man's Land. During this time the Germans continually rained shells on the Pals and many were hit by machine-gun bullets. The cost to the Pals was 21 dead and nearly 100 wounded during the day.

One of the Pals' wounded was Nathaniel Sowerbutts, a postman and a regular attendee at the Wesleyan Church who had served with the 5th battalion before the war. In a letter to his sister, he wrote:

> "I saw some of our men go over and the sight thrilled me. It would have made anybody feel proud to belong to the British race. They had been singing and joking in the trenches, waiting for the order to go over, and by the way they went they might have been doing manoeuvres in Sherdley Park. There was no lagging behind, and each man seemed to be eager to be the first to get to close grips with the enemy."

Sowerbutts was hit by a piece of shell that went through his helmet and injured his head. He was helped into a shell hole where Private Alcock bandaged him. While he was waiting he saw Lieut. Fletcher, his platoon officer, injured and being led back. Supporting each other they made their way back to a dressing station. His letter to his sister concludes with:

> "I am doing champion, walking about. I was knocked down by a piece of high explosive shell a piece four inches going right through my steel helmet. Thank God (or the helmet). I may want you to send me a nice shirt, drawers, and socks; these are very much stained red. … Never say die but keep the old flag flying!"

After evacuation to England he spent some time at Huddersfield War Hospital before going to a convalescent camp at Blackpool, from where he wrote his letter. Lieut. Fletcher, the son of solicitor from Eccleston Park, had a fractured jaw and was sent to a hospital in Manchester.

Another of the wounded was Private Harry Dennett, an employee of Sherdley Colliery. He was shot in the leg and evacuated to England where the leg was amputated in a Warrington hospital. He was only 19 years of age. Private Robert Bradshaw had enlisted under age in the middle of 1915 and went to France after only 6 months training with the battalion. After recovering from his shrapnel wound he went back to France, being posted to 7th South Lancs, and was killed after only a month, in November of the same year.

Sergeant John Small, of 'A' Company, was killed while he was writing a field postcard for a fellow soldier he had met who was suffering from shell shock. He had been a tailor's cutter before the war, having served his apprenticeship at the Co-op. The son of a policeman, he was unusual in that he had never been a private. He was made a sergeant on enlisting, having been trained privately by officers at Prescot.

Private William Bryan, age 33, was killed by shrapnel. He was the manager of the Cowley Hill Lane branch of the Co-op and one of his staff from the shop was with him when he died and assisted with his burial. Private James Hodgins of 'A' Company, a boilerman at the Hardshaw Brook Chemical Works also died. He had enlisted at the very start giving his age as 32, when in fact he was 44.

Sergeant Jimmy Flanagan, who played at threequarter-back for Saints, wrote to his wife to say he was:

"… in the land of the living, and in good health, after our terrible experience … the sights I saw were heartbreaking. … had many a lucky shave during the bombardment, for many times shells burst only four yards from me and never touched me".

His luck was to run out in May 1918 when a piece of shell struck his chest and he died of his wounds.

Lance-Corporal Bert Allender, aged 24 of Peter Street, was killed in action. He had written to his parents only a couple of days earlier:

"Just a few lines to let you know I am still in the pink ... You must not be surprised or anxious if you don't receive any word from me for a few days as I shall not have the chance of writing for a matter of about four or five days as we are going to be very busy, but will write as soon as possible so don't get thinking anything."

Sergeant Thomas Cousins, aged 24 of Greenfield Road was wounded in the knee by shrapnel. Before the war he had worked in the offices of Pilkington's and was well known as the scoutmaster of the 2nd St. Helens Troop. He had already had several narrow escapes, including being buried by shellfire. He wrote to his mother from a Brighton hospital:

"Shrapnel wound in knee. Not serious, and in the pink of condition."

Earlier in the day a piece of shrapnel had gone through the end of his rifle, missing him completely. Later, after tea, he was bringing water up for his company when his party was shelled. Only Cousins was hit. After about an hour a stretcher-bearer found him and went for help. He then followed the standard route of dressing station, casualty clearing station, and hospital at Boulogne before being evacuated to England.

The walking wounded lay down in a field for several hours. While they were there a minister helped them to bread and butter and tea, after which they all sang the hymn, "I need Thee every hour." It was started by the minister, and all the men seemed to know the words so they joined in, accompanied by the sounds of artillery and gunfire.

There can be little doubt that 30th Division was the most successful of the day anywhere on the Somme battlefront. Their right flank was secure, being formed by the French Sixth Army that had learned its lessons the hard way at Verdun. Also, the French had many more medium and heavy howitzers, whose shells actually penetrated dugouts and cleared barbed wire. Despite today's public image of what happened on 1 July 1917, 89th Brigade captured all of their objectives and 18th King's didn't lose a single man on the day.

In St. Helens at 2.30 p.m. on Sunday 2 July, the 2nd day of the Battle of the Somme, a group of 24 Sutton men gathered in Rolling Mill Lane to chat and entertain themselves. They were mainly neighbours from that street, with others from Watery Lane and Sutton Moss. They were unaware that they were under surveillance from the Sutton bobbies with Police Sergeant Bate and his constables concealed in a position overlooking the road. He observed the "gang", as they were referred to in court, for over two hours playing pitch and toss and handball. Around 4.40 p.m. Frederick's ice cream cart drove up and all the men bought ice cream. Sergeant Bate seized the moment and with his quarry distracted he moved in with his constables and raided the unsuspecting group. In court all but two were convicted and fined 30 shillings or 14 days.

That same day the Thatto Heath police were in action at the Labour Club in Elephant Lane. Three days earlier, Constable Garrett had seen some women go to the club with bottles that were filled with beer for them. Because of this he had gone to the club with another man and said he wanted to join. While there he was invited to take part in a draw and observed someone "treating", what we would now call buying a round, which was illegal. Worse still he saw others playing dominoes for money; a halfpenny a game! It ended up at the Police Court mid-month. The magistrates thought that while there had been some laxity, the club was not being run improperly. They allowed it to remain open provided the regulations were more strictly adhered to in future. The steward pleaded guilty to allowing "treating" and was fined 20s (£1).

Back in France, on 2 July the 9th Division relieved the working parties on two of the main communication trench extensions. Work continued on the other two and in the evening the C.O. reported that all four trenches were usable for 500 yards beyond the old German front lines. By 8 p.m. the Division's artillery had fired more than 120,000 high explosive and shrapnel shells from its 72 18-pounders and its 16 4.5" Howitzers. The largest expenditure had been in the 24 hours from 8 p.m. on 30 June when over 30,000 shells had been fired. The same day, Corporal Harry Preston, of Central Street, died in No. 45 Casualty Clearing Station from the wounds he had received the previous day. He had suffered gunshot wounds in the leg, arm and face. Another Pilkington's employee at Bottom Works, he had enlisted aged only 17. After midnight the C.O. of 201st Field Company R.E. reported that he had just returned from Montauban and that it no longer existed as a village. The scheme for the defence of the village had to be modified as a consequence.

On 3 July the Division was reporting there had been no difficulty maintaining their ammunition and ration dumps. Water had been a problem, however, with the supplies at Talus Boise and Four Willows being failures. The Royal Engineers had organised four 400 gallon tank trucks and these had been a success, as had two canvas tanks at the junction of Bronway and the Peronne Road. These were kept full by means of 20 tank wagons obtaining water from Maricourt and Carnoy. The water was distributed using petrol cans as these proved to be the handiest. The trenches were policed so that prisoners could be escorted through to the Corps cages at Boise des Tailles. It was noted there was a marked absence of stragglers, only 7 having been reported. The area between Etinehem and Bray was handed over to the French. This involved the clearance of Bray and Etinehem and the removal of the camps at Etinehem. The evacuation of the wounded was thought to have gone well. There had been some delay with the walking wounded due to the large numbers but the Military Police had diverted some lorries and helped the situation.

By noon on the 3rd, over 1,350 German prisoners had been moved through Grovetown Camp. One of the N.C.O.s wrote to the *St. Helens Reporter*:

> "One cannot help but feel sorry for the poor fellows, even though they have caused us so much trouble. On the other hand it is hard to feel any regret for their officers; they seem hard and cruel, and give a vivid impression of what Prussian militarism means."

By noon on the 4th, the battalion's casualties since 24 June were 1 officer and 23 other ranks killed, 4 officers and 80 other ranks wounded, and 4 officers and 6 other ranks missing. After working under almost continual German shelling for four days the battalion went out of the line to Grovetown Camp and then to rest billets in the Bois des Tailles. The battalion's strength was reported as 24 officers and 948 other ranks, down from the previous week by 4 and 100 respectively.

The following day, 'A' and 'C' Companies were sent on preparatory work, cutting lanes from West to East through the southern part of Bernafay Wood. The clearing of the battlefield also began on the 5th under the supervision of Captain Downes Powell, one of the Staff Officers. Areas were allotted to 21st and 89th Infantry Brigades. The 90th Division was to send a party to help out the following day. The two brigades also began the work of recovering and burying the dead. Dumps were arranged by brigades and the material was then taken to the Advanced Ordnance Dump in the northern Bois des Tailles. The Division compiled a list of German equipment captured and sent back to the railhead. This was very detailed, ranging from 5 artillery pieces, through 6 machine guns, down to "Boots, odd 11" and "drinking cup 1"!

The battlefield was reported as cleared in 30th Division's area on the 7th and they went back into the line. Two companies were ordered to move during the night to assembly trenches between Oxford Road and Cambridge Copse. They were put at the disposal of 21st Brigade which was to attack the Southern end of Trones Wood. A third company was at the disposal of 2nd Battalion Yorkshire Regiment, with the fourth held in reserve in the assembly trenches.

From 8 to 13 July the Division's operations concentrated on Trones Wood. During the night of 8th/9th 21st Brigade was relieved by 90th Brigade. 2nd Yorkshires and 2nd Wiltshires had been detailed for the assault on the wood. The situation for the R.E. and the Pioneers remained the same and no work was done except for repairs to bridges on the Maricourt to Montauban road. Another company of 11th South Lancs was moved to reinforce those already with the brigade. At 9 p.m. on the 9th five sections of R.E and three companies of 11th South Lancs proceeded to dig and wire a trench from the southeast corner of Bernafay Wood. They also fire-stepped and wired the Sunken Road running from the Briqueterie to Hardicourt. The following day 3 companies went forward to work under 90th Brigade when they completed and wired a trench from Bernafay Wood to Sunken Lane. The work was constantly interrupted by shelling. Work continued on the 11th but during the night there was a heavy German counter-attack on Trones Wood and all troops were standing to and no R.E. work was possible.

On 12 July, the battalion was moved to Grovetown Camp, near Bray, for a week of rest from where it moved to Happy Valley on the 20th. Casualties in the Somme fighting had amounted to 1 officer killed and 190 other ranks killed or wounded.

Once again the provision of water had proved difficult but not so for rations or ammunition. It had been possible to send up 20 wagons every night with materials for repairing the Maricourt to Briqueterie road. A Forward Divisional Dump, containing about 4,000 Mills Bombs and 80 boxes of ammunition, had been established in Chimney Trench. The dump was kept full by the transport conveying supplies from the Divisional Dump at Napier Redoubt. Another dump was formed at the Briqueterie and a new Supply Railhead opened called "Edgehill". The evacuation of the wounded had proved difficult due to the bad state of the roads. In this period the battalion had 5 other ranks killed and 1 officer and 49 other ranks wounded. One of the dead was Private Ralph Kay, of Duke Street. He had enlisted in September 1914 under age and had only been back with the battalion for a month after being wounded in May.

Between the 20 and 29 July the battalion had various works in the area. Cable trenches 6 feet deep were dug from the Briqueterie to Trones Wood. A trench was dug from Glatz Redoubt to Signal Station at the Briqueterie and on to the Sunken Road. 'C' Company cut a track through Trones Wood south of the railway. Cobham Trench was completed, as was the trench leading to the dugouts in the Briqueterie. They also dug four assembly trenches on the east side of Trones Wood and one on the right of Guillemont road. As well as a trench between Trones Wood and Bernafay Wood. Four Rides (paths that could be ridden on) were cleared through Trones Wood and marked with strips of calico. One platoon worked with the R.E. on Divisional Headquarters dugouts near Billon Farm. Reliefs worked on dugouts in Sunken Road near the Briqueterie. During this period some of the casualties were men who had been gassed, including Major Potter, and others suffering from shell shock. Despite the casualties the battalion's strength was up to 901 other ranks at the end of the month as drafts had been arriving from base. It was reported that 600 steel helmets had been collected from walking wounded during the month.

On 28 July, Company Sergeant-Major Charles Norbury, of 'D' Company, was killed aged 28. A married man from Windle Street, he had been a clerk at Sutton Heath Colliery before the war. Norbury had married Ruth Woods, a teacher, at Dorrington in Wiltshire only a month before leaving for France. He was the son of Colour-Sergeant Norbury the well-known crack shot of the 5th Battalion. He was also well known in junior rugby having been player and Secretary to the Dentons Green Club. Norbury was in charge of a party digging a new communications trench and had remained at the exposed post under heavy fire when a shell burst in it, killing him. Major Potter, his company commander, had had a very high opinion of him, and R.S.M. Harrison wrote to his widow:

> "Charlie was one of the few bright spots in our lives out here. Always
> ready to be a pal to anyone, doing his best to cheer everyone up".

The *St. Helens Reporter* noted that the King had visited a War Hospital at Epsom. While there he had sympathized with a soldier who had lost an arm. The King received the reply "I don't mind your Majesty". When asked his regiment, the man replied "the Lancashires". "They have done very good work indeed" said the King, who didn't often visit the wounded in hospitals as it "upset him".

Operations again took place on 29 and 30 July when the Division attacked Guillemont. The battalion had officers at both 89th and 90th Brigades Headquarters and waited for orders, but in the end it was kept in Divisional Reserve at Talus Boise which was about 2 kilometers southwest of Bernafay Wood and south of Montauban. Reliefs were constantly working on dugouts in the Sunken Road near the Briqueterie while they awaited orders. Cobham

Trench was completed as were four assembly trenches, each 120 yards long, on the East side of Trones Wood. Nearly 500 Liverpool Pals were killed during the failed attack on Guillemont; the day later became known as Liverpool's blackest day. During the month the Division had received reinforcements amounting to 170 officers and 4,700 other ranks.

Private Peter Maloney was reported missing on 30 July. He had paraded with 'A' Company on the evening of Saturday 28th before the company went up to dig two assembly trenches in front of Trones Wood. When they were in the open near the Railway in front of the wood, the Germans opened a heavy bombardment. The men took what cover they could in various shell holes during the shelling which lasted about 40 minutes. Lance Corporal Dingsdale said he'd seen Maloney on the road from Trones Wood to Guillemont within about 50 yards of the work. The enemy started to shell and he saw Maloney going in the direction of the enemy apparently looking for cover in a shell hole. When the shelling stopped he went to the shell hole but no-one was there. Private Maloney was never seen again.

Lord Derby, the new Under-Secretary for War, wanted made known his opinion of the work which the Pals had done in the fighting. He had only just returned from France, and said "there was nothing but admiration of their bravery and courage, not only in attack, but in defence. They had been fighting close by the French troops, who had not only joined in the general commendation, but expressed the hope that in any future fighting the "Pals" would be by their side".

At the end of the month the people of St. Helens read how the Pals of 'D' Company had taken advantage of a rest from the fighting to have a sports day followed by a concert. Under the heading of "We Are Not Downhearted" one of the sergeants described how:

> "At the first opportunity we took full advantage of the chance of having some sport, by arranging a company gymkhana, which duly took place on our old lines, where, previously, it was nothing less than suicide for a man to show himself; that was before July 1st. The actual scene of our sports was once a pretty valley, and the only drawback to the complete success and enjoyment of our programme was that the enemy's guns would not keep silent; in fact, 'Jerry' shot more than one or two 'Krupps' to show he was still alive and kicking. Still, they did not stop the programme."

Equipment Race - 1 Pte. J. M. Edwards, 2 Pte. J. Speakman, 3 Lce.-Corpl. T. Tully.

Gas Bag Race – 1 Pte. W. Critchley, 2 Pte. J. M Edwards, 3 Lce.-Corpl. W. Ford.

100 Yards – 1 Lce.-Corpl. H. Owen, 2 Pte. H. Maylin, 3 Pte. T. Rigby.

Gretna Green Race - 1 Ptes, McCooey and B. Roberts, 2 Lce.-Corpls. McEwen and T. Gormley, 3 Ptes. McGee and G. Milsop.

100 Yards N.C.O. Race - 1 Sergt. J. Large, 2 Lce.-Corpl. H. Owen, 3 Lce.Sergt. H. Wilde.

Boot and Puttee Race - 1 Pte. T. O'Donnall, 2 Pte. J. Swindles, 3 Pte. J. Bradshaw.

Three-legged Race - 1 Lce.Sergts. T. Jones and J. Flanagan, 2 Ptes. J. W. Tickle and H. Maylin, 3 Lce.-Corpl. Southern and Pte. W. Foster.

Sack Race - 1 Lce. Sergt. J. Flanagan, 2 Pte. J. W Tickle, 3 Pte. J. Swindles.

Potato Race - 1 Pte. H. Maylin, 2 Pte. J. Swindles, 3 Pte. T. Rigby.

Wheelbarrow Race - 1 Sergt. J. Large and Pte. A. Winstanley, 2 Ptes. R. Melling and A. Derbyshire, 3, Corpl. W. Leyland and Pte. J. W. Tickle.

The evening saw a concert with the stage and seats improvised from fuse boxes obtained from the artillery. The sergeant went on "Unfortunately, the piano was 'absent without leave,' so we did our best to provide accompaniments out of the roar of the guns – which, I am bound to say, did not give us satisfactory results, from a musical point of view, as a piano would have done." The programme for evening was presided over by Lance Sergeant Taylor:

Song – "Greed of Gold" Sergt. W. Thornburn

Song – "Thora" Pte. G. Pearce

Song – "The Last Roll Call" Pte. C. Thompson

Song – "Whilst the Dance Goes on" Pte. J. Duffy

Song – "Cassidy V.C." Lce.-Sergt. T. Jones

Song – "The Old Arm Chair" Pte. H. Johnson

Song – "Mona" Pte. J. Webster

Song – "Killy, Dear" Pte. H. Maylin

Interval for Rum Ration

Song – "If I could only make you care" Pte. A. Cunningham

Song – "I am wearing my heart away for you" … Pte. Pearce

Recitation – "Napoleon" Second-Lieut. R. Struthers

Song – "Let not his name be spoken" Pte. B. Roberts

Song – "Another One Off for America" Pte. E, Finney

Song – "One of the Light Brigade" Pte. C. Thompson

Song – "When the Midnight Choo-Choo leaves for Alabam" Sergt. Thornbury

Song – "Leicester Square" Pte. H. Maylin

Song – "When you know you're not forgotten" Pte. G. Pearce

Song – "Paddy O'Leary" Corpl. J. Wright

Song – "Yarns, True and Untrue" Major Potter
Song – "Old Bill Kaiser" Lce.-Sergt. T. Jones (and Co.)
"God Save the King"

At the beginning of August the battalion was resting in Happy Valley having had about 190 casualties during the previous month. It then moved away from the fighting area to rest in a back area at Hallencourt. The rest was a short one and the battalion moved to Gorre for work in the Festubert and Givenchy areas. One company was attached to each of the R.E. Field Companies for maintenance work. The fourth company was employed on drainage of the Divisional Area. The Divisional Dump was established at Gorre Brewery. On their first day in the line 'A' Company had 6 men wounded and 'B' Company had 5 men wounded and one killed by shellfire. This was Private Thomas Naylor, a married man from Grafton Street who had worked at Pilkington's Cowley Hill Works before the war.

On the 24th the General Officer Commanding, First Army, presented Private John Frodsham of 'A' Company with the riband of the Military Medal. It was awarded for gallantry and devotion to duty in the previous month's operations. In his diary Major Alan Champion had recorded that on 1 July:

"Frodsham was very cool & told his men to keep cool & got them to working alright."

Two days later a further 41 Military Medals were awarded to NCOs and men of the Division for acts of gallantry during operations on the Somme.

In August the 13th South Lancs battalion at Prescot was absorbed into 69th Training Reserve Battalion, severing all links with the old regiment and breaking up the Pals Reserve Battalion. The Colours of the Pals had been presented by the officers of the battalion, and when the unit went out to France in 1915 they were removed for safe-keeping to the Reserve headquarters at Prescot. When the Reserve Battalion was broken up the Colours, somewhat dilapidated from lack of proper care, were placed in the St. Helens Parish Church. Lieut. Struthers, an ex-Everton footballer, represented the Pals. The battalion temporarily left 30th Division on 27 August and moved to the 15th Corps area near Dernancourt. After two weeks it was moved to 17th Corps area as a matter of urgency. They entrained at Bethune and after arrival at Aubigny, marched to Ecquvres arriving on 10 September.

A couple of days earlier the local newspapers had reported that Sir John Harrington, the previous C.O. now serving with the Rifle Brigade, had been wounded. A week later Private John Lee was posted to No. 6 Infantry Base Depot in Rouen after it was discovered he was under age. He had enlisted at Prescot with 'F' Company in May 1915 at the age of 16, and landed in France in

July the following year. From Rouen he was sent to the Depot in England from where he deserted in 1917.

At Ecquvres 'A' Company had been working at Fort George, 'B' at the Empire and Pylones, while 'C' and 'D' were at Neuville St. Vaast. After only a week they were on the move again, this time to Havernas to rejoin 30th Division. A week of training and they moved again by bus to Dernancourt and from there marched to Montauban. Much of the month had been taken up with preparing to move and actually moving. At Montauban the Germans, using an observation balloon, saw them erecting their tents and shelled them during the night. Luckily only one man of 'A' Company was injured. The battalion was at Montauban to work on roads at Bazentin under the orders of 41st Division. It was 69 other ranks under strength and, more seriously, 14 officers short. The work involved clearing obstructions and laying duckboards in Fish Alley, Goose Alley and Turk Lane, as well as work on roads in the area. Much of the work had to be done at night.

On 1 October, 30th Division took part in the Battle of Transloy Ridges. This would be the final battle of the Somme Offensive. Since the offensive started in July the Germans had built a fourth defensive line along the Transloy Ridges. Fourth Army's objectives involved the taking of Eaucourt L'Abbaye which was not achieved until the 3rd. In worsening weather on the 12th, Fourth Army launched a major assault that floundered in front of Le Transloy.

The Division was to take part in the Battle of Flers-Courcelette which lasted from 15 to 22 September. The bombardment began on 12th and the infantry advance on 15th. XV Corps was in the centre of attack against the 6th Bavarian Reserve Division and the 6th Active (Brandenburg) Division. In 30th Division, 89th Brigade would be on the left and 90th Brigade on the right, with 21st Brigade in reserve. The Pioneers were kept in the assembly trenches until late in the evening when they were sent forward. 'A' and 'C' Companies were to dig a continuation of Fish Alley, a main communications trench of 90th Brigade. Two platoons were to dig a communications trench from the end of Goose Alley, used by 89th Brigade, to a strong point held by 17th King's that had been formed in advance of the original front line. The remaining one and a half companies were with Advanced Headquarters along with the Lewis gunners.

14 October saw 'A' Company and two platoons of 'B' on night work in Fish Alley extending it so as to be clear of Factory Corner avoiding all German trenches were possible. This was to avoid the possibility of enemy artillery knowing the exact range of their old trenches and shelling them thinking they were being used for assembly. The following night, 'B' Company continued the work on Fish Alley, clearing it out and extending it by 250 yards. Goose Alley was also cleared and deepened for 450 yards. The final assault was on the morning of 18 October when only minimal gains were made. The battalion's

Advanced Headquarters were moved up to Crest Trench and 500 yards of fire trench was traversed and dug from the end of Turk Lane. On 20 October the Lewis Gunners were ordered to report to 21st Brigade to be attached to one of their battalions to assist in the line. The last attack was a failure with only minimal gains. Lt-Col. Pinwill, commanding 18th King's, wrote his "Reasons for Non-Success". He said the failure of the operation was due to loss of morale brought about by persistent shelling, tiredness of the troops due to being employed on carrying parties the night before, and the state of the weather. The men were soaked through and chilled the whole of the night. One of his recommendations was that units about to attack should be given adequate rest beforehand.

The battalion left the vicinity of Montauban on the 22nd for Dernancourt Camp, North of Dernancourt. The previous day had seen five men killed including 2nd Lieut. Edgar Parr, a 24 year old from Nottingham. Just before leaving Montauban there was another casualty when one of the Lewis Gunners, Private Frank Hartley, was killed on the front line. Two days later they were back near Montauban in Caterpillar Wood for railway work. This would continue until the battalion rejoined 30th Division on 6 November and were billeted at Humbercamp.

On 1 November Private William Brotherhood was with a working party in Railway Cutting near Bazentin-le-Petit when he suffered a fit. Nobody saw him fall; he was discovered unconscious and frothing at the mouth. He was carried back to his tent from where the stretcher bearers took him to the water point at Montauban. From there he was taken to No. 21 Casualty Clearing Station where he died. His death was attributed to an epileptic fit. Brotherhood had been a soldier since 1901 when he had enlisted with the South Lancashire Regiment at the Depot in Birmingham. On his transfer to Army Reserve before the war Captain Herbert, his company commander stated he was "not really as bad as his conduct sheets show".

The battalion stayed in billets until 9 October when they went to a forward area to take over from a battalion of the Monmouths. Two platoons of 'A' Company, and 'B' and 'D' Companies were billeted at Berles-au-Bois, about 1,800 yards from the front line. The other two platoons of 'A' were with the Quartermaster stores and the Transport at La Cauchie. 'C' Company was at Bailleulval. The battalion was responsible for the defence of Berles-au-Bois in case of attack by the Germans. The rest of the month was taken up with work on the Divisional Lines and the defence of the village along with work on the roads in the area. There were gas alerts frequently during the month as the wind was blowing towards them from the German lines, and owing to the bad weather each Infantry Brigade was issued with 2,000 pairs of wellingtons.

Around this time there was a discussion at Divisional level on the practical day to day things. It was noted that in October there had been a failure to give the men hot food when in the trenches. It was decided that cookers must be pushed further forward even at the risk of losing them. Winter vests and drawers had been issued but supplies of socks and shirts to form the working stock of the laundry had not yet arrived. The Brigade Baths, particularly those at Bellacourt and Berles needed to be improved and more Geyser Showers had been asked for. Each bath also needed an ironing room where the seams of clothes could be ironed, to kill the lice and their eggs, while the men were being bathed. 50 irons were ordered for these rooms. The supply of fuel was not sufficient for the lamps, stoves and braziers and they were trying to get more. However, satisfactory progress was being made with regard to providing steel helmets, gum boots, and soup kitchens.

On 12 November the Mayor, Alderman Bates, paid his official visit to St. Helens Parish Church. Accompanied by members of the Corporation, Magistrates, Friendly Societies and Boys' organisations, he led an imposing procession to church in the fine weather. It was notable that the military were practically absent so far as local regiments were concerned and their place was filled by 300 Boy Scouts and 70 members of Church Lads' Brigades. The other unusual feature was the carrying of the Colours of the St. Helens Pals. On arrival at the church the Colours, carried by an escort of Scouts and Cadets, were handed over by the Mayor to the Vicar, the Reverend Albert Baines, for safe keeping who said:

"We gladly receive the Colours of the 11th South Lancashire Regiment from your hands ... We shall keep it as a symbol of the loyalty of the men of St. Helens, and we shall prize it as a hallowed memory of the men who have given their lives for the cause."

The Vicar took as his text "Lift up a banner" (Isaiah – 13-2) and concluded with "If God is with us or, rather, if we are with God, our steps will not be backward, but forward to a lasting peace."

Two days later on the 14th the first sentence of death in the Division took place when Private W. Hunt of the 18th Manchesters was shot for desertion.

On 2 December, in the early hours of the morning, there was a fire at the Parish Church, believed to have been caused by an electrical fault. Sadly the church burnt down and the congregation had to worship at the Town Hall for ten years. The battalion's original colours, presented by the officers, were lost in the blaze.

The battalion remained in and around Berles-au-Bois during December continuing the same work as in November and also building a new strong point. Even in billets at Bienvilliers it wasn't safe, as Private James Rigby found when he was struck by shrapnel. After the dressing station he was taken to Boulogne where the shrapnel was removed, then hospital in Chatham. After his convalescence at Sittingbourne he was only fit for light work as he walked with a limp and couldn't flex his knee properly.

On 9 December Sergeant Harold West died in 97th Field Ambulance from an accidental gunshot wound that happened in his billet that afternoon. A Court of Enquiry was held four days later to decide (a) what orders existed with regard to revolvers being loaded, (b) who loaded the revolver, and (c) who was responsible for hanging up the revolver in the billet. Eight witnesses all claimed that the revolver wasn't loaded when they handled it. Private Robert Saxon said he'd taken his revolver out of his equipment to clean it and found it was dirty and going rusty. He wanted to know who had been using it without his permission. Private Ernest Tatlock asked to have a look at it. He tried to open it but it was very stiff. He was holding the Webley by the barrel and trying to break it open when it went off. Sergeant West shouted "Oh" and "I'm hit" and jumped up from the table where he was writing. He was helped onto his bed and a field dressing put on the wound. A doctor was called and Sergeant West was taken to a dressing station. Tatlock said he didn't know the gun was loaded and must have accidentally touched the trigger when he was trying to force the catch to break open the weapon.

Private Saxon had been working on a sap for the last fortnight and hadn't worn the weapon in that time. He had given permission to some of the other privates to borrow the revolver when they were acting as No. 2 in a gun team, as they had no revolvers of their own. Private Winstanley had it on the 7th. He claimed that although he had worn the revolver on the 7th, he hadn't examined it and had never loaded or fired it. Sergeant Percy Robertshaw told the enquiry that 2nd Lieut. Ridsdale had given verbal orders previously that all rifles and revolvers were to be inspected before going up to positions and on returning to billets. All of the men in the billet denied loading the revolver.

The Court decided that ample orders had been issued about loaded weapons, that there was no evidence about who had loaded the revolver, and that Private Winstanley was responsible for hanging up the weapon but was unaware it was loaded. The C.O.'s opinion was that Private Tatlock was principally to blame. When the case was referred to Major General Shea, commanding 30th Division, he decided that Private Tatlock and Private Winstanley who left the revolver loaded were both to blame and ordered the two privates to be tried by Field General Court Martial.

There were artillery operations by the British on 13 December and the battalion had to be ordered to Bombardment Stations in Berles for much of the day in case there was German retaliation on the village. Work continued until the end of the year when the German artillery was very active on Christmas Eve, shelling Berles-au-Bois heavily. The next day being Christmas Day the battalion was allowed to rest and no work was done.

By the end of the Somme fighting the German Army was of the opinion that it couldn't withstand another offensive like that so prepared to withdraw to the Hindenburg Line several miles to the East.

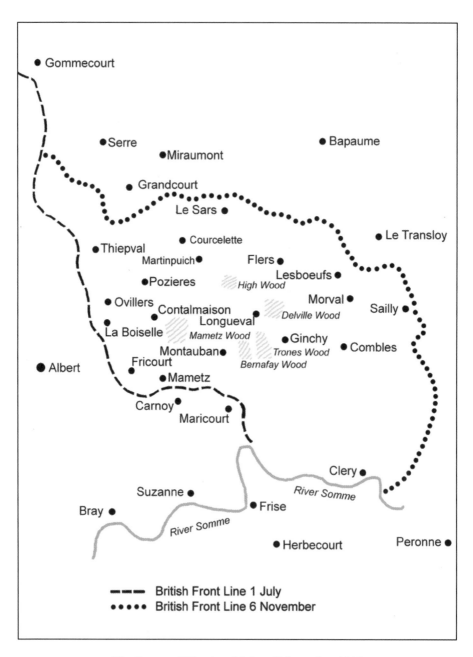

The Somme Offensive, 1 July - 6 November 1916

The village of Montauban before the war
[Ste Murgatroyd]

Montauban, July 1916
[Imperial War Museum, © IWM (Q 4003)]

The wrecked Briqueterie near Montauban, September 1916
[Imperial War Museum, © IWM (Q 1160)]

The Virgin of Montauban, the only thing untouched by the shellfire
[Imperial War Museum, © IWM (Q 4426)]

Road-making near Bernafay Wood, September 1916
[Imperial War Museum, © IWM (Q 1157)]

Working party in the mud near Bernafay Wood, November 1916
[Imperial War Museum, © IWM (Q 1616)]

Arras

The Divisional strength on the first day of 1917 was 529 officers and 18,304 other ranks, with headquarters at Le Meillard, about 12 miles northeast of Abbeville. The 11th South Lancs were still in the area of Berles-au-Bois, southwest of Arras. 'A' Company was at Agny and would be joined there by 'D' towards the end of the month. January was notable for severe weather. 18 January saw a break in five weeks of frost and restrictions had to be placed on road traffic, taking some off the roads because the camber became easily cut up and roads became impassable.

The Concert Hall at Halloy, about 12 miles north of Amiens, burned down on 22 January. It was being used by 'The Optimists' a concert party troupe who dressed as Pierrots. The Optimists had originally got together at Prescot Barracks for the benefit of 17th King's and had become 89th Brigade's concert troupe in 1916. Popularly known as 'Billy Bray and his Gang', Billy is thought to have been their comedian. As well as losing their piano in the fire they had to pay damages for the building and both government and civilian property. As well as The Optimists, 30th Division also had a concert party troupe, known as 'The Bluebirds'.

On 29 January Private Hugh Lewis was sent back to England and posted to the Depot for being under age. Eleven months later he went back to France and was posted to 2nd South Lancs with whom he served for only four months before being killed in action. Ten men of the Pals had been wounded during the month.

St. Helens Hospital and the Providence Hospital had been treating casualties since 1914, while in Rainhill the Tower Hospital, later Tower College, was also in operation. The Towers had been built by Mr. R. H. Baxter of Baxter's Chemical and Copper Works at a cost of £80,000. In 1914, Mr. Ernest Baxter, who owned the house at the time, loaned it to the war effort rent free. An appeal raised funds and in February 1915 it opened with 35 beds. The hospital was staffed by V.A.D.s and had an operating theatre. It was later enlarged so that 100 patients at a time could be treated. At the end of 1914, Mr. Henry Gamble loaned Oakdene in Rainhill and this opened as a hospital in March 1915. Again staffed by V.A.D.s, it later expanded to have 65 beds by 1917. Sir David Gamble loaned Oaklands which became a 40 bed hospital. Lord Derby had Knowsley Hall equipped with 120 beds as early as August 1914.

In 1916 the local press was not slow to appeal for support for soldiers hospitalized locally, encouraging the ladies of St. Helens to visit them with gifts. Apparently stamps, cigarettes and smiles were vastly therapeutic. To be fair, most of the ladies were probably already doing their bit for the wounded.

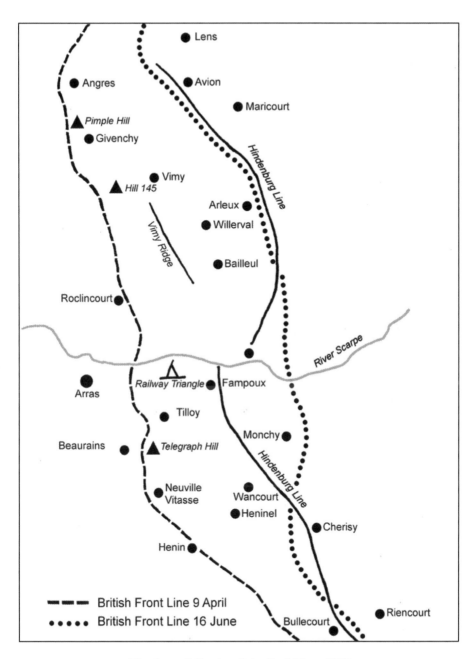

The Arras Offensive, 9 April - 16 June 1917

Throughout the war, the War Hospital Supplies Depot at The Elms on Cowley Hill Lane received staggering amounts of dressings, swabs, splints, jackets, and slings, all supplied by the ever-busy ladies of the borough. Now Pilkington Bros. were to add to the town's facilities for the wounded.

The Pilkington Special Hospital, founded by Messrs. Pilkington Bros., was opened in February 1917 on the Ravenhead site in Borough Road where an old grinding shed had been refurbished. Part of the Cowley Hill works had been turned into a shell factory and the firm decided to use excess profits from munitions for the hospital. The firm's Medical Officer, Dr. J. R. Kerr had been sent to France in 1916 to study facilities there and on his return the hospital took in its first intake of patients. Kerr had been chief surgeon at a French war hospital and nine of the staff at St. Helens had worked with him there. The hospital became an orthopaedic and limb-fitting centre for a large area of Lancashire and the whole of Westmorland, providing 300 beds, mostly occupied by discharged soldiers undergoing treatment. It also had 8 side wards for cases after operations and a ward for women and children. In addition, upwards of 250 out-patients attended 5 days a week. Facilities also included baths, massage, electrical and hydro treatment, remedial gymnastics, curative work-shops, and what was regarded as the finest X-Ray equipment in the country. There was also a recreation room with a piano and billiard table. The medical staff consisted of three resident medical officers and a visiting surgeon who was also the medical officer in charge. Nurses were accommodated at Ravenhead House. By the end of the year more than £40,000 had been spent by Pilkington's on this hospital. It remained open until 1925 when the demand for specialized treatment of ex-servicemen declined.

For the first half of March the battalion was employed on the defence of Agny, preparing dugouts, first aid posts, and collecting stations in the forward trenches. The Pals first heard of the German withdrawal on the morning of 18 March. Two days earlier the German army had withdrawn to the Hindenberg Line some miles to the East of their previous positions. It had been constructed in secrecy as a new, much stronger defensive position. The Germans adopted a "Scorched earth" policy. Roads, bridges and buildings were destroyed, and wells were poisoned as they withdrew. Mines and booby traps were left behind to delay the Allied advance. The roads and bridges had to be rebuilt before the Allies could resume the fight, giving the Germans time to consolidate their positions. Villages were razed to the ground and 150,000 civilians were forcibly evacuated to work in the rest of occupied France and Belgium.

Once 11th South Lancs had been informed of the withdrawal it was stood to, awaiting fresh orders. As the battalion was near to the front it was soon rushed forward to begin repairing roads and filling in craters. 'A' and 'B' Companies went out from Agny to the Arras-Bucquoy, Agny-Bucquoy and

Mercatel Switch roads to prepare them for guns and transport. These roads had been behind Germans lines and had been blown up in places. Temporary tracks were made round these spots while the craters were being filled in. on the Arras-Bucquoy road a very large concrete barrier had to be removed. During this work, several booby traps were discovered and made safe. 'C' and 'D' Companies relieved 'A' and 'B' during the night and the work continued. By 22 March the battalion was in new billets in Blairville, which had been evacuated by the Germans, and remained there until after the Arras Offensive. The following day, Private Samuel Dalton died in No. 20 Casualty Clearing Station. The cause of death was given as being pneumonia due to exposure on military duty.

During the war so far, the opposing armies were at stalemate with both sides entrenched and with little movement in the frontline. The Allied objective had been to break through the German defences and engage the German Army on open ground. The Arras offensive was to be part of this plan. The British were to attack on a front between Vimy in the northwest and Bullecourt in the southeast. The French would simultaneously open the Nivelle Offensive about eighty kilometres to the south. At Arras the British objective was to take the German-held high ground that overlooked the plain of Douai.

The battalion was involved with the Arras Offensive from the beginning, taking part in the First Battle of the Scarpe. After the Somme Offensive the German Army had been forced into a salient, an outward bulge in the front line extending into enemy territory and surrounded on three sides; this one being formed by the River Scarpe and the River Ancre. Haig's priority in 1917 was to attack both shoulders of the salient and cut it off, causing large German losses. Once this was accomplished Haig would be able to turn his attention to the salient in the North, Ypres, where he thought the war could be won.

The French town of Arras, like Belgium's Ypres, had the misfortune to lie very close to the front line for most of the war. Despite suffering extensive damage from bombardment, it remained a key Allied strong point because of one major advantage – it was built on chalk. For centuries the inhabitants of the town had dug tunnels and hideaways. When the British discovered this they too excavated the chalk to provide miles of tunnels. In November 1916 the 446-strong New Zealand Tunneling Company moved to Arras. Recruited in 1915, they had arrived in France in March 1916 under the command of 33-year-old regular soldier and Boer War veteran Major J. E. Duigan. Most of the tunnellers were quarrymen, gold miners or labourers from the Railways and Public Works departments. Others were coal miners from the West Coast of the South Island. Over the next five months the New Zealanders extended the two existing underground systems and created new tunnels. They constructed a complex system of galleries, subways, kitchens, headquarters and hospitals – facilities capable of housing 20,000 men.

With an offensive planned for April, the tunnellers had been shifted to a more offensive role early in the year. They tunnelled towards the enemy lines and laid three mines under the German trenches for detonation when the attack began. Tunnels were also dug to positions just short of the German trenches so that when the offensive was launched, troops could rapidly break through to the surface and man covering machine-guns, while others attacked the German positions.

The battle began on 9 April; it had been preceded by a bombardment, lasting three weeks, to cut the enemy's wire and destroy his strong points. Lessons had been learned from the Somme and overall the barrage was a success. 30th Division faced a part of the Hindenburg Line west of Neuville Vitasse and its frontage constituted a salient, as it jutted out exposing three sides. The attacking Divisions on the left needed to succeed before it could move forward. Although these Divisions were to attack at 5.30 a.m., 30th Division was not scheduled to move until the afternoon.

'A' and 'B' Companies were kept in reserve at Blairville, being held in readiness to move at one hour's notice. 'C' Company under Major Beal formed No.1 Road Party. They had assembled at the billets in Blairville by 1 p.m. waiting for orders. They were to ensure wheeled traffic could get through on the road from Boiry Becquerelle through Henin to Wancourt, and on the road from Henin through St. Martin to Wancourt. If the roads needed a great deal of work then the party was to open a new road through to Wancourt first. Major Beal was to send 2 officers and 4 other ranks to reconnoitre the roads first and report to battalion headquarters by 12 noon. 'D' Company under Captain Hodges formed No. 2 Road Party. They too were to assemble at the billets in Blairville by 1 p.m. and await orders. They were to ensure wheeled traffic could get through on the road from Mercatel through Neuville Vitasse to Wancourt. As with 'C' Company, one officer and 2 other ranks were sent to reconnoitre the road and report to battalion headquarters by 12 noon.

Each company had sent a man to battalion headquarters at 9 a.m. to synchronise watches. Each man had to carry a shovel and 6 sandbags as well as his rifle and 50 rounds of ammunition. Every fourth man carried a pick instead of a shovel. In addition every man carried his iron rations, a full water bottle, a waterproof sheet and a haversack. Each company also had to carry axes, saws, wire cutters, hammers, notice boards and rope for moving trees; all shared out between the men. More equipment and materials were available from the R.E. Dump. The road parties had to send reports on the state of the roads to headquarters at Blairville every 3 hours and whenever the roads had been opened up for traffic to Wancourt. The messages were sent using cyclists. Headquarters was also to be informed when casualties exceeded fifty.

30th Division only managed to take its second objective. 21st Brigade had been held up by the German wire, as was 89th Brigade who followed. What the British had seen from their lines and shelled was not the German front line but their support line. The front line was hidden behind the crest of a small rise in the ground and the wire was intact. Only after the fighting was it seen what an obstacle had been before them. Huge dugouts, great bands of wire, and for the first time they saw concrete emplacements, 'pill boxes'. The Canadians took Vimy Ridge, but at the cost of more than 3,500 killed and 7,000 wounded. The German line had been pushed back over 6 miles. The following day, 3rd Army estimated it had taken 10,000 Germans prisoner.

11 April saw the Division relieved by 33rd Division, and a couple of days later the Pals moved to the railway embankment near Boisleux-au-Mont. Again they moved after a few days, this time to Neuville Vitasse. Despite the frequent moves they were still in the vicinity of Agny, south of Arras.

On 26 April, Private Henry O'Reilly of 'A' Company was killed in action. He had been wounded in the Somme Offensive, suffering gunshot wounds to his back and neck on the first day. His return to France was in February, eight days after marrying Margaret Stubbs. She was the widow of another St. Helens Pal, Private Arthur Stubbs, who had been killed in June 1916. After 2 months of marriage she was a widow again and her four children had lost a second father.

During April the Division had seen 41 officers and 503 men killed, 108 officers and 2,124 men wounded, and 17 officers and 771 men were missing. A total of 166 officers and 3,398 men had become casualties.

There had been a great deal of air support during the Arras Offensive and the Royal Flying Corps had suffered very heavy casualties. For those involved in the air support it became known as "Bloody April". The life expectancy of a new pilot was only a few days.

At the beginning of May, the battalion was stationed at Beauvois near St. Pol. Later in the month they moved to Palace Camp near Dickebusch in Flanders working on light railways and corduroy roads. These were roads made by placing sand-covered logs at right angles to the direction of the road, often over a low or swampy area. The result is an improvement over impassable mud or dirt roads. These roads were pretty bumpy even in the best of conditions. They were a particular hazard to horses as any loose logs could shift.

The Ping Boys Concert Party, France, April 1917
[St. Helens Reporter]

Battle of the Scarpe. Working party going up to the forward area, April 1917
[Imperial War Museum, © IWM (Q 2030)]

Fixing scaling ladders in a trench near Arras, 8 April 1917
[Imperial War Museum, © IWM (Q 6204)]

Working party moving through Arras, 9 April 1917
[Imperial War Museum, © IWM (Q 5114)]

Messines

In mid-May 30th Division was ordered to move to the dreaded Ypres Salient. On the 18th they moved to Hazebrouke, and the day after by lorry to Poperinghe, referred to as 'Pop' by soldiers, and about 7 miles to the west of Ypres. It was the centre of a large concentration of troops. The town was the home of the famous 'Talbot House'. Known to soldiers as 'Toc H' as 'Toc' was signaller's code for 'T' and 'H' was 'H'. It had been opened on 11 December 1915 after Army chaplain the Reverend Philip "Tubby" Clayton saw a use for a place where soldiers could meet and relax regardless of rank. The club was named after the brother of padre Neville Talbot, 6th Division's most senior chaplain. His brother, Lieut. Gilbert Talbot, was buried in Sanctuary Wood Cemetery. On the same street was Skindles café. A notice was hung by the front door of Talbot House saying "All rank abandon, ye who enter here" and there was always an urn of tea on the go. For the more religious, the loft was used as a chapel.

At the end of the month they moved to Ypres, where Richard Hesketh recalled they were billeted in the cells under the ruins of the Cloth Hall. After a couple of days they moved again to a slightly safer location, an Ecole (school) East of Ypres. Their first task was to dig a fire trench in Zouave Wood to the South East of the Menin Road. The battalion was to be heavily involved in the preparations for the defence of Zouave Wood.

On the night of 3rd/4th June the battalion was detailed to dig a new fire trench. 'D' Company would be on the left, then 'A', 'B' and 'C' to the right. The work on the left started work about 11 p.m. but on the right it was delayed until about midnight. The trench was to consist of a series of firebays, each 9 yards long, with 4 yard traverses between. Only the firebays were to be dug. 'D', 'A' and 'B' were to dig 20 firebays each with 'C' Company digging up to 17 firebays and 2 strong points. Between them they dug a trench 3 feet deep with 77 fire bays and two strong points.

'D' and 'A' Companies went up via Bond Street, turning north when they reached the Front Line, until they reached the end of the wood. 'B' and 'C' Companies went up via Vince Street and Lovers Walk. The men were told to move forward in shirt sleeves, carrying rifle, bayonet, bandolier, respirator, a shovel and 15 sandbags. Every fourth man was to carry a pick. A reserve of 10 men per Company was held back under Lieut. Ridsdale. The work went well so they continued and dug 24 traverses. The company on the left was subjected to heavy shelling with up to 60 shrapnel and high explosive shells landing. On the way back from the work they were hit by a gas shell barrage.

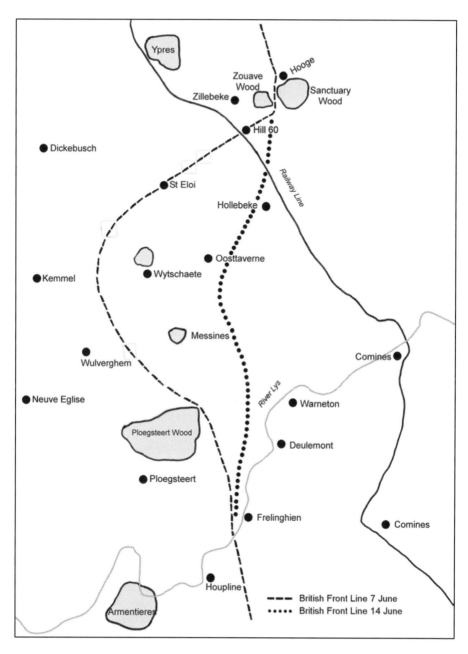

The Battle of Messines, 7 - 14 June 1917

Alan Champion wrote:

"Got past Hellfire Corner & found they were plastering Ecole with gas. I tried the railway cutting - that was full of gas."

Although they put on their respirators the men still inhaled the gas and several had to go to hospital. Most could not work for the next 24 hours. Alan Champion again:

"Stinking night but men stuck it very well indeed."

The German shrapnel had caused one casualty in 'A' Company; Private Richard Hesketh. He hadn't been back with the battalion long after being hit in the thigh by shrapnel at Givenchy not long after the Somme action. While billeted at the Cloth Hall he had attended a short sermon given by the Chaplain, followed by a hymn. During this, a piece of plaster dropped on to his elbow. It was this elbow that was shattered by the shrapnel. Hesketh always thought it a strange coincidence. He was evacuated from Ypres and spent some months in a Reading hospital before being discharged as no longer fit for war service. It took several years for him to get the strength back in his arm.

Hesketh's wound was known as a 'Blighty One'. These were wounds that were serious enough for the man to be sent to England but not life threatening. 'Blighty' came from the Hindu word bilayati, meaning a foreign land, and was used to refer to Britain. It was yet another word brought back from India by soldiers before the war. In England the wounded soldier would wear a special hospital uniform known as 'Hospital Blues'. This consisted of a blue single-breasted jacket with a white lining and facings. It was worn open at the neck with blue trousers, a white shirt and a red tie. Curiously there were no pockets. The uniform was completed by the man's own service cap with its regimental badge. Once fit enough, the man would be sent to a Base Depot in France, often at Rouen or Etaples. After refresher training he would be sent to a battalion, frequently different from the one he had previously served with. Those that did not recover sufficiently were discharged and issued with a Silver War Badge. This was worn on civilian clothes to show they had served and to protect them from women with white feathers.

The French Nivelle Offensive in April had failed to achieve its ambitious aims. The offensive at Messines would force the German Army to move forces to Flanders, away from the Arras and Aisne fronts, and relieve the pressure on the French. The objective was to capture the German defences on a ridge that ran from Ploegstreet Wood through Messines and Wytschaete and deprive the Germans of the high ground south of Ypres. It would be a prelude to the much larger Third Battle of Ypres. The front of the attack ran from St. Yves to Mount Sorrel, a distance of about 10 miles.

On the opening day of the Battle of Messines, 7 June, John McCormack, the Frank Sinatra of his day, recorded a song that was to become very popular on the Western Front. Called "There's a Long, Long Trail" its chorus went:

There's a long, long trail a-winding
Into the land of my dreams,
Where the nightingales are singing
And a white moon beams.
There's a long, long night of waiting
Until my dreams all come true;
Till the day when I'll be going down
That long, long trail with you.

The battle was to begin with the detonation at 3.10 a.m. of 19 huge mines in tunnels dug under the German lines. The Germans had been counter-mining in the same place but didn't reach the British tunnels in time. Over a million pounds of explosives were used for the mines. Immediately after, the artillery barrage began and the infantry went forward. By 7 a.m. New Zealand troops had captured Messines. Before midday Irish Divisions had fought their way through the defences of Wytschaete. The final attack took place in the afternoon when the village of Oosttaverne was captured. In all 7,200 Germans were taken prisoner and 67 guns captured.

The battalion spent June digging assembly trenches and maintaining the roads in the Divisional Area. This was a considerable task, as the roads were continually being damaged from being heavily shelled with high explosive and gas from 8 to 13 June. On the 12th they had suffered 26 casualties in their billets and the battalion moved out to the Railway Dugouts. These were about 2 Km southeast of Ypres and 2 Km west of Zillebeke, where the railway ran on an embankment overlooking a farmstead known to the troops as Transport Farm. Around this time a number of men returned to the battalion after being attached to the New Zealand Tunnelling Company for work on the Arras Caves.

Before the war Private James Heyes had lived at Coal Pit Lane Farm in Bickerstaffe where he worked for his parents. He'd already had a lucky escape in the Somme Offensive when a shell fragment hit him on the breast pocket. The pocket contained a notebook that took the force of the blow and saved him from serious injury. On 26 June he was on duty at the railway embankment when he was caught in a heavy artillery bombardment and killed. That same day Carl Champion recorded they had been shelled in the afternoon and the corner of the mess hut had been hit. He wrote in his diary:

"Stove and dinner gone west - also my pyjamas."

The next day the battalion moved to an area near Chateau Segard. This was between Dickebusch and Ypres. The chateau had been used as H.Q. for many units fighting at Polygon Wood and was now a ruin.

At the end of June, the battalion War Diary records:

"During the month the Battalion suffered a very large number of casualties, one Officer being killed, one wounded and died of wounds later, and three other Officers wounded, one of whom is still on duty. Other Ranks: killed 17, wounded 88, wounded still on duty 38. These figures do not include gas cases or shell-shocked cases."

The entry was signed by Carl Champion; the officer who had been killed was his brother Eric.

The beginning of July was occupied with the usual work. 'A' Company cleaned, repaired and drained 310 yards of trench in Zillebeke Street and Vince Street. 'B' Company dug 270 yards of trench between the junction of Vince Street and Border Lane and the junction of Lovers Walk and Goulrock Street. 'C' Company was finishing a communications trench from Wellington Crescent to 'D' Trench. 'D' Company was finishing off the trench named Fenn Lane which needed an extra parapet 4 sandbags high and the trenchboards laying.

The following week was more trench digging between Bite Street and Wellington Crescent, and 300 yards of Vince Street were dug. 'A' Company had a change from trenches as they were put to work on roads; filling 138 shell holes and 6 craters as well as erecting and repairing screens.

On 7 July Lieut. John Culshaw heard that his sentence of dismissal from the Army had been commuted to a severe reprimand. He had been court-martialled earlier in the year.

12 July, 1917, saw the first use of mustard gas, fired by the Germans at the British near Ypres. More than 50,000 shells were fired, affecting more than 2,000 Allied soldiers and killing 87. In the next three weeks the Germans fired a million gas shells, killing 500 more soldiers and incapacitating several thousand, but they were unable to break through the British lines. The British retaliated on 17 July, firing 100,000 gas shells containing chloropicrin, and causing 75 German deaths. This retaliation led to no breakthrough either.

Haig was now able to turn his full attention to the Ypres Salient.

The 13th century Cloth Hall in the ruined city of Ypres, September 1916
[Imperial War Museum, © IWM (Q 29056)]

The captured village of Wytschaete, 8 June 1917
[Imperial War Museum, © IWM (Q 5460)]

The destruction of Oosttaverne Wood, 11 June 1917
[Imperial War Museum, © IWM (Q 2304)]

German trenches on the ridge at Messines, 11 June 1917
[Imperial War Museum, © IWM (Q 2311)]

A German shrapnel shell explodes in Ploegsteert Wood, 20 June 1917
[Imperial War Museum, © IWM (Q 2313)]

The ruins of Chateau Segard
[Imperial War Museum, © IWM (Q 546)]

Passchendaele

For much of July the battalion was engaged in tasks connected with the coming Third Battle of Ypres, now commonly known as Passchendaele. The month had begun badly with the men being shelled in their billets on 3 July and the Dump being blown up the day after. On 21 July 'C' and 'D' Companies moved to Chateau Sigard.

The coming battle was for control of the ridges south and east of Ypres. Passchendaele was on the last ridge east of Ypres, and five miles from a railway junction that was important to the German supply chain. Haig had wanted a major offensive in Flanders for a long time and the success of the attack at Messines Ridge provided encouragement. There was a two week bombardment prior to the attack during which 4½ million shells were fired at the Germans. Once again aircraft had been used as spotters to improve accuracy. The bombardment and the flatness of the ground meant that the Germans knew an attack was coming.

On 27 July the German forward defences were found to be unoccupied at one point in the line. This allowed Allied troops to cross the Yser Canal and take up positions in the enemy's old trenches near Boesinghe. During the night, a number of bridges were put across the canal which assisted the troops on the 31st. From 31 July to 2 August the Division was involved with the first stage of Third Ypres, the Battle of Pilckem Ridge. 30th Division was to assault the enemy on their front.

Three platoons of 'D' Company were to work on strong points under Major Clavering of 200th Field Company Royal Engineers. Each strong point had to hold two platoons. The other platoon of 'D' Company was to maintain the artillery track from Zillebeke past Yeomanry Post and back to Zillebeke. This platoon would have to leave their billets three hours before the attack to be in place in time.

'B' Company was to prepare a track for artillery from Observatory Ridge Road to a forward area. A reconnoitering party had to start out an hour earlier to find the best way. No Man's Land was waterlogged and the track needed to be kept below the sky line. The company was to leave their billets an hour after the attack began.

'A' Company was to work on Light Railways under the orders of Fifth Army, while 'C' Company were kept in Divisional Reserve.

2nd Lieuts. Corman and Mercer, along with Privates Longworth and Thompson of 'B' Company, Private Henderson of 'C' Company, and Privates

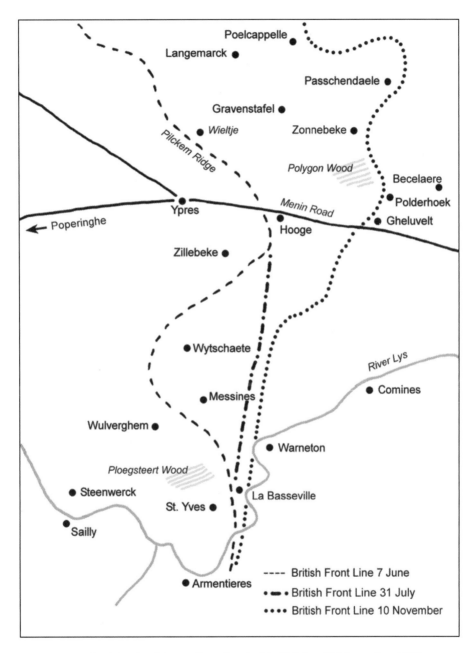

The Third Battle of Ypres (Passchendaele), 31 July - 10 November 1917

Finney, Martin and Johnson of 'D' Company were detailed to signpost the German trenches under Lieut. McCallum of the Royal Engineers.

The parties had to carry picks and shovels as well as 5 sandbags and 2 grenades per man and, of course, their rifles. The officers were instructed to wear private's tunics with pieces of red ribbon on the shoulder straps to identify them as officers. This was to make them less of a target for German snipers who were always on the lookout for officers. The parties had to report progress every two hours, and 'B' Company was to report as soon as the track was open for artillery. A relay system of runners was set up for reporting, with posts in Railway Dugouts, in a Sap near the old headquarters, and near the centres of the brigades.

Royal Engineers' Dumps had been set up at Border Lane and Valley Cottages. The Advanced Dressing Stations were at Dorny, Valley Cottages, Woodcote House, and forward areas. Water points were established at Zillebeke Lake, Maple Copse, and wells at Crab Crawl Dugouts. The forward areas also held ammunition dumps and bomb stores, with a reserve ammunition dump at Bedford House.

Major Carl Champion was in command at the time and he ordered Major Beal, Captain Dixon, Captain Hodges and 2nd Lieut. Ridsdale, the Lewis Gun Officer, to remain in the Advanced Corps Reinforcement Camp.

The Pioneers were tasked with opening up tracks so that transport and guns could move up to the captured ground. They were also to assist the Royal Engineers in the construction of strong points just behind the new British front line. Normally, making and maintaining tracks would be no problem, but this time there was torrential rain and the tracks became quagmires. A shortage of hard material to fill in shell holes and trenches added to the difficulties. Little could be done except mark out the tracks and bridge old trenches. Added to this, the working parties were also shelled constantly.

'B' Company was working on a track from Observatory Ridge Road to Stirling Castle. All along this track the mud was over the boot tops, but by 7 p.m. it was open for light guns as far as the old German front line. Owing to heavy fire from German machine guns and snipers, attempts to work beyond the ridge in daylight had to be abandoned. 'C' Company, which had been in reserve, continued the work on the track while 'B' Company slept in trenches near the work. The intention was to push it as far forward as they could for use by mules. Both companies continued the work the next day, returning to camp the following evening. One man had been killed, and one officer and 30 men wounded.

'D' Company was split between working on an artillery track out from Zillebeke and constructing strong points with 200th Field Company of the

Royal Engineers. The track was successfully opened and put into use, and three strong points were built despite heavy shelling. During the course of this work, 20 men were wounded.

On 31 July, the attacking brigades had fought their way through Shrewsbury Forest and Sanctuary Wood, capturing Stirling Castle, Hooge and the Bellewaarde Ridge. Scottish troops took Verlorenhoek and Frezenberg. By 9 a.m. the second line of objectives had been achieved with the exception of a strong point near Frezenberg, known as Pommern Redoubt. A little later this was taken by 55th Division, the West Lancashire Territorials that included the St. Helens Battalion, 1/5th South Lancs. The first day had gone well with objectives achieved and over 6,100 Germans taken prisoner.

The battalion stayed in the Chateau Segard area, working on forward tracks, until 5 August when they marched to Reninghelst. From there they went to Strazeele, staying there until 11 August when they marched to Epsom Camp for some training. On 16 August the battalion moved to Vierstraat to begin work on the Messines Ridge Defences. Six days later and they moved again; this time to Spy Farm, for work on Manchester Street (a forward communications trench), forward roads and camouflage. Around this time Major Carl Champion saw Ypres from a new perspective when he flew over at 6,000 feet. Two weeks or so later Carl Champion heard he was now a Lt-Col.

Between 24 July and 4 August, the battalion's casualties were 4 other ranks killed, and 2 officers and 70 other ranks wounded. On 1 August Sergeant Edward Ashby died of wounds. Originally from Leicester, he was working as a Picture Operator when he enlisted in September 1914. He left a wife, Emily, and four children.

The weather now began to worsen, with rain falling heavily. It continued without respite for four days, turning the clayey soil into a sea of mud. This was impassable except for a few tracks that were targeted by the enemy. To leave a track meant to risk death by drowning, and men were lost in this way. The offensive ground to a halt until the middle of August when the weather improved a little. On 15 August, Canadian troops attacked and took the strongly fortified Hill 70 near Lens. On the following day the outskirts of Langemarck were reached. Wet weather again set in, reducing operations to small attacks near Ypres.

The beginning of September saw an improvement in the weather and preparations for the next attack proceeded. At 5.40 a.m. on the 20th the assault was launched. On the right, 19th Division achieved their objectives, 39th Division pushed through the valley of Bassevillebeek, while 41st Division advanced up the slopes of Tower Hamlets. 23rd Division captured Veldhoek. On the left Australians took Glencorse Wood and then Polygonveld. From 13

September 11th South Lancs were erecting Nissen Huts near Kemmel, and on 17 September one platoon began preparing winter quarters for the battalion. On 26 September, Australian troops took Polygon Wood, while 3rd Division took Zonnebeke village. On 30 September the Germans had reorganised and launched counter-attacks using flame throwers. These were repulsed at great loss.

Early October saw the weather worsen again. 9 October saw the British attack on a 9 mile front from Zonnebeke to the junction with the French near Langemarck. By early afternoon the Allies were on the outskirts of Houthulst Forest. The push towards Passchendaele continued.

During the month, one of the men was informed that the Army would no longer issue separation allowance to his wife as she had been convicted the previous month of assisting in the management of a brothel. The allowance for their child would continue but would, in future, be issued in trust to another person. The man was also informed that he no longer had to give any of his pay to his wife if he didn't want to. Sadly, this wasn't the first time she had been convicted while he'd been away.

The same month saw the accidental death of Private Richard Melling, a 25 year old single man from Billinge. Although not married he had a fiancée, Margaret Cunliffe, living with their daughter Gladys on Rainford Road. On the afternoon of the 21st Melling had gone with Lance-Corporal Derbyshire to watch a football match at the Divisional ground. Afterwards they had gone to Danoutre for tea and some drinks. About eight o'clock they set off back to camp. After about a quarter of a mile, Melling stopped to relieve himself and told Derbyshire he'd catch him up. Derbyshire didn't see him again and told the subsequent Board of Inquiry that Melling "was far from drunk". Some hours later Corporal Carter of the A.S.C. was in charge of three lorries going from Bailleul to Lindenhoek via Danoutre and about a quarter of a mile from Daylight Corner saw a body lying in the road. The lorries pulled up and Carter finding the man was dead moved the body to the side of the road. He sent to Daylight Corner for someone from Traffic Control. The man who came was Private Creswell, who seeing the body was of a man from 11th South Lancs sent a report to the battalion. The body was examined by Captain Giles, an R.A.M.C. officer attached to the battalion. He concluded that Melling had been struck from behind and knocked down by a heavy vehicle, and that death must have been instantaneous. Lt-Col. Fenn decided that Melling himself was to blame but he was overruled by Major-General Williams who thought it was simply an accident when he reviewed the findings.

On the night of 26 October, near Kemmel, 2nd Lieut. Holmes and 5 men went out on patrol to reconnoitre an enemy post at Bang Farm. Leaving at 12.30 a.m. they moved towards the German lines. When they approached the

German wire they saw Germans only 25 yards away carrying materials and digging in very muddy ground. The patrol remained stationary until sometime later when they examined the trenches, finding many of them had fallen in and were disused.

The following night, Lieut. Owen and his party had a lucky escape when out on patrol. They had gone out from Post No. 13 to reconnoitre the ground towards the Verne Road where they came across a double belt of concertina barbed wire, each belt about 3 yards apart. Seeing a German working party only 30 yards ahead, they had to quickly and quietly retreat.

On the night of 28 October, 2nd Lieut. Holmes with one N.C.O. and 9 men went out again to reconnoitre Bang Farm and if possible take a German prisoner. When they had got about 20 yards past the British wire they saw an enemy party, 15 to 20 strong, moving to and fro near Verne Road. Holmes and the N.C.O. advanced to get a closer view with the men protecting their flanks. As they were outnumbered nothing much could be done except observe that the German party was protected by 3 groups of double sentries behind trees on the Verne Road.

At the end of October 2nd Lieut. Alexander D. Walker had written to the Military Secretary asking for news of his brother, Lieut. George. H. Walker. His brother had left the Pals in the middle of 1916 when he was attached to the Royal Flying Corps. While flying a Sopwith with 45 Squadron in July he had been seen going down near Polygon Wood and had been reported missing. Alexander Walker received a reply telling him that there was no definite news but a German aeroplane had dropped a message into the British lines which stated that he was "Wahrscheinlich Tot" (probably dead) but this was unconfirmed. He was never found.

At 6 a.m. on 6 November, Canadian troops captured the village of Passchendaele. In his report, Haig said:

> "The Field, Signal, Army Troops and Tramway Companies, together with Pioneer and Labour Battalions, from home and overseas, have played an increasingly important part, not only in preparation for our offensives, but also during the latter stages of the battles. The courage and enduring self-sacrifice displayed by all ranks, whether in the organisation of captured positions or in the maintenance of forward communications under heavy shell fire, are deserving of the highest praise."

The battalion moved back to the familiar Zillebeke sector on 8 November; then on the 13th to Salvation Corner, between Ypres and the infamous Hellfire Corner, where they took over from the Canadians. The following day work began on forward roads in the Passchendaele Sector to prepare them for moving artillery forward for a possible operation.

On 20 November Hugh Thomas, of 'C' Company, was killed in action. A miner from Elephant Lane and aged 26, he had married Mary Chisnall at St. John's, Ravenhead, whilst on leave in January. Hugh's brother, Robert, had been killed with 2nd Battalion South Lancs in 1915.

In early December families in St. Helens were once again invited to visit Santa's Grotto in Blacklers Stores. Parents were advised to take their children early before the big rush. The seasonal display was to be entitled "Somewhere in France" with tanks moving into action. This would "please their children immensely, and be a scene which will live long in their memory". The advert didn't say if Santa would be in military uniform.

In France, 28 December revealed the results of a salvage competition held by the Division's three infantry brigades. The idea was to salvage any articles they came across and value them at their cost price. The winners were 90th Brigade with salvage valued at £47,084. 89th Brigade had managed £42,446 and 21st Brigade £41,114. The total came to £130,618, the equivalent of about £7.5 million today.

On the last day of the year, Lance-Sergeant John Potter heard he had won the Distinguished Conduct Medal. It was for devotion to duty on many occasions, but mainly for when he had volunteered to lead a party to rescue four men buried in a tunnel. The rescue succeeded despite heavy enemy shelling.

Shelled ground over which troops went in the Passchendaele attack, 1917
[Imperial War Museum, © IWM (Q 10498)]

British stretcher bearers in the ruins of Pilckem, 31 July 1917
[Imperial War Museum, © IWM (Q 2630)]

Operation Michael

1918 began with sugar rationing in Britain. In the last weeks of 1917 food stocks had been getting low because of the German U-boat blockade. In the coming April rationing would be introduced for meat, bacon, butter and margarine.

The Pals were occupying dugouts at Zillebeke Bund and Railway Dugouts, with the Transport at Dickebusch. On 4 January they started moving again, first to Amiens where they entrained for Longeau; then a march to Nelse, arriving on the 19th. They were to take over part of the line from the French, working under the orders of C.R.E. 5th Army. The sector was astride the River Oise and in front of the St. Gobain Massif. On 25 January, one officer and six Lewis Gun Teams were moved to Villers-St-Christophe and Ham for anti-aircraft duties.

Sport came to the fore again in early February when 'D' Company arranged a football tournament. In the first round No. 15 Platoon beat No. 13, and No. 14 beat No. 16. The final took place on a fine day and drew a crowd from all of the neighbouring units. Even some of the local "belles" turned up. Excitement ran high amongst the more partisan spectators when the teams lined up by the referee, Sergeant-Major Harrison.

14th Platoon: In goal, Lieut. J. R. Cole; full backs, Privates E. Wilmore and I. Edwards; half-backs, Privates J. Moran, R. Pilkington and Davies; forwards, Privates R. Melling (captain), T. Fenlon, Evans, Barnes and Connor.

15th Platoon: In goal, Private A. Winstanley; full backs, Lance-Corporal Hughes and Private J. Pye; half-backs, Lance-Corporal D. Sumner, Private A. Woods and Lieut. B. F. Mackenzie; forwards, Corporal Price, Privates B. McCue, W. Swift, J. Gallagher and Tickle.

The *St. Helens Newspaper & Advertiser* reported the game:

"The sphere was given the initial kick by No. 15 Platoon, who opened out an attack in masterly style on the left. A well placed cross pass deceived the defence, and Pte. Tickle looked like going through, but Pte. Wilmore just managed to save and set his forwards going. "14" again pressed, and it was only the splendid saves of Pte. Winstanley which kept the "15" goal inviolate. The spectators were now treated with another good example of goal keeping, for Pte. Swift, getting possession, caught the "14" defence napping, got through and sent in a beautiful drive which, however, was smothered and cleared in the approved Roose style by Lieutenant Cole. Corpl. Price at outside left for "15" repeatedly gave "14's" defence trouble by tricky work, and from one of his centres a scramble took place in front of "14's" goal, and the back was penalized. The resultant penalty, however, proved unfruitful. The "15" backs, Lce.-Corpl. Hughes and Pte. Pye did some sturdy work, and the latter relieved with a huge kick just as the whistle tootled for a well-earned rest, the score board reading: 14th Platoon, 0; 15th Platoon, 0.

After "lemons" the game re-started with renewed vigour. "14" again taking the initiative with a sparkling movement down field. The attack was again nipped in the bud by Pte. Pye, who once again proved himself a tower of strength. The situation looked ominous for "14" when they were awarded a free kick. This relieved matters somewhat, and "14's" forwards got going nicely, but ruined what would have been a good opportunity by over-eagerness. Pte. Woods changed the zone of action with a well directed kick, and this put "15" in an offensive position. The game was hotly contested in the vicinity of "14" penalty area for a few minutes, and eventually Pte. Tickle, from a melee, netted with a fast shot. The excitement was now intense, and on the resumption "14" made a determined assault, but found the defence solid. A splendidly fought game thus ended with 15th Platoon the victors by one goal to nil.

It is indicative of the spirit of sportsmanship displayed when the various players of rival sides left the field congratulating one another on the splendid game played. St. Helens should be proud of producing such splendid sportsmen and fighting men."

In mid-February, 'A' Company H.Q. and one platoon were at Roupy, one platoon at Dury, one at Aubigny and the other in a forward area. 'B' Company H.Q. and all platoons were at Savy Wood. 'C' Company H.Q. and three platoons were at Roupy, and one platoon at Fluquieres. 'D' Company was at Savy Wood. The Savy-Roupy area was opposite St. Quentin. 'C' and 'D' Companies would spend the second half of the month working with the R.E. preparing a defensive line. At this time the average strength of a pioneer battalion was 28 officers and 760 other ranks, which was higher than many infantry battalions.

On 23 February, 30th Division took over the front line near St. Quentin in the area of Manchester Redoubt. The redoubt at Manchester Hill had been named after its capture by 2nd Battalion of the Manchesters in 1917. The redoubt commanded a field of fire overlooking St. Quentin. The front was held by two brigades, each utilising one battalion for the front, with the other two digging trenches in the battle zone and in training. A German attack was expected and the battalion, if attacked, had orders to fight under the nearest unit if they were in the Forward Zone; otherwise they were to withdraw to Etrevillers. In the Division, up to 1,800 men were on leave on any one day due to an increase in the leave allotment. Others were away on courses, leaving the fighting strength depleted. None of the infantry battalions had over 600 men on the day of the attack.

By the end of February the forward zone trenches were nearly complete but the battle zone tranches had only been marked out. All battalions in the Division were at work each day in the trenches. As well as digging they had regular training, either attacking or defending the very same trenches.

Not long after, the Army reorganised infantry brigades and battalions reducing the numbers each comprised. In 89th Brigade, the 20th King's was disbanded and the men distributed amongst the three remaining battalions of Liverpool Pals. In 90th Brigade, the 17th Manchesters left and the 18th Manchesters was disbanded, leaving 16th Manchesters who were joined by 2nd Royal Scots Fusiliers and 2nd Bedfords. 21st Brigade retained 2nd Yorks and 2nd Wilts. These were joined by 17th Manchesters to complete the new brigade. On 8 March, 11th South Lancs was reorganised from four companies down to three. No personnel were withdrawn as surplus men were "to be absorbed by natural attrition". In other words, casualties would take care of any excess numbers!

The Germans had been massing in St. Quentin and were about to launch the Kaiserslacht Offensive, also known as Operation Michael. This was their last chance of breaking through before the Americans started arriving in large numbers. The German objective was to capture the strategically important area of Amiens. This would divide the British and French armies and make a combined counter-attack impossible. While the Germans no longer expected to win the war, they wanted to be in a stronger position when the inevitable peace negotiations began. Sixty three German Divisions attacked along a 60 mile front held by 26 British Divisions. The St. Helens Pals were to be at the centre of the German attack. In the skies above was the legendary 'Red Baron', Manfred von Richthofen, flying with his squadron, Jagdstaffel 11, part of his 'Flying Circus'. Little more than a month later Richthofen would be shot down and killed near Amiens, aged 25.

On the morning of 21 March one company was in Savy Wood dug-outs, one company in Roupy, and one company split up between L'Epine de Dallon, Roupy and the back area. The German attack began at 4.30 a.m. in fog which helped them and lasted for five hours. At 4.40 a.m. 'Man Battle Stations' was ordered. Just after daybreak there was furious bombardment all along the front and in accordance with a pre-arranged plan, 11th South Lancs was concentrated in the village of Fluquieres. The company in Savy Wood lost heavily from high-explosive and gas shells. Manchester Hill Redoubt was held by 'D' Company of 16th Manchesters and H.Q. staff under the command of Lt-Col. Elstob. By 2 p.m. they were completely surrounded and engaged in hand to hand fighting.

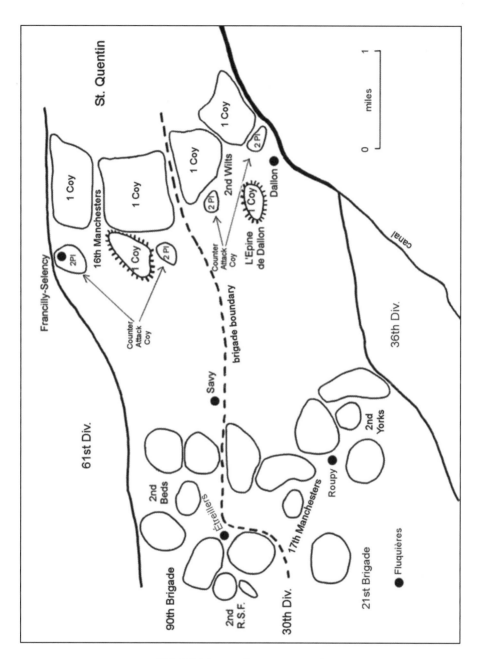

30th Division positions, 21 March 1918

At 3:00 p.m. the 11th South Lancs was ordered to withdraw to the quarry behind Aviation Wood. This was done and picquets posted on the east side. Shortly before 4 p.m. Elstob informed his Brigade the fight was all but over. Most of the men on Manchester Hill were dead or wounded. Three men of 11th South Lancs were in the redoubt, working as signallers; Private James McComas of 'B' Company, and Privates Stainsby and Walker. They maintained communications until the last moment when the redoubt fell. McComas was taken prisoner and sent to a camp at Giessen in Germany. When the war was over he returned to play for St. Helens Recs for ten seasons and was the landlord of the Queen's Arms on Higher Parr Street.

The Division ordered 200 men from the infantry battalions to move to Pithon for duty as additional stretcher bearers. By 7 p.m. the estimated casualties incurred by 21st and 90th Brigades, Pioneers and Machine Gun Sections was about 50 officers and 1,300 other ranks. About 7.30 p.m. Lt-Col. Fenn was informed that he was responsible for the battalion's defence; so a line was dug between Hill Wood and Aviation Wood.

On 22 March the battalion was placed at the disposal of 21st Brigade with orders to cover their retirement if necessary. Nothing was to be left for the Germans use if it could be prevented. The Division ordered the destruction of the Officers Clothing Store and the Corps Cartridge Dump was set on fire. 89th Brigade threw their spare clothing into the canal as there was no time to start fires. Infantrymen who had been attached to 172nd Tunnelling Company were recalled and attached to 89th Brigade for the defence of Ham. At 6:00 p.m. orders were received for 11th South Lancs to retire to Ham. At that time the enemy was just coming into view on the crest southeast of Aviation Wood On arrival at Ham the battalion was ordered to bivouac in one of the suburbs, Eppeville.

At 4:30 a.m. on the morning of 23 March, enemy machine-guns were heard. The Germans were in Ham and the Royal Engineers were waiting for the last troops to come through so they could blow up the bridge over the Nesle canal. Fenn sent to 89th Brigade for orders but by 7 a.m. none had been received. A large number of units had withdrawn down the Ham to Eppeville road including the 23rd Entrenching Battalion who said they had been holding the front line. Fenn then started the battalion down the same road. Shortly after he was informed that Canizy was being held and that 11th South Lancs was to hold the line of the canal. Before the battalion could get into trenches along the canal Fenn heard from 19th King's that the enemy had crossed the canal. He posted two companies on high ground to protect the right flank and one on the embankments of the Amiens railway. One Platoon was sent as a covering party to the Royal Engineers at the bridge; one Platoon was sent to the front to take up a position near the canal north of Eppeville and one platoon on the left towards Canizy while the remainder of the Battalion had breakfast on the road.

At 8 a.m. one company of 11th South Lancs was attached to each of the Division's three infantry brigades. About 10 a.m. Fenn heard that the enemy was massing on the north of the canal. Large numbers of enemy were now observed and there was heavy rifle fire. Just before 2 p.m. the company on the railway embankment reported the enemy was advancing on their right rear and on three sides of them, so was withdrawn to its former position. In the evening Fenn met the O.C.s of 182nd Brigade, the 23rd Entrenching Battalion, and a Composite Battalion. Between them they agreed to reorganize to hold a consecutive line. The Composite Battalion was holding a line near the Sucrerie. An attempt was made to get in touch with them by the right flank but this was unsuccessful. There was heavy machine gun fire straight down the railway line and shell and mortar fire on the railway cutting. Carl Champion later wrote in his diary:

> "23rd Made & manned trenches Eppeville - Canizy. Fought good fight about 1pm."

Carl Champion took charge of 'A' and 'C' Companies for the night. Estimated casualties for 30th Division were now 128 officers and 3,800 other ranks.

At 5 a.m. on 24 March it was considered too late to dig a new trench so the battalion was to withdraw to their old positions. By 7 a.m. troops were falling back on both flanks and two companies were nearly surrounded. Their only line of withdrawal was across a stream lined with barbed wire. At 8:30 a.m. the battalion withdrew and crossed the Nesle Canal near Moyencourt where they held trenches. Half an hour later the Germans attacked and broke through. The withdrawal continued during the day until noon when the battalion was ordered to hold a line near Libermont. About 3 p.m. they occupied the Ramecourt bridgehead. This was done until 6.30 p.m. when they were ordered to withdraw again and take up a line between Moyencourt and Cressy. By the evening of the 24th most troops were across Nesle Canal. By 10:00 p.m. the battalion was on its way to Roiglise which was reached by 5 a.m. on the 25th.

On the night of 24 March, Captain Harold Hodges had been sent out with his Company to get in touch with a battalion that had reported their position as being the Sucrerie on the outskirts of Ham. Hodges had been transferred to 11th South Lancs after his previous battalion, 3rd Monmouths, had been disbanded after its mauling in July 1916. He had been severely wounded at Ypres in 1915 and returned to duty even though not all the shrapnel had been removed from his body. The 24th was a misty night and it appears he left his company in a railway cutting and went on to the Sucrerie with only one of his subalterns. He entered the building by himself expecting to find British troops but came upon Germans. He used his revolver on them until he was shot down. His subaltern was also wounded but managed to get away in the darkness, reaching the railway cutting. Hodges was reported as missing believed killed, and in September information was received from the Germans confirming his death.

It was also during this fighting that Corporal John Davies won the Victoria Cross. This occurred near Eppeville, about 11 miles south-west of St Quentin. 21st Brigade and 11th South Lancs were dug in in front of the village of Esmery Hallon. After heavy shelling, the Germans advanced from Ham; crossing the river at Canizy. By 8.30 a.m. two of the South Lancs companies were almost surrounded. To escape they had to retire across a stream barricaded with barbed wire. They were saved by the heroic actions of the battalion Lewis gunners. During this, 22 year old Davies remained behind with a Lewis gun to provide cover for his comrades and hold up the enemy as long as possible. To gain a better field of fire he mounted a parapet, fully exposing himself to the enemy. In later years when Davies was asked for his reaction to being left behind he said it was "Oh sod off you lot". This was the last the battalion saw of him, on Palm Sunday, 24 March. He had already been wounded twice prior to this. According to the citation he was presumed killed but, in fact, he had been taken prisoner and was freed on New Year's Day 1919. It is believed that John Davies is the only man to have been awarded a posthumous V.C. and to later receive it in person. His medals are now on display in the Imperial War Museum, London. They were a gift from his daughter, Mrs. Eunice Swift. Carl Champion was awarded the D.S.O. for his work on the same day.

On 25 March the battalion withdrew to Roi Eglise and Lt.-Col. Fenn was ordered to take command of a Divisional Composite Battalion made up of men from several units including 11th South Lancs. At 5 p.m. the Composite Battalion was ordered to make a 15 mile march to Plessier where it was billeted at 1 a.m. At 10 a.m. on the 26th Fenn took the Composite Battalion to take up a line between Rouvroy and Le Quesnel, staying for a short time in trenches with 89th Brigade. Along the way as many men as possible were returned to their units. On arrival the O.C. 89th Brigade ordered Fenn to hold a line in old trenches with his left flank in front of Rouvroy. By 2 p.m. 19th King's had arrived on his right. Soon after, a battalion of the Royal Warwickshire Regiment was in touch on his left. At 8 p.m. 150 men of 17th King's were sent to help hold the line in front of Rouvroy. Fenn realised that a number of old communications trenches ran between the enemy and his front line so he had them filled in for 100 yards. Patrolling had to be carried on all night. The Brigades were moved back; 21st Brigade to La Neuville, 89th to Le Plessier, and 90th to Arvilliers.

At 8.50 a.m. on the 26th, 30th Division was ordered to take up a line from Rouvroy to Le Quesnoy, with strong points on the Amiens to Roye road near Buchoire. 11th South Lancs were attached to 89th Brigade. At 5.40 p.m. Divisional Order No. 160 was issued. 90th Brigade was to be on the right, 89th Brigade on the left and 21st Brigade in reserve. The intention was to delay the enemy for as long as possible. The order stated "Present positions must be held at all costs".

27 March saw 17th King's withdraw behind Rouvroy about 10 a.m. without informing Fenn. He ordered his left Company to form a defensive flank and then reported to 89th Brigade. Support was needed as enemy snipers had occupied Rouvroy and were enfilading, firing along the length of, 11th South Lancs' trenches. Orders came for 11th South Lancs and 19th King's to withdraw in extended order, giving each other covering fire, until they reached a point south of Folies. There they got into Artillery Formation and withdrew to the quarry on the Roye to Amiens road, west of Folies. At the quarry Fenn was told the withdrawal was a mistake. The 11th South Lancs then joined several other battalions, including King's and Manchesters, in a counter-attack. They advanced to a line running from in front of Folies towards Arvillers, where they were held up by machine gun fire and trench mortars coming from Arvillers. The infantry battalions occupied old trenches while 11th South Lancs dug a support line about 300 yards behind.

On the following day, the Germans began to shell these positions and some men had to be moved to the left. At 11.30 a.m. the Royal Irish Rifles, on Fenn's right, withdrew and Fenn had to send men to defend the flank. Not much later all of 11th South Lancs and some of 19th King's were needed on the right to prevent the enemy moving forward from Arvillers. At 1.30 p.m. Fenn was informed they had been relieved by the French and were to withdraw to Rouvrel. The infantry brigades and the field companies were also concentrated at Rouvrel. 50 Lewis guns had been obtained by lorry from a gun park at Poix and were issued to the units at Rouvrel in anticipation of the Divisions being sent forward to support the French.

On 29 March, after a show by the Optimists, the battalion stayed the night at Rouvrel. The following day, the Division received orders to move and the Pals entrained at Saleux. From there they went to St. Valery sur Somme, arriving about midnight, and stayed at a rest camp. The Division was temporarily reorganised as one brigade with each of the former brigades making one composite battalion. The infantry brigades were reported as averaging only 500 strong. The casualties for the Division were now estimated at 218 officers and 5,245 other ranks. Mullaly's history of the South Lancashire Regiment records, for the 11th Battalion, that:

"... in the slowing down and eventual halting of the German advance [the Battalion] had played a very gallant part, and its magnificent fighting qualities are seen to be thrown into even brighter relief when it is remembered that its men had been for so long employed on solely pioneer work."

Whalley-Kelley in his history of the regiment said:

"Their magnificent fighting during these critical days is especially creditable when it is remembered that for the previous three years the unit had been engaged solely on "navvy" work; nevertheless, these men were first and foremost soldiers of the Prince of Wales's Volunteers, and, when there was need, they rose nobly to the occasion in accordance with the best traditions of the Regiment to which they belonged."

A week's fighting had cost the battalion 3 officers and 28 other ranks killed; 8 officers and 169 other ranks wounded; and 210 other ranks missing. The battalion had been reduced by about half its strength. Despite a Victoria Cross, one D.S.O., three M.C.s, two D.C.M.s and nine M.M.s, the battalion would be reduced to a cadre; a small group used for training others.

Private Lawrence Hannon, of Widnes, was killed on the 24th. He had enlisted with 'E' Company in May 1915 giving his age as 19 when it was in fact 16. He had been killed by gunshot wounds to his chest and "fell back into the arms of his mates".

One of the men taken prisoner was Private George Webster, a single man of Crispin Street. George found himself behind enemy lines during the retreat. He was with the Signals Section posted to a station at L'Epine de Dallon, a redoubt southwest of St. Quentin held by 50 men of the 2nd Wiltshires. They held out until 2.30 p.m. before being overrun. Nearly all were killed or captured with only half a dozen getting away to Roupy to carry the news. When the redoubt fell Webster was sitting in a dugout; noise and voices told him there were Germans outside. Sitting in near darkness, with only a small candle, a hand holding a revolver appeared in the doorway. He was ordered outside, rounded up with other prisoners, and transported to a camp in Germany. Other men taken prisoner were sent to Silesia, now part of Poland, to work in the salt mines.

A third signallers station at Savy dugouts with 5 Pals was captured by the Germans and the men taken prisoner. However, 17th Manchesters made a successful counter-attack and the men were freed.

During the fighting Captain John Pethick won the Military Cross for managing to withdraw his company across difficult ground while outflanked.

Later he had led a counter-attack, regained some ground, and held it under heavy trench-mortar and machine-gun fire. At some point he was injured and fell into water. Lance-Corporal Albert Atherton, a small man, jumped in under shell-fire, pulled Pethick out and carried him to safety. Atherton was awarded a Military Medal. Pethick did not forget this, and after the war he set Atherton up as manager of the Eureka pub off Scotland Road in Liverpool. It was a rowdy pub and Atherton would often jump over the counter to deal with the trouble-makers. He used to feel sorry for ex-soldiers and would give them free drinks, which led to him losing the pub. Atherton returned to St. Helens and a job as a glass blower at Pilkington Bros. Pethick would visit him at his Smithie Brow house, and his posh accent gave the neighbours something to talk about.

Another Military Cross was won by 2nd Lieut. John Acton, for setting "a fine example of courage" when during a counter-attack he went forward in the face of heavy machine gun and trench mortar fire. A third Military Cross was awarded to Lieut. Sydney Boulton. When the part of the line held by his company was heavily shelled and enfiladed by machine gun fire, he took command, moved his company forward and held the position. He had earlier withdrawn his company in the dark and under heavy gas and high explosive shell fire.

Two men had won the Distinguished Conduct Medal. The first was Regimental Sergeant Major John Harrison for setting a fine example of high courage and coolness under fire. He had reorganised and fought scattered troops throughout the whole battle. The other was Lance-Corporal William Twinning who had jumped up on the parapet of his trench when the enemy had got to within 10 yards, and shot one of them. Later he killed several others in hand to hand fighting. Eventually, when they were nearly surrounded, he withdrew his platoon with great skill and coolness.

The battalion received an official German list of dead that named men fallen and buried on 25 March 1918 near La Folie Ferms, South West of Ham. This was followed on 24 April by the men's identity discs sent in by a German Grenadier Regiment. The discs were accepted as "sufficient evidence of death for official purposes". In 1919 these men were exhumed and reburied in Ham British Cemetery, Muille-Villette. This cemetery began in January-March, 1918, as an extension of Muille-Villette German Cemetery, made by the 61st (South Midland) Casualty Clearing Station. In 1919 these graves were regrouped and others were added from the German Cemetery and from other burial grounds. There are nearly 500 1914-18 war casualties commemorated on this site. Of these, almost half are unidentified.

On 29 March, Private Frederick Pendlebury died of his wounds at a Red Cross Hospital in Rouen. He had been in Savy Wood on the 21st when the attack began. After an hour long barrage finished, he and others started to vomit, and put on their respirators. The barrage continued and men started making their way to a clearing station in Ham. A few hours later they began to vomit again and were put into lorries for Albert. By late evening Frederick was in hospital in Rouen, where he seemed comfortable and cheerful. His brothers separately managed to get passes to go and see him. His younger brother, Harold (in the Field Artillery) went to see him on the 24th. Harold spent the day with him but had to return to his unit. A nurse told Harold she thought he would recuperate and be sent to England. Frederick's other brother, Les, arrived on the 28th. He told his family that Frederick had looked very sick; having large blisters, and difficulty breathing. Even the slightest movement was painful. Les, too, had to return to his unit. Frederick died on the morning of Good Friday and was buried at St. Sever Cemetery in Rouen. Before the war Frederick had worked at Pilkington Bros. sheet works. He had been a devout Anglican, and a pianist, playing regularly at church. During his time in France he had made it to Paris twice.

That same day there was a show by the Optimists concert party to lift everyone's spirits. The next day they entrained for a rest camp near St. Valery sur Somme where they spent a few days reorganizing before moving to a camp just north of Poperinghe.

In the last ten days of March 30th Division's casualties were 218 officers and 5,245 other ranks. The fighting strength of the infantry units was now estimated at only about 3,000. On 11 April Field Marshall Douglas Haig issued a Special Order of the Day that included:

> "There is no other course open to us but to fight it out. Every position must be held to the last man; there must be no retirement. With our backs to the wall, and believing in the justice of our cause, each one of us must fight on to the end."

The following day Zeppelin L61 bombed Bold. This was the second of only two Zeppelin raids on Lancashire. The pilot reported to his superiors that he had bombed Sheffield!

Although Operation Michael had looked like succeeding, the British 3rd Army had held. The Germans had recaptured all of the ground they had lost during the Battle of the Somme the previous year and moved even further forward. However, they had been prevented from capturing Arras and Amiens which were their main objectives.

On 16 April some German soldiers resting near Esmery-Hallon about 15 kilometres southeast of Ham heard that the body of a British soldier was lying nearby. In the afternoon they found the body in a field. From his uniform they realised he was a British officer, and found his name sown on some of his clothing. The body had wounds to the head and right leg. They dug a grave for him and put up a wooden cross. The British officer was Lieut. John Cuthbert Lidgett, aged 32. Lidgett's family found out about this in 1919 when they received a letter from the Germans involved that came via the Red Cross in Geneva. The Germans had also sent a map they had drawn so the burial place could be found. Lidgett's body was recovered and reburied in Ham British Cemetery.

22 to 27 April was Tank Week in St. Helens; part of a national campaign to raise money for tanks, as each one cost £5,000. The Mayor had arranged the event saying:

> "Many Lancashire towns have each subscribed over £1,000,000 during their week of the current Tank campaign, and arrangements have been made for a Tank to be in St. Helens."

It came into the town by train and was kept in the goods yard until the Monday when it proceeded to some vacant land at the top of Bickerstaffe Street. Here there was a display of "the weird and wonderful things that Tanks can do", culminating with "the great event was its perambulation over a sandbag parapet". The Tank then moved to Victoria Square to take up its position for the week. It was named "Drake" and the people of St. Helens were told it had been over the top three times in France. If fact the tanks used as travelling tank banks were training machines from Bovington Camp in Dorset. Normally identified by numbers, they had been given names as this was thought to have more propaganda value. Lieut. Rennick M.C. was in charge of 'Drake', and it had "a strong military guard" day and night. At 12.30 the Mayor opened Tank Week and everyone was invited to being their friends and their money. A travelling postal hut accompanied the tank. Here the public could invest in War Bonds and War Savings Certificates. A person making an investment took his book to the tank and inside the tank the book was stamped.

Tank Week ended with a huge parade on the Saturday. Over five thousand munitions girls, followed by tableaux on foot and on vehicles. The most elaborate came from Cowley Hill Works with themes such as "Our Fallen Heroes" and "Death of Nelson". Forsters Works' procession was headed by a steam lorry with a load of 13-pounder shells. The Ministry of Munitions Inspection Bond 1201 had over 2,500 employees there. With Boy Scouts and bands the procession ended up over a mile in length. It ended as "a sea of faces" in Victoria Square where the Mayor addressed the crowd from on top of the tank, thanking them. In all over £500,000 was raised.

On the last day of April the battalion strength was recorded as 23 officers and 494 other ranks. Major Carl Champion had been invalided to England and Captain, soon to be Major, Pethick took over as second in command.

Local newspapers were now printing requests from wives and mothers for news of their loved ones missing since the German attack in March.

"Lance-Corporal W. Atherton, 20795, of the St. Helens "Pals," is missing, and any information concerning him would be gladly received by his wife, who resides at 35, Atherton-street, St. Helens."

During the first week of May a meeting of the St. Helens and District Victuallers Association decided to stop the sale of pints in an effort to ration beer. The alternative would have been compulsory rationing to meet the wishes of the Ministry of Food.

The battalion moved from Rouvrel to a rest area near the coast at St. Valery sur Somme. From there they were sent to the Ypres Salient. On 10 May, near Lederzeele, the battalion heard that it was to be broken up, retaining only 10 officers and 51 other ranks. Two days later 300 men were transferred to the 19th Lancashire Fusiliers, with 300 men moving the other way. The men received by 11th South Lancs had come from several battalions of the Lancashire Fusiliers and been brought together in the 19th battalion shortly before the exchange.

Two days later, 7 officers and 381 other ranks of 11th South Lancs were transferred to the Base Camp at Etaples for dispersal to other units as reinforcements. The other ranks would include all of the men recently transferred in from the Lancashire Fusiliers. The officers were Captain Alan Champion, Captain Dunthorne, Lieut. Bretherton, Lieut. Symon, Lieut. Mackenzie, 2nd Lieut. Hurley, and 2nd Lieut. Harpur. The following day 11th South Lancs was reduced to a training cadre and Lt-Col. Fenn was sent to take over command of the 19th Lancashire Fusiliers. This was originally an infantry battalion of Salford Pals that had been converted to Pioneers at the end of July 1916. It now had 300 St. Helens Pals in its midst who were the survivors of the March fighting.

A few days later 11th South Lancs, now under the command of Major Pethick, moved from Beaumont Chateau, near Eu, to Touffreville where the American 110th Engineer Regiment, part of the U.S. 35th Division, was billeted. The remnants of the battalion were there to train the Americans. Work started on a G.H.Q. sector near Amiens. The Americans did not get on with the British. They didn't like British soldiers or officers. They didn't like British rations and they loathed tea at breakfast. It was almost impossible to get the men from Missouri and Kansas to drink tea at breakfast. A British mess sergeant said "but WE have ALWAYS drunk tea for breakfast". The American reply was "Maybe that's what is the matter with you". There were occasional fights, one of them caused by a joke doing the rounds at British headquarters and repeated by an N.C.O. to some Americans in Eu. "Did you know the next war is to be fought between the two yellow races? Yes, the Japanese and the Americans". The N.C.O. ended up in hospital. Perhaps because of these problems the battalion was then attached to 66th (2nd East Lancashire) Division when the American Division left for a French Army area.

On 30 June the battalion embarked at Boulogne, to return to England with 75th Brigade of 25th Division. This Division had itself been broken up to reinforce other Divisions, and was returned to England for rebuilding. On arrival at Folkestone they entrained for Aldershot. Some familiar units were also to join 25th Division as it rebuilt; 17th King's, 20th and 21st Manchesters.

In July the 6th Battalion South Wales Borderers became the Pioneers for 30th Division. Some of the 11th South Lancs men are known to have been transferred to the Borderers so it would seem that a number of men may have been retained by 30th Division perhaps to aid continuity.

The disease known as the Spanish Influenza had started to appear in the battalion. It also appeared in St. Helens at the beginning of July and disappeared about eight weeks later. Thirty seven people died from the disease or its complications. During the first weeks in October, the disease reappeared in a more virulent form. Although fatalities amongst children were small, it seemed that the infection was spread in the schools, and on 16 October all public elementary schools in St. Helens were closed. The influenza pandemic was worldwide and lasted until 1920. It got its name from the early affliction and large numbers of deaths in Spain in May 1918. All told as many as 500 million people may have been infected, with many more people dying than did in the Great War.

By now many of the Pals taken prisoner at St. Quentin were being forced to work in German salt mines. Thomas Rigby, a miner from Ellamsbridge Road, was one of these. He returned home, at the end of the war, with a heart weakness. Another was Timothy Cunningham, a miner of Boundary Road, who came home with Bronchitis and had difficulty working. Several men did not survive their captivity, dying in Germany either from their wounds or illness. After the war John Kenwright said they were not treated well as prisoners. All they had to eat was bread crusts, potato peelings and any leftovers from the Germans' meals. He also said that the Germans in the camp liked to make them run by shooting at their feet.

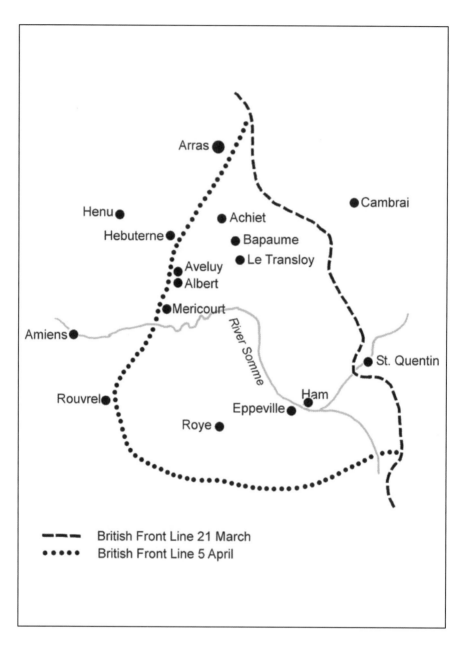

Operation Michael, March 1918

German Troops concentrating in St. Quentin prior to the March Offensive
[Imperial War Museum, © IWM (Q 55479)]

British Prisoners of War near St. Quentin, March 1918
[Imperial War Museum, © IWM (Q 51460)]

German pioneers bridging a crater in the battle area between St Quentin and Ham
[Imperial War Museum, © IWM (Q 55241)]

Harry Oswin Adams (centre) wearing Hospital Blues,
No. 3 General Hospital, Rouen, April 1918
[Norrette Moore]

The Road to Victory

On 3 July, 1918, 11th South Lancs was in the North Camp at Aldershot with Major Pethick in command. Major Carl Champion had rejoined the Regiment at Barrow after illness. The 3rd Battalion had been at Barrow for much of the war and it was used as a staging post for men returning to the regiment from sickness or wounds. While there the C.O. sent Carl Champion on a flying course at Worthy Down near Winchester. He was flying each day learning to spot shell bursts. In the middle of August, Champion was sent to Aldershot to take over command of 11th South Lancs from Pethick. The 18th Battalion South Lancs had been formed at North Walsham in Norfolk, largely from 'B' category men. The battalion was only in existence for about a week when it was absorbed by the re-formed 11th battalion. 11th South Lancs had been brought up to strength with men who had had no Pioneer training at all. According to local newspapers over 250 of the men in the 18th battalion were from St. Helens, so the re-formed 11th could still be considered to be a St. Helens battalion. It joined the 25th Division, 4th Army, under General Rawlinson, as Pioneers.

On 7 October the battalion sailed for France and moved to St. Riquier near Abbeville to join 25th Division. This Division was itself a reconstituted unit, having been broken up in June, and the Divisional H.Q. returned to England to begin rebuilding. Due to its involvement in the heaviest fighting, 25th Division was no longer in a fighting condition. Its remaining infantry were all drafted to other units and it needed to raise 10 new battalions. Its Pioneers, 6th South Wales Borderers, had been transferred to 30th Division to replace 11th South Lancs, the St. Helens Pals. 25th Division returned to France in September, moving to St Riquier, and was now engaged in the advance across Picardy. In the first four weeks at the front the Division suffered 46 casualties.

During the German retreat in autumn 1918, which was semi-open warfare, the British desperately tried to keep up with the Germans to prevent another defensive line of trenches being formed. That is exactly what happened on a 20 mile stretch of the Sambre-Oise Canal in Picardy. It became the last set piece battle of the war with more men going into battle than on the first day of the Somme.

In October the 19th Lancashire Fusiliers took part in an action near the village of Naves about 3 miles northeast of Cambrai. The village had been liberated by the Canadians on the 10th. Operating as infantry rather than as Pioneers, on the 13th, two companies, with a half company in reserve, went over the top at 8 a.m. on a misty morning. Their objective was Sauloir but they came under heavy machine gun fire and the advance was halted. Many of these men were ex 11th South Lancs men who had been transferred to the Fusiliers earlier in the year. Of the 320 men who took part, 260 became casualties. Of these 1 officer and 54 other ranks were killed with a further 7 other ranks later dying of their wounds. The casualties included 24 ex St. Helens Pals who are buried at Haspres Cemetery and another who is buried at York Cemetery, Haspres. All were killed in action on the same day, 13 October. The action was part of the Pursuit to the Selle where a battle would be fought on the 19th.

13 October also saw 11th South Lancs join up with 25th Division, moving to Premont that day. Its three companies were now commanded by Captains Taylor, Boulton and Askew. Work began the following day, together with the three Royal Engineers field companies, repairing bridges blown up by the enemy near Le Cateau. This was in preparation for the coming operations. There were a number of road and rail bridges crossing the River Selle and all had been destroyed. The objective was to get three forward routes through or near to Le Cateau and at least two tank bridges over the Selle. That day and the following one saw heavy rain and the roads became very muddy. Work started on clearing the roads from Premont to Serain, Serain to Elincourt, Elincourt to Avelu, and Avelu to Maretz. A Bridging Dump was established where the bridges were laid out and assembled. And launching gear made ready. One company of 11th South Lancs assisted the Engineers in the building of four permanent road bridges across the River Selle. The bridges had to be capable of carrying tanks. On the 16th, the battalion had two companies in Railway Cutting south of Mourois and one east of Reumont, preparatory to work in connection with operations by 13th Corps in the Le Cateau Sector the following day.

4th Army attacked on 17 October, with 50th Division making a crossing of the Selle. The enemy was still holding Le Cateau Station. A second attack on them failed. At the same time 66th Division took Le Cateau, though it was not yet clear of the enemy. The engineers made several attempts to work on the bridges but could not due to heavy machine gun fire. One company of Pioneers was clearing debris and the other two working on the Maretz to Le Cateau road. The attack was renewed the next day and Le Cateau taken and mopped up. 50th Division advanced and 74th Brigade took Bazuel. It was now possible to start work on the bridges. Working day and night, five bridges were ready by the afternoon of 19 October. A company of Pioneers had been working on No. 1 Bridge in half-company reliefs while subject to bursts of heavy shelling and much gas. Another company was clearing a passage to this bridge, making it passable for lorries. There was a violent bombardment and 1 man was killed and 2 officers and 11 men wounded and the company had to withdraw. 11th South Lancs were moved to St. Benin on 19 October with No. 1 Bridge being completed the next day.

On 20 October, the Division was holding the front from East of Le Cateau to East of Bazuel. They now had a lorry route on the Le Cateau road to

Honnechy and onwards. The road from Busigny to Honnechy was also open. 11th South Lancs were now improving a crossing the Engineers had made where the railway bridge on the route to Bazuel had been blown up. The road on from there became impassable to heavy traffic though as the rain fell.

From 20 to 22 October one company was clearing a blockage on a corduroy road going forward, working in 6 hour reliefs, to make the road to Bazuel practical for all transport. The blockage was finally free and the road open to lorry traffic on the 22nd. Another company was detailed to open a road for lorry traffic between Bazuel and Pommereuil. The third company was to open a road from a forward area to Pommereuil. A section of 182nd Tunnelling Company was searching the forward areas for mines especially looking for tank traps along the road out of Pommereuil and towards Fontaine. While this was happening, 11th South Lancs supplied a reconnaissance party to closely follow the advance and report back on the condition of all roads in the area.

On 23 October the Division attacked again. Pioneers were detailed to repairing roads in the forward areas. They did this successfully, clearing the road from Bazuel to Pommereuil, and the one from Le Cateau to Pommereuil. The enemy had failed to blow some bridges and the roads further forward were in better condition so the Pioneers had lighter work than before and in calmer conditions. The roads were kept open for all traffic during the day. The same day, 2nd Lieut. Robert Carr went missing whilst reconnoitering forward roads. He had been taken prisoner only 17 days after joining the battalion. He would be repatriated in December. Lance-Corporal Sydney Lord, a baker from Colne, was also taken prisoner and sent to a camp at Cassel in Germany.

This work continued through into 28 October. During this time the clearing of roads involved clearing unexploded mines. Repairs were made to a fallen girder bridge. The main obstacle was a railway bridge that had been cleverly blown lengthways onto the main road between Le Cateau and Bazuel. As it was 70 feet long and weighed about 400 tons, it took four days and 12,000 lbs. of explosives to remove it. Headquarters moved from St. Henin to Le Cateau. A good deal of work was put into defensive positions. Two days earlier had seen work start on a defensive support line to enable troops to be withdrawn and rested. This line was west of the Malgarni Road.

In Prescot the munitions workers at BICC had gone on strike. They wanted their working week reduced from 53 hours to 47, without a reduction in pay. Over 2,000 workers were affected and the management said the dispute would have to be settled by the Ministry of Munitions. The strike, which was the first at the works since it was opened in 1891, was over after one day when workers delegates came to an agreement with the Ministry.

On 30 October, orders came that, as part of operations commencing on 4 November, 25th Division was expected to cross the Sambre-Oise Canal; capture Landrecies; establish a bridgehead; and drive the enemy towards the Leval-Avesnes Railway. Work on the support line was stopped, and because of the strenuous time ahead, the Pioneers were withdrawn into rest billets. Battalion H.Q., the transport and one company were at St. Henin; one company was in a forward position near Pommereuil; the third company was at Honnechy. Apart from 'A' Company, who were keeping the Pommereuil to Fontaine road open, the battalion was rested and involved in training for the coming operation. The tasks for the Royal Engineers and Pioneers were: forward roads; passage of the canal by the leading infantry without delay; passage of the canal by guns and transport; passage of the canal by heavy guns and tanks.

The canal was known to be over 50 feet wide and 6 feet deep. The infantry would have to fight through enclosed country for more than a mile to get to the canal. The problem was how to cross the canal as normal bridging equipment could not be brought up with the infantry in the face of shell fire. A further difficulty was that there was a river on the other side of the canal which itself was 20 feet wide. On top of that the ground in between was marshy and could not be used by wheeled traffic.

It was decided to cross the canal using rafts. The only available rafts were made of cork and each could carry only one man so these could not be used. Rafts using petrol tins for buoyancy were designed and 3,000 tins asked for. These rafts were to carry 200 infantry across in one wave. The construction of 80 rafts was detailed to 105th Field Company Royal Engineers assisted by one company of Pioneers. A second company of Pioneers was to repair roads, and the third to be in reserve. A demonstration was put on near St. Henin to show the infantry how the crossing was to be made. The method for the crossing got the thumbs up even though there was a general feeling of doubt, with one infantry C.O. saying it would be a "Sporting Event".

The R.E. officer in charge was nervous about the Pioneers as they had only been in France for a short time. Many of the men now with the battalion had not been to the battle front before, had not seen a barrage before, and had not worked with infantry before. Also, they had had no opportunity to practise. Afterwards he would say that his misgivings were unfounded and that Captain Boulton must have briefed them thoroughly.

On 3 November Advance Battalion H.Q. opened at Pommereuil and materials were drawn from the advance dumps prepared by 'A' Company. 'B' Company together with 105th Field Company Royal Engineers moved from Honnechy to their forward positions and at dusk to their assembly positions in the front line. 'C' Company moved from St. Henin to the Railway Cutting in front of Le Cateau. Three supply tanks at Bazuel were to be used to bring bridging materials forward. Although one broke down, the other two arrived with all of the materials at the appointed rendezvous on time.

The Battle of Landrecies started at 5.45 a.m. on 4 November. There was thick fog that morning and some of the carrying parties got mixed up with the infantry as they moved towards the canal. Instead of being about 300 yards behind the infantry, they were in front, and in some places were taking Germans prisoner. A few minutes after the battle started the poet Wilfred Owen was killed during the crossing of the canal. He was leading 'D' Company of 2nd Manchesters, part of 32nd Division, further along the canal at Ors.

There were three bridging parties; No. 1 to bridge the river using three floating bridges supported by rafts; No. 2 to bridge the canal between the lock and the right side of the Division using 30 rafts; No. 3 to bridge the canal between the lock and the left side of the Division using 35 rafts. The rafts weighed 95lbs each and had to be carried over and through hedges for more than a mile. On nearing the canal, the groups spread out so the rafts were about 20 yards apart along the canal. The rafts were launched, each with a sapper in it, and paddled across pulling a line behind. On reaching the other side another line was secured. This way the rafts could be pulled back and forth across the canal carrying an infantryman each time. Once the first wave was across the rafts were brought together to form a floating bridge.

'B' Company under Captain Boulton assisted the sappers of 105th Field Company Royal Engineers in ferrying the covering parties across the canal under heavy fire. Lieut. Henshaw was wounded during this but carried on. Once the initial crossing was completed, the company was moved back towards Pommereuil. 'C' Company were working on forward roads; Pommereuil to Malgarni, Malgarel-le-Faux to Fontaine-aus-Bois to Boyennes and on to Landrecies. They also worked on approaches for the two pontoon bridges across the canal near the Landrecies Lock. This had been done under heavy shelling. 'A' Company, in reserve, had to send men to help with the bridging of the canal. A platoon was sent to maintain and keep open the road from Pommereuil to Fontaine, particularly in the areas of Foresters House and Malgarai which were being heavily shelled. The company was told to keep another platoon in readiness for work bridging the Petite Helpe river. At 8 p.m. the battalion, except for 'B' Company, moved to Fontaine-au-Bois near headquarters. 'B' Company remained in bivouacs for the night near Pommereuil. At night, one platoon of 'A' Company was ordered to report to 130th Field Company Royal Engineers to work under them.

An artillery barrage supported the crossing but there was still heavy fighting before the German rearguards were driven out of position. During this fighting Private Victor Redstone single-handedly captured a machine gun that was holding up the advance. He went forward by himself, killed or wounded most of the gun crew, and took others prisoner. Later he collected several of the infantry together and cleared a number of houses of the enemy. Redstone was awarded the Distinguished Conduct Medal for his actions.

The success of 75th Brigade on the day was the crossing of the canal, the capture of the town of Landrecies, and the establishment of a bridgehead. Over 800 Germans were taken prisoner and 40 guns captured. The Engineers and Pioneers part in this was two floating bridges over the Ancient River, two floating bridges near the canal lock, two foot bridges constructed near the lock, and a company of 1/8th Warwickshires rafted over the canal near the lock. The lock house was taken intact. Casualties were considered to be light.

Apart from Private Redstone's D.C.M. there were other awards for actions during the crossing. A Military Cross for Lieut. Henshaw. The Military Medal was awarded to Sergeants Owen and Ions for leading their sections with great skill and dash; to Privates Eglington and Dawson who were invaluable as runners under very difficult conditions, Dawson being wounded while helping to ferry the infantry across; and to Private Stephen Rumble for his disregard of danger when obtaining information about the progress of the crossing. Captain Boulton was awarded a bar to his Military Cross for his fine example and leadership.

With the infantry across, the canal had to be bridged to take guns and transport across. By night time two pontoon bridges were taking traffic across despite heavy shelling. 'A' Company of 11th South Lancs assisted the Engineers in repairing a heavy transport bridge. Two artillery pens had also been excavated on the bridge approaches. The next day a bridge that could take the weight of tanks was completed by the lock and three were moved across.

On the 5th 'A' Company moved forward to Fontaine-au-Bois. 'B' Company was rested for a day. The three companies were now filling in craters and draining and repairing the main Landrecies to Maroilles road. They were also making a corduroy track to the west of this road. By the following day one company was through Landrecies and moving west to Maroilles. One company was making approaches to pontoon bridges at Les Hill Despres, one working on bridging, and the third was at Landrecies working on craters and roads. Once again unexploded mines were found and removed. In the afternoon, battalion H.Q. and two companies moved to Maroilles. The next couple of days were spent continuing this work and on a bridge and new road at Raisnieres. It had rained night and day since the afternoon of the 5th, making the work harder and the roads very muddy.

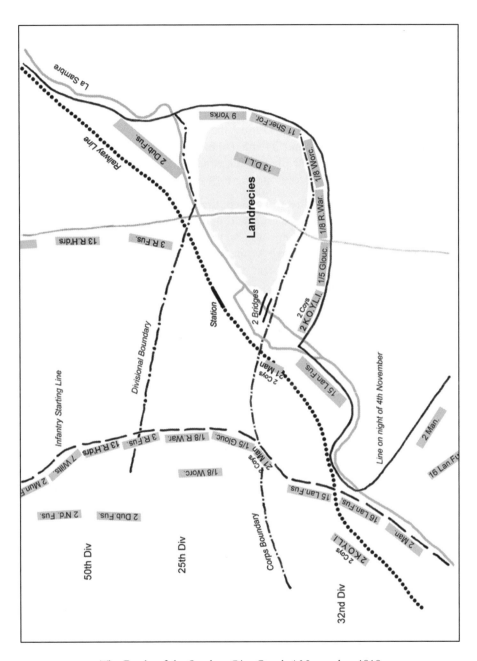

The Battle of the Sambre-Oise Canal, 4 November 1918

On 7 November the whole battalion moved up to the advance position near Avesnes. One company worked on the Maroilles to Marbaix road, one moved to Dompierre and the third was working on craters. That night 30th Division was relieved by 66th Division. During the recent operation the Division had moved forward 12 miles in difficult country. The crossing of the Sambre-Oise Canal and the capture of Landrecies was the last time the battalion was involved in heavy fighting. During the battle, the battalion had 8 other ranks killed, and 5 officers and 34 other ranks wounded. One of the officers, 2nd Lieut. Hebert Jones, later died of his wounds. 2nd Lieut. Robert Carr had been taken prisoner while reconnoitering forward roads.

While the Division had been relieved, there was so much work to be done that the Engineers and the Pioneers could not be spared and were placed under the orders of XIII Corps. There was an urgent task to ensure a lorry route through Taisnieres and Dompierre. While one company was at Landrecies filling in craters, another was at Taisnieres working on the approaches to a trestle bridge, the third working on a lorry diversion at Dompierre Station. The work was finally completed on the evening of the 10th, so on the morning of the 11th there was an open lorry route from Maroilles through Taisnieres to Dompierre.

At 5 a.m. on the morning of 11 November an Armistice was signed in the Forest of Compiegne. It was to come into effect at 11 a.m. that same day when hostilities would cease on all fronts. Although the fighting was over the war was not and it would take six months of negotiations at the Paris Peace Conference to conclude the peace treaty. The Armistice had to be renewed every thirty days until the war was formally concluded by the signing of the Versailles Treaty on 28 June 1919.

There was a rumour in St. Helens early in the morning and official news arrived at 10.30 a.m. Business at the Police Court had been interrupted in the morning when the Chairman, Alderman Martin, asked those present to rise while the Mayor made a statement:

"You will join me in saying how pleased we are to learn that the Armistice has been signed by the Germans. The splendid fighting that has been taking place by our townsmen, our countrymen, and our Allies has at last succeeded in attaining that object for which we went into this terrible war. I hope that our town will remain peaceable, that we will show our appreciation of the splendid efforts that have been put forward by our troops and by our Allies; but we will remember that we owe a deep debt of gratitude to those who have done so much for us, and in memory of the fallen heroes that have left us, I would say: Let us enjoy ourselves as much as possible, but keep within all reasonable bounds."

As soon as he had received the news that the armistice had been signed the Mayor sent congratulatory telegrams:

"To General Haig, Allies Headquarters, France. People of St. Helens send congratulations on the successful issue of the struggle, and warmly thank you and the forces for the gallant victory."

"To his Majesty the King, Buckingham Palace, London. Inhabitants of St. Helens, Lancashire, send heartfelt congratulations of the glorious victory of your forces."

"To Marshall Foch, Allies Headquarters, France. People of the Borough of St, Helens, Lancashire, England, most warmly congratulate you and the forces on the splendid results obtained by your strategy."

"To the Prime Minister, 10 Downing-street, London, S.W.1. People of St. Helens heartily congratulate you on the victorious results of your energies."

Flags and banners appeared on most public buildings in the town, and streamers criss-crossed many of the roads. Crowds flocked onto the streets and rejoiced. Pilkington Bros. closed their works for two days, and many other companies followed suit. The crowds gravitated to the Town Hall where the Mayor appeared on the steps saying:

"Citizens of St. Helens, I have the honour to announce that the Armistice was signed by the representatives of the German Government this morning at five o'clock and the officer in charge of the Allies forces on the Western Front, the renowned General Foch, gave the order for firing to cease at eleven o'clock this morning. The Allies have completed the tremendous tasks they set out to do, to free humanity and to put Christianity and civilisation on a sound footing. They have proved the doctrine that might is not always right and that the freedom of small nations must be observed. They have beaten some of the greatest criminals that the world has ever known. On behalf of this town I give my sincere thanks to the inhabitants for the splendid manner in which they have rallied to their country's call."

Short speeches were then made by the Rev. Canon Baines, the Rev. Father Riley, and the Rev. Luke Beaumont. The Doxology, a short hymn of praise to God, was then sung, and the cheering crowd then dispersed. In the evening a crowded thanksgiving service was held in the Town Hall, and a similar service was held at Lowe House Church, the "Te Deum" being sung by the choir. The Free Church Council held their service at Ormskirk Street Congregational

Church. There was a very large attendance with several ministers taking part. A rendering of the Hallelujah Chorus brought the service to a close.

The streets were crowded all evening and in parts of the town bonfires were lit and fireworks set off. A group of soldiers from Knowsley Camp were seen dancing round a tramcar, and children were marching up and down, waving flags.

Despite the Armistice there was still work to be done in France to ensure troops could move forwards towards Germany. 11th South Lancs were ordered to Sars Poteries to work on craters blocking the roads. Influenza was becoming more of a problem with the epidemic getting serious. It became difficult to carry on with the work. The epidemic was put down to living in unhealthy cellars, prolonged battle strain without rest, and exposure to bad weather. Large numbers of officers and men went down with influenza. In the Engineers, the only officers fit for duty were subalterns who had only just joined as reinforcements.

On the 16th, 11th South Lancs finished their work on the road from Sars Poteries to Bas Lieux and moved to the neighbourhood of Avesnes. The following day both the Royal Engineers and the Pioneers were ordered to rejoin 25th Division at Le Cateau. They marched to Dompierre, then to the Divisional Area with 11th South Lancs billeted at Ors. They were back now with 25th Division under Armistice Conditions.

The long period of battle was over but there were still casualties. Abraham Jervis died at his home in Traverse Street while on sick leave. Sydney Lord died whilst a prisoner of war at Cassel. At least 8 men would die after the Armistice.

King George V. passed through Quievy in the afternoon on 4 December. The battalion, along with 7th Infantry Brigade, formed up at the side of the road and gave three cheers. The King stopped, walked along the line, and spoke to both officers and men. December was also a month when sport came to the fore again. There was a boxing match against 21st Manchesters on the 2nd and 'A' Company beat 21st Manchesters H.Q. 3-0 at football. Boxing Day was celebrated by 'B' Company with a "funny football" match in fancy dress, followed, of course, by a concert.

As the war was ending there was gossip amongst the prisoners of war in Germany that the tide was turning and the British were making significant gains. Their German guards now started to desert, leaving them unattended, and encouraging them to make their way back towards France. Private George Webster remembered being roused from his bed and being told he was free to go. He said it was a chaotic situation and they had great difficulty getting lifts. The German economy was ruined and coins had become worthless. At one point he found 100,000 Marks, which before the war would have bought a railway engine, and was now worthless. Somehow he met up with the main force in France and was repatriated. He lived in Freckleton Road until he died in 1946.

On 13 December Private Alfred Cooper was with a party of men from 'A' Company returning from salvage work when he lit a cigarette and suddenly smoke started to come from his clothing. Private Albert Tierney threw him to the ground and tried to extinguish the fire by rolling him in the mud. By this time his clothes were burnt through to the skin and Lieut. Lea was trying to get them off him. While this was happening Private Cooper pulled a handful of cordite out of his trouser pocket. He was searched but no more was found. A passing ambulance was stopped and Cooper was taken to the regimental doctor. The Board of Inquiry the next day decided that as "Precautionary Orders" relating to the handling of explosives and shells had been read out to the working party Private Cooper was to blame. The Board determined that he was "wrongfully in possession of cordite" and that he did not appear to realise how inflammable it was. Men were also still dying; Private John Stanley, of Ramford Street, died of his wounds, leaving a wife and three children.

December also saw five German guns on display in St. Helens. They had been captured by Canadian troops and loaned to St. Helens for exhibition. After arriving at the station, troops from Knowsley Camp brought them to Victoria Square. The Mayor and his party received the guns; four 77mm field guns and a 105mm howitzer. The guns and their carriages were all camouflaged, rather battered and showed signs of being hit by Allied fire. The 77mm guns fired the shells known to the troops as whizz-bangs.

Captain Cooper, of the South Lancashire Regiment, asked the Mayor to accept the guns on behalf of the municipality. The Mayor replied, saying it was a proud moment for the people of the town to be given the temporary exhibition. The Mayor and others inspected the guns before the soldiers departed for Knowsley. Large crowds came to see the guns afterwards.

The battalion had remained pretty much intact until 18 December when 100 men, all miners, were transferred to the Army Reserve and sent home. The battalion then began to "melt away".

St. Helens Tank Week, April 1918
[St. Helens Reporter]

St. Helens Tank Week, April 1918
[St. Helens Reporter]

Orderly Room, Aldershot, 23 September 1918
[C. C. Champion Collection]

Lock No. 1 on the Sambre-Oise Canal
[Paul Reed]

After the War

On 7 January 1919 an appeal was placed in the St. Helens Reporter for local men who had been Prisoners of War to contact the St. Helens War Service Association. There was to be "an entertainment" at the Town Hall for these men. By the end of the month over 600 had returned. Their names and addresses were collected by the Prisoners of War Depot of the St. Helens War Service Association and 640 invitations issued for an event at the Town Hall later in the month. At the event, an "excellent tea" was provided at tables decorated with plants and flowers, with a large banner saying "Welcome Home" prominently displayed. It was reported that the men spent a "very pleasant social evening". The Mayor, Alderman Bates, welcomed the men and spoke of the privations they had suffered saying that:

> "... when he looked round on the smiling faces before him he realised once more that it was an impossibility for the Germans or any other of their enemies to overcome British pluck and dogged perseverance. In meeting the men who had been prisoners from the very early days of the war, he found that they would not talk about their privations, or complain of their lot, but he felt that it was the duty of every Britisher to do whatever was possible to see that those privations had not been suffered in vain, and that those who were responsible for the dastardly treatment that had been the feature of some camps were brought to book as quickly as possible."

The Mayor went on to thank the ladies of the town who for four years had sent out parcels to the prisoners, without which many would have starved. Lady Gamble, on behalf of the War Service Association, replied that the only reward they wanted was the knowledge that the parcels brought comfort to them and reminded them that they were not forgotten by the people at home. She then received a memorial scroll signed by many of the men thanking the association for the work they had done. The evening concluded with smoking and entertainment.

Pilkington Bros. advertised that any former employees who were serving in the Forces and who wanted information on demobilization and employment should contact Captain Spruce at Canal Street.

On 18 January, Private John Robinson, of Hope Street, died of pneumonia that he had contracted as a result of exposure while on duty.

Also in January, Frederick Crick claimed disability due to his dentures being broken; caused by eating Army biscuits. The examining Medical Officer agreed this was due to service during the war but declined any payments stating the dentures only needed repair. There was also an appeal for money to cover the costs of replacing the battalion band's instruments which had been lost in the German offensive in March. A new set of instruments had been sent out to the battalion at a cost of £250. The officers themselves had contributed £64 and Pilkington Bros. had promised £100, but some £60 or £70 had still to be recovered. The Mayor promised to hold a concert at the Town Hall to help secure the balance.

The Mayor also held a meeting at the Town Hall to discuss publicly recognising Corporal John Thomas Davies' gallantry in winning the V.C. A Town Recognition Fund was set up to gather public subscriptions. The fund progressed well with ex-soldiers of the battalion contributing generously. Lt-Col. Carl Champion gave £10; four of the Captains gave 12 Guineas between them; and N.C.O.s gave varying amounts. There were collections in works and pubs; drinkers at the Grey Horse gave 10s and the patrons of the Bridge Street Picturedrome £18 7s 6d. The proceeds of the fund totaling £650, the equivalent of about £23,500 today, were used to buy War Bonds that were given to Davies on 21 January at a public presentation in the Town Hall. He was also presented with an illuminated certificate that read:

> "Presented to Corporal J. T. Davies, V.C., No. 20765, 11th South Lancashire Regiment, St. Helens, in recognition of the honour he has brought to his native town by his conspicuous gallantry and devotion to duty in the field at St. Quentin during the great European War, for which he was awarded the Victoria Cross by His Majesty King George V., on the twenty-fourth day of March, 1918. On behalf of the Mayor, Aldermen and Burgesses, Henry B. Bates, Mayor"

The presentation was made by Sir John Harrington, the ex-C.O. of the Pals. After presenting the certificate and War Bonds he said:

> "I hope that this re-union between myself and those of my old regiment present to-night can be turned into an annual one and that at least as long as we live that one day a year we will manage to have a meeting, because, whatever you may think about your old colonel, he has a very soft spot in his heart for the 11th South Lancs. Davies, you are an honour to your old regiment and an honour to your town and, I consider it an extremely great honour that I have been given the privilege of presenting you with this address."

Davies had returned home to Peasley Cross after nine months as a prisoner at Sagan in Germany. Before the war he worked at the Ravenhead Sanitary Brick and Tile Company, and was a student at the St. Helens College of Art. He was one of the original Pals, joining when he was 19, and had been wounded in the arm and leg earlier in the war. During his captivity he had to work in the mines in Silesia. Replying to Sir John, he said:

"I have very great pleasure in showing my gratitude to you for the great reception you have given me. I think of the old battalion, the 11th South Lancashires, and as you know when the battalion was first formed a great many people were under the impression that we would never see France, but when the battalion did go out the Pals made a great name for themselves both as workers and fighters when the occasion arose. As regards the honour I have won I am going to say very little, because like the rest of the boys I only did my duty. I know the lads of the 11th South Lancashires who are here to-night are just as pleased as I am to see our old colonel present, for he is one of the best colonels that ever came to a battalion. I should like to thank all those who have worked so hard raising the different subscriptions on my behalf and tender my sincerest thanks to the officers and men of the 11th South Lancashire Regiment, especially those who are in France at the present time. Wishing the people of St. Helens and district the best of luck and happiness in the future, I thank you."

Colonel Thomas moved a vote of thanks which was seconded by Sir David Gamble and supported the Hon. Edward Cozens-Hardy. The vote of thanks was accorded with three cheers and the meeting concluded with the National Anthem.

The beginning of the year had seen a sharp increase in the numbers of men being demobilized and others trying to claim pensions. The first three months saw nearly all of the men in the battalion discharged, with priority given to miners who were urgently need back home.

In February the battalion moved to Escaudoeuvres on the 16th; the same day that Sergeant Herbert Kenyon, of Haydock, died after an appendicitis operation at Warrington. In March Private John Murphy tried to claim a pension for the disability of varicose veins caused by cycling on duty.

At the end of March, 170 other ranks were available for the Army of Occupation and were awaiting disposal. Seven officers had volunteered for the Army of Occupation and 2 more were detached from the battalion. This left the battalion at cadre strength of 4 officers and 41 other ranks.

By the end of April more than 40 men had re-enlisted under Army Order IV of December 1918. This continued in May, when Private Thomas Burke, one of the Pals, re-enlisted in the Labour Corps and was posted overseas for exhumation work. He was returning to France before the battalion cadre came home, and would himself only return in 1920. David Williams and Matthew Hayes (in June) did the same. Clearing the battlefields and recovering bodies for reburial would take a long time. William Grimes re-enlisted, this time with the Royal Horse Artillery, and was still serving in 1923.

In June the battalion cadre was still at Escaudoeuvres. On the 6th, Lt-Col. Champion was ordered to form a Battalion Equipment Guard. Two days later the cadre entrained for Cambrai and with the exception of those detailed for the Equipment Guard were sent back to England. The last entry in the battalion War Diary reads:

"June 8th, the Cadre entrained for the U.K. at Cambrai. Strength 6 officers and 38 other ranks."

On Friday afternoon, 13 June, the Mayor was informed that the cadre of the 11th South Lancs would arrive back in St. Helens the following day. Despite the short notice he arranged for posters to be put up asking the inhabitants to join in the reception.

More than an hour before the train was due crowds began to assemble in the streets, especially round Victoria Square and the railway station. The approaches to the station were especially congested, thousands of people having assembled there. The Discharged Soldiers Federation marched down to the station. About 200 strong, dignified and disciplined, they gathered at the arrival platform under the command of Sergeant-Major Bates. The surging of the crowds besieging the station revealed the depth of feeling towards the men who were coming. Amongst the crowds were the somber clad women who mourned the heroes who would never come back.

Shortly before four o'clock the Mayor of St. Helens, the Mayoress, the Town Clerk and the Mayor of Wigan arrived. The Mayor addressed the Discharged Sailors and Soldiers. He said he wanted to take the opportunity of thanking them one and all for assisting him in welcoming the cadre of the 11th South Lancashire Regiment. The crowd was to understand it was in honour of the whole battalion that they were meeting the cadre that afternoon. It was not to the individual man that the honour of that reception was given, but to the regiment of which they were all so proud. Just as the Mayor finished speaking the train steamed into the station. After the passengers alighted the cadre got off the train. They had returned to St. Helens just after four o'clock, to be greeted by cheering crowds. The cadre consisted of 2 officers and 21 other ranks. Of these, only 3 were St. Helens men, two of whom had been in the original battalion that went to France.

Captain Taylor was in charge of the cadre, with Lieut. Lea in charge of the Colours of the battalion. The cadre consisted of Company Quartermaster W. Diggle (of Rochdale), Sergeant James Gee (of St. Helens), Sergeant Reg. Trafford (of Leek), Corporal W. Prescott (of St. Helens), Corporal C. Clark (of London), Lance-corporal J. Holden (of Eccles), Privates Dick Collins (of

London), J. Inglis (of Liverpool), J. Fenney (of St. Helens), A. Davies (of London), Edward Fountain (of Widnes), Walter Mason (of Lincoln), R. Adderley (of Manchester), W. Oram (of London), S. Kirt (of Syston), E. O'Shaugnessy (of Leek), W. Oakley (of London), J. H. Smith (of Urmston), C. Wall (of Birmingham), G. E. Brown (of Hitchin), and G. Collier (of Hemel Hempstead). So different from the more than 1,000 men who left the town in 1915.

The officers approached the Mayor, shaking hands with his party and having a brief conversation. The men were then formed up in fours and moved off the platform, followed by the Discharged Sailors and Soldiers. As they left the station there was more cheering from the great numbers of people. The procession was formed of Mounted Police, the Band, Men of the 11th South Lancs, Sailors' and Soldiers' Federation, the Mayor's party including the Mayor of Wigan, John Davies V.C., a landau bearing the Colours, and more Mounted Police. It proceeded along Shaw Street, Church Street, Baldwin Street and Corporation Street to the Town Hall. All along the route were crowds of people cheering.

The cadre came to a halt in front of the steps of the Town Hall with the colours unfurled. The band of the Federation was on their right and members of the Federation behind them. The four sides of the square was a solid line formed by the crowds in the sunshine. A silence spread over the square and the Mayor welcomed them back.

> "Officers and men of the 11th South Lancashire Regiment, On behalf of the town of St. Helens, I welcome you back home again after the arduous time spent on the battlefield. We realise, those of us who have remained at home, all you have done for us and what we have gained by your noble sacrifice. It is in honour of the regiment that you represent that we give you, on behalf of the town of St. Helens, our welcome to-day. We will always remember those who have gone never to return. By their sacrifices they have secured for us freedom and justice, and in their name I ask you to go forward to make this country a happier and brighter place for heroes to live in."

The Mayor then had the sad duty of presenting a Military Medal to Mrs. Ellen Frodsham, the widow of Lance-Corporal John Frodsham who had been killed on 24 March, 1918, during the German attack. John Frodsham had been presented with the riband of the medal by the G.O.C. 1st Army on 24 August 1916 for his bravery during the Somme Offensive.

After an address by the Mayor, the cadre and the Mayor's party then went into the Town Hall. In the Assembly Room, used at weekends for the services of the Parish Church, the colours were handed over into the custody of the

Parish Church. The Reverend Hinde, who was in his khaki uniform of an Army chaplain, received the colours and promised they would be held in memory of the 11th South Lancashires and would be placed in the church.

The Mayor then entertained the members of the cadre, and some others, to dinner in the Town Hall. After toasts of "The King" and "The Royal Family", the Mayor then proposed a toast to the health of the South Lancs saying:

"… they knew the qualities of the St. Helens Pals, a name by which they would ever remain in the memory of the townspeople. When the terrible crisis of the war was looking at its blackest, when that "contemptible little Army" was being thinned out to a thin red line, when his Majesty and the late lamented Lord Kitchener appealed for volunteers, and Lord Derby visited the town, they knew how readily St. Helens men came forward to form the battalion, the 11th South Lancs"

Captain Taylor replied, expressing hearty thanks for the great reception. He said that every man and officer of the battalion had only done his duty. They were proud of their V.C. and glad to see him looking so well after his "sojourn" in Germany. He apologised for the absence of Lt-Col. Champion, who was still in France. Sir John Harrington had sent a telegram to the Mayor saying he, unfortunately, could not be there. Lastly the Mayor said that the 1/5th South Lancs were expected back in the town at any time and asked the townspeople to have their bunting ready. The proceedings concluded with the National Anthem.

The final members of the Pals to leave France, the Equipment Guard with the baggage, equipment and wagons, entrained at Cambrai and arrived at Le Havre on the 14th, moving to Harfleur the same day and staying at No. 2 Despatching Camp. On the 19th they embarked for Southampton, arriving the following day. From there they went to the camp at Prees Heath where they were demobilized. Carl Champion drove the 149 miles home in his Singer car on the 24th. The next day he was back at Haileybury School to resume teaching when term began the day after.

The Commonwealth War Graves Commission traces its origins to Fabian Ware who became a commander of a British Red Cross unit after being told he was too old for the army. His unit began recording and caring for all the graves they came across. In 1915 his unit was given official recognition and renamed the Graves Registration Commission. In 1917 the Imperial War Graves Commission was established and Ware became its vice-president. At the end of the war land was secured for cemeteries and the enormous task of recording the dead began. By 1918 over half a million graves had been recorded and more than half a million men as having no known grave. Sir Edwin Lutyens, Sir

Hebert Baker and Sir Reginald Blomfield were employed to design and construct cemeteries and memorials. Rudyard Kipling was employed as advisor for the wording on inscriptions. Frederic Kenyon, director of the British Museum, brought their ideas together. Three cemeteries were built to try out the ideas. The one at Forceville in France was thought the best, being a small walled garden style setting with a uniformity of headstones. This became the template for all the cemeteries going forward. In cemeteries with more than forty burials the Cross of Sacrifice by Blomfield was added and in ones with more than a thousand a Stone of Remembrance was placed. St. Helens Cemetery has a Cross of Sacrifice.

Lloyd George wanted to stir public feelings by a Victory Parade, and one was arranged to take place on Britain's official Peace Day, 19 July 1919. He also proposed that a temporary structure be erected as a tribute to the dead. The structure would stand beside the route of the parade so that the marching soldiers could salute the dead. Sir Edwin Lutyens was commissioned to design the structure. He took his inspiration from the ancient world and produced a design for a cenotaph or 'empty tomb'. The chosen inscription was to be "THE GLORIOUS DEAD", a commemoration of the fallen not a celebration of victory. As it was not intended to be permanent, it was constructed from wood and plaster, painted to look like stone. It was erected the day before the parade and people immediately began laying flowers around it. During the parade on the following day, some 15,000 soldiers marched past in silence to salute the dead. After the parade, thousands again began laying flowers and wreaths. The idea of a permanent memorial began to take shape. Despite government opposition, the press took up the theme and pressed for a memorial on the same site in Whitehall. The Daily Mail argued that the site had been "consecrated by the tears of many mothers". The temporary cenotaph was left in place for the commemorations on 11 November 1919. The crowds then were even bigger than for the Victory Parade. Lutyens was commissioned to design a permanent memorial that would be unveiled by King George V on 11 November 1920. The design was almost the same as for the temporary structure. On that day came the 'Great Silence' lasting two minutes. The first minute for those who fought and came home, and the second for those who did not come home. It rained all day but the queues grew longer as the day went on. At one point it was reported to have been seven miles long. The police estimated that over 100,000 people had passed the Cenotaph by noon. The mountain of flowers grew ever larger. By the following Monday, 15 November, it was estimated that a million and a half people had filed past. Other cities, such as Manchester and Sheffield, soon followed suit and erected their own cenotaphs but it was not until 1926 that St. Helens had one.

September 1919 had seen a smoking concert, held at the Town Hall, for men who had won honours during the war. About 370 St. Helens men had been awarded gallantry medals. At the concert they each received a present from the town's Heroes Fund. A full list of the men's names was published in *The Reporter*.

The mining industry was privatised on the 1 April 1921 and the new mine owners immediately threatened wage reductions. The Miners' Federation of Great Britain planned a coordinated response with its allies in the rail and transport unions, known as the Triple Alliance, on Friday 15 April. This triggered a 90 day emergency call up for ex-soldiers. One of these was ex-Pal Michael McMenamy who was called up for service with 5th P.W.V. (Defence Force). This must have been difficult for him as he had been a miner himself before the war. His call up papers note his distinctive marks as "Shrapnel wound top right arm Bullet wound in back". It was reported that twenty thousand miners in and around St. Helens went on strike and as they were idle due to a trades dispute they were not entitled to unemployment benefit. In St. Helens the Central Children's Care Committee decided that arrangements had to be made to feed school children during the stoppage. They were to be supplied with three meals a day, seven days a week, in cases where it was necessary. Following some confusion over what terms the Miners' Union would be prepared to accept, the transport workers' and railwaymen's unions decided not to call their members out on strike in sympathy with the miners. This was subsequently remembered as 'Black Friday' by many socialists and trade unionists, who regarded it as a betrayal of solidarity and a major defeat for trade unionism. The miners returned to work in the July for conditions much the same as the mine owners had proposed at the start of the strike. McMenamy was released from duty on 4 July.

Also in April a 'Victory Bazaar' was held at the Town Hall. Running for several days, it netted close to £4,000 for Lowe House Church. It was opened by Lord Gerrard and goods from various nations were exhibited. In a light hearted prologue to the brochure, Father Riley explained the origins of bazaars, adding:

> "... the slave trade obtained in the Oriental bazaars and women are not infrequently sold. In the Western bazaars converse holds good, men being invariably sold by women."

The money was to be used towards the new church and, in particular, a memorial chapel dedicated to the fallen of the parish. Plans for the new church dated to before the war. In 1917 a shallow trench had been dug along the lines of the proposed outer walls and borings taken to test for old mine working, but it was decided to leave the rebuilding until after the war. In 1920 work resumed and during excavations for the tower a large amount of coal was brought up. This was sold to cover the cost of the digging. A start was also made on the memorial chapel. There was no contract for the work; it was done by direct labour. Three Catholic builders in the parish, Messrs. Middlehurst, Yearsley and Forber, formed a company conceding all discounts to the church. In this way the cost was reduced by two-thirds.

The ceremonial erection of the Celtic cross over the Memorial Chapel took place on 5 November, 1922. This was followed by a reception and a concert in the Volunteer Hall. There had been a connection between the church and the Volunteer Hall since the church had leased the land it stood on to Sir David Gamble in 1861. Since then the hall had been used regularly by parishioners for teas and public events. In 1911, 750 children sat down to a meal of tea, pies and buns, with apples and oranges to follow. The opening of the Memorial Chapel took place on 15 July, 1923. It was performed by Archbishop Keating and the Mayor, with men of the 5th South Lancs in attendance. The statue of St. George was unveiled by Colonel Pilkington, followed by a bugle salute, the National Anthem, and hymn to St. George. 176 men of the parish had died in the war.

1921 also saw the Prince of Wales make a tour of Lancashire towns, and on Wednesday, 6 July, he visited St. Helens. Outside the Town Hall the 5th Battalion of the South Lancashires marched behind their band and drums to form a guard of honour with fixed bayonets. The band took up a position near the Gamble Institute. The column of Queen Victoria's statue had been scrubbed clean. The square had been decorated with rows of pink geraniums. A platform had been built outside the Town Hall for councillors, officials and local dignitaries. It was covered with a red baise and ferns that had been brought from the parks. Prominent on the platform was the chair that had been used by King George V when he and Queen Mary had visited the town in 1913. Arriving at the Town Hall the Prince was greeted by a throng of people who had waited patiently, as had those lining his route from Blackbrook where he entered the town.

After being welcomed by the Mayor, the Prince sat on the same chair his father had used next to a small table on the platform and signed the mayoral visiting book. He then left the platform and inspected the guard of honour, stopping here and there for brief words and handshakes with some of the soldiers. There was a burst of cheering to which the Prince responded by raising his hat several times. Then he returned to the platform for the civic greetings and to be presented to the dignitaries. The Mayor then called for three cheers which met a great response. After this the Prince returned to his open car and, accompanied by Lord Derby, was driven away. As the car was driven from the square, the Prince stood with his hat raised, nodding to each side. Near the end of Duke Street, opposite the Y.M.C.A., a group of soldiers who had met the Prince in France took advantage of the car's slowness to renew their acquaintance.

The next stop of the visit was at City Road where crowds waited at the football ground. He was there to meet ex-soldiers. The band of the British Legion and the Nutgrove Band played the National Anthem, and then broke into "God Bless the Prince of Wales". The ex-soldiers were then asked to march round in a single rank as the Prince wanted to shake hands with all of them. The first to be presented were the Victoria Cross winners, John Molyneux and John Davies. The Prince spent several minutes chatting to these two men, asking when they won their medals. They were followed by Master at Arms H. J. Heighway of the Cunard Line. He had been torpedoed twice, on the Lusitania and the Franconia. As the line passed by the Prince he chatted with each man. By the end he had shook hands with over 300 men, inquiring of the disabled if they were well cared for, and whether they suffered much pain. He then mounted an improvised rostrum and spoke a few words before being driven away.

The final stop was at Victoria Park where the town's schoolchildren had been assembled in eight groups stretching from the King's Gate in Bishop Road to the Cowley Hill gates where a hundred disabled children were with their nurses; nearly 8,000 schoolchildren in all. The Prince was driven through all of the groups of cheering children, not stopping anywhere, and five minutes after entering the park he left by the Bishop Road gates. About half-way down the road some 300 Boy Scouts and a number of Girl Guides were assembled. The car now went more quickly up Dentons Green Lane and down Kiln Lane passing the Borough boundary and on to Knowsley.

The start of the 1920s saw two more phenomena resulting from the war. No French farmer in northern France was surprised that the crop yield was much higher than in 1913, the last year that there had been a harvest at Montauban. Apart from lying fallow for at least six years, the ground had been fertilized by the huge amount of blood that had been spilled over the years. In Britain the Daily Mail sensationalized the results of the 1921 Census with the story of the 2 million "surplus women". It claimed these women were never likely to marry as their men had been mowed down in France. The statistics showed that for those aged between 25 and 29 there were 1,209 single women for every 1,000 men. The next Census, ten years later, showed that 50 percent of those women were still single. The end of the war also created problems for women who wanted to work. The 1921 Census also showed that there was a lower percentage of females working than had been the case in 1911. Indeed, over 750,000 women were made redundant in 1918 as women were expected to stand aside and release jobs to demobilised soldiers. The end of the war also saw marriage bars in many occupations, including teaching, nursing and the civil service. This was in spite of the Sex Disqualification (Removal) Act of 1919 which was supposed to prevent discrimination due to sex or marriage.

House of Commons debates in the 1920s reflected the public's questions over whether an amnesty would or should be granted to men who had deserted during the war. In July 1920 Mr. Palmer asked the Secretary of State for War, Winston Churchill, whether he would "grant a general amnesty to all men who are now serving reduced sentences for desertion". Churchill's answer was "No, Sir". Three years later Mr. T. Griffiths asked Churchill what was being done in the case of men who had deserted. Churchill replied he was:

"... not prepared to dispense altogether, by a general amnesty, with the right to try and punish men, in serious and special cases, for the grave military offence of desertion. The normal practice, however, has for long been to discharge the deserter without resorting to trial and without withdrawing him from his civil employment."

In 1924 he was asked whether any amnesty had been granted to deserters and whether it was his intention to offer an amnesty. In both cases Churchill's answer was no. There seems to have been no active pursuit of deserters after the war. Those ex-soldiers who admitted their desertion often had the liability of a Court Martial dispensed with and were granted a Certificate of Protection. They did however forfeit their campaign medals.

In 1923, Thomas Johnson, of Doulton Street, was finally awarded a pension after years of visits to hospitals. For the loss of use of his right arm and a weak right leg, while serving with 19th Lancashire Fusiliers, the medical board decided he could have a 60% pension for life.

On Easter Sunday, 4 April, 1926 Mrs. Elizabeth Davies, of Chancery Lane, unveiled the St. Helens War Memorial in Victoria Square. She had been given the honour due to her having five of her seven sons killed in the war. The memorial had been paid for by public subscription, and had cost £2,000. It was designed by Messrs. Biram and Fletcher, and Messrs. William Rigby and Sons were the contractors. Twenty thousand people attended the ceremony. Mrs. Davies and the Mayor, Alderman Thomas Hamblett, each took a corner of the purple cloth, pulled, and revealed the memorial to a subdued crowd. After hymns and the National Anthem, the Mayor proceeded to place a wreath on the memorial. This was followed by more official wreaths, and then the great crowd began placing their own tributes to their loved ones. The buglers of the 5th Battalion South Lancashire Regiment sounded the "Last Post", and the "Reveille". The memorial originally had 2,270 names on it of men who never returned from the war and space was left for additions. More names from the Great War have been added over the years.

'B' Company Fancy Dress Football, 26 December 1918
[C.C. Champion Collection]

'C' Company Mess at Roupy
[C. C. Champion Collection]

25th Division Sports, 8 May 1919
[C. C. Champion Collection]

Loading Tanks at Cambrai, 13 June 1919
[C. C. Champion Collection]

The 11th South Lancs Cadre in Victoria Square, St. Helens, 14 June 1919
[St. Helens Reporter]

The Pals' last crossing from France entering Southampton Water, 19 June 1919
[C. C. Champion Collection]

The Prince of Wales at City Road Football Ground, 6 July 1921
John Molyneux V.C. and John Davies V.C.
[St. Helens Newspaper & Advertiser]

The unveiling of St. Helens War Memorial, Easter Sunday 1926
[St. Helens Reporter]

Reunion

Ten years after the unveiling of the War Memorial a meeting was held at the Swan Hotel to arrange a battalion reunion. About 30 ex 11th South Lancs men attended and a committee was formed with three men representing each company. G. Waring, H. Fairclough and J. Kirkham for 'A'; W. Swift, J. Lowe and W. Molyneux for 'B'; J. Hutton, J. Lea and T. Grimes for 'C'; J. Davies, V.C., J. Large and W. Fairclough for 'D'. Mr. H. Collins was appointed chairman, and R. Abberley honorary secretary. The reunion was to take place on Saturday 7 November. The committee appealed for as many men as possible to parade at the Parish Church at 3.55 p.m. to receive the Pals' Colours.

More than 350 men turned up together with three of their former officers; Captain W. Bretherton, M.C., and Lieuts. A. D. Walker and J. H. Bishop. Walker took charge of the parade and formed the men up in fours. Inside the church, a service was conducted by the Rev. E. D. Buxton who read The Soldier's Prayer. During the singing of "Fight the Good Fight" the members of the colour party formed and the colour bearer, J. Davies, V.C., went to the communion rail to receive the Pals' colours from Rev. Buxton. At the end of the service the colour party marched to the head of the column of Pals and the parade moved off to the sounds of Parr Public Prize Band.

They marched via Church Street and Cotham Street to the War Memorial. There Mr. H. Collins placed the wreath, a "Pick and Rifle" made up of red poppies, with the inscription "In everlasting remembrance of our fallen comrades, officers and men, 11th Battalion South Lancs Regiment, St. Helens Pals". The band played the first verse of "Abide with Me". Three uniformed buglers of the 5th South Lancs sounded the "Last Post" and "Reveille", and then the National Anthem was played. The parade then marched off via Corporation Street and Duke Street to the Volunteer Hall for the tea and social.

At the Volunteer Hall a large number of ladies served tea after the buglers had sounded "Come to the Cookhouse". One of the guests was Colour Sergeant W. J. Milligan who had helped to form the battalion in 1914. Another was John Molyneux, V.C. After tea, Lieut. Walker read telegrams from Lord Cozens-Hardy and Captain Bolton, and one from the 17th Battalion King's Liverpool. Three toasts followed; "Fallen Comrades", "The Colonel-in-Chief, His Majesty the King", and "The Regiment". Before leaving, each man left his name and address with the committee. The following day, the colour party retuned the Colours to the Parish Church.

In November 1937, Church Street once again rang with military commands and 300 men marched down the street singing "It's a long way to Tipperary". They paraded outside the Parish Church in the afternoon. Church of England members of the battalion attended a short service, while those of other denominations waited outside. The service was conducted by the Rev. E. D. Buxton, and the colour party, consisting of Corpl. Davies, V.C. Sergts. Keeble, Latham, Thornburn and Hughes, and Privates Gilligan, Eddowes and Lea, waited at the foot of the chancel steps to receive the flag of the battalion from the hands of the senior curate, who was assisted by Sergt. Molyneux, V.C. After the service the colour party marched to the head of the waiting men, then all marched Church Street accompanied by the Parr Public Brass Band.

The men were cheered by a large crowd which was waiting at the War Memorial. They formed four deep round the memorial with their former officers, Capt. W. Bretherton, M.C., Lieut. E. D. Walker, and Lieut. J. H. Bishop. Heads were bared as the opening bars of "Abide With Me" were played and they sang the hymn so often sung during the war. After a short silence, the buglers of the 5th Battalion Prince of Wales's Volunteers sounded the "Last Post" and Lieut. N. Collins placed a wreath in the form of the regimental badge at the base of the memorial. They then marched to the Volunteer Hall where the men were served tea. Volunteer Street rang with French greetings pronounced in broad Lancashire accents. Cheers greeted more of their old officers; Woolcock, Dixon, A. T. Champion, and the old soldier who was the first to help train the Pals, Colour Sergeant Milligan.

During tea, tunes were thumped out on a piano and "The Man Who Broke the Bank at Monte Carlo" and "Mademoiselle from Armentieres" could sometimes be heard over the hubbub. There was talk of obstinate mules, German prison camps, "Blighty ones" and "Jerry's" activities but very rarely of death. That was best forgotten. A minute's silence was held in memory of fallen comrades, and the toast was drunk silently. After more toasts, the men had the evening to themselves, and it was getting late when the Pals were dismissed, with the assurance of another meeting next year.

In 1938 the third reunion was preceded by a trip to Bangor on the August Bank Holiday. About 90 of the original members of the battalion made the journey by coach. Nearly all of them hadn't been back since they left 23 years earlier. Before entering Bangor the party was taken through the grounds of Penrhyn Park, where they had learned to dig trenches all those years ago. Then into the town itself where acquaintances of those days, and some landladies who used to billet them, were soon recognized among the crowd that had gathered at the War Memorial. One ex-Pal walking along the street saw a young woman, whom he recognised as the daughter of his former landlady, and for whom he used to buy toffee when she was four years old. One of the landladies learned that three of the men who billeted with her had been killed in action. Lunch was at the Rotary Club as guests of the local branch of the British Legion. The men then paraded back to the War Memorial, wearing their medals and led by John

Davies V.C. carrying the colours. There they were given a civic welcome by the Mayor of Bangor who expressed his pleasure at their visit. He read out the visitors' names to help the people present recognize them. After words from the British Legion, a cross of poppies was placed on the War Memorial by Carl Champion, the 'Last Post' was sounded, and the ceremony ended with the singing of 'Abide with Me'.

The reunion that year was held at the Nag's Head on 12 November. It was attended by 125 ex-Pals including 5 of the officers. In a speech during the evening, Colonel Champion mentioned that although the regiment had been rechristened the Prince of Wales's Volunteers, the King had given permission for the battalion to revert to its old name of 11th South Lancs. He also suggested that they should organize a pilgrimage to the old battlefields during the following summer. Of course this wasn't to be, due to the outbreak of the Second World War. After an address by the chairman, Richard Hesketh, the rest of the evening was spent telling war-time stories and singing songs that were popular during the war. Entertainment during the evening was provided by H. Watkinson (concertina player), A. Turner (baritone), H. Sanderson (comedian), Charles Dacre (illusionist), and W. Blythe (versatile artiste). Mr. H. Greenall accompanied and also played for the community singing.

The committee chairman, Richard Hesketh (1896-1993), is believed to have been the last of the Pals. He was interviewed for the *St. Helens Star* in 1980 and said that the parades stopped when their old Captain died.

The whereabouts of the battalion's Colours, last known to be at the Parish Church in 1938 are now unknown.

"On Parade Again", the Pals Reunion, November 1936
[St. Helens Reporter]

Appendix 1: The Volunteers

The St. Helens Reporter published the following list of names on Friday, 11 September, 1914. It was of men who had passed the medical for the new battalion.

F. Addowes	J. Ashcroft	Thos. Banks	J. Bickerstaffe
C. Anders	A. Appleton	John Benyon	J. Bedley
J. J. Atherton	G. Atherton	Ed. Berry	J. Briers
W. Anderton	H. Abbott	Wm. Bracken	W. Bullock
J. Ashall	J. Aspinall	Wm. Bryan	D. Bright
H. B. Ashcroft	T. Appleton	Thos. Baines	T. Bracken
W. T. Atherton	J. Ashcroft	Mich. Bowes	W. Brinco
J. Appleton	H. A. Busby	Francis Brynn	J. Brooks
J. Anderton	H. Brown	J. Burrows	H. Brooks
John Aspinall	John Blakoe	A. Benbow	H. Bradbury
Jos. Atherton	H. Burrill	G. Boardman	E. Barrett
Wm. Appleton	T. Bailey	H. Berry	W. Burgess
Jno. Ashcroft	W. Bilby	Edwin Beesley	H. Barnes
R. L. Abberley	T. Bowkis	J. Barnes	J. Bibby
W. Ashby	W. Battersby	H. Buckley	H. Brighouse
J. Ashcroft	J. Blaney	J. Bloomfield	W. Boardman
A. Anders	T. W. Bott	T. Bonceby	N. Burns
T. Appleton	W. Bell	J. Billing	A. Bedford
W. Abbott	O. Bate	W. Briers	G. Burrows
H. Atherton	A. Bignall	J. Brown	D. Bond
A. Appleton	G. O. Bunyan	P Byrne	O. R. Bagley
J. Ashcroft	T. H. Bradbury	B. F. Black	J. Barber
A. Ashall	W. J. T. Birks	T. Bridge	H. Briers
A. Alexander	J. Bellis	J. Briers	H. Brownbill
C. Arnold	R. Brown	P. Barry	W. Brown
T. Alcock	E. Balfour	W. Barrett	D. J. Bates
J. Addison	S. Bagnall	M. Broderick	W. N. Booth
J. A. Adams	F. Bloomfield	S. Bate	H. Banks
G. Atherton	H. Brown	J. Burrows	P. Bowe
J. Almond	W. Burrows	R. Bowes	J. Birchall
T. Ashford	F. Bolton	G. Bulger	J. Beard
E. Alcock	A. Butterworth	J. T. Brown	T. Butter
H. Atherton	W. Boardman	H. Beard	A. Bamber
H. Archbold	Jas. Brown	J. J. Bridghorn	W. Bonghey
A. Anders	E. Billington	J. Burke	A. Bullock
J. Armstrong	Rd. Booth	J. Byall	J. Bartley
T. Anders	A. M. Barton	H. Bailey	W. Beech
W. Atherton	H. Billington	J. Bowden	T. Berry
J. E. Ashton	Henry Bennett	S. Bailey	J. Brown

A. J. Ball
T. H. Burdekin
E. Byrom
P. Buckley
E. Brown
J. F. Bell
E. Balmer
S. Brown
W. Burgess
T. Beesley
W. Bott
W. Briers
J. Burrill
W. H. Blake
J. Burrows
F. Byrne
W. J. T. Birks
O. Bate
J. A. Beard
T. Broderick
J. P. Bagley
H. Burrell
J. Beard
P. Brennan
J. Baxter
J. Briers
D. J. Bates
W. Burgess
W. N. Booth
J. Bickerstaffe
M. Brodrick
T. Byrne
G. Barrow
G. Billington
W. Boardman
A. Billington
H. Ball
J. Bebbington
S. Brooks
J. Barker
P. Byrne
O. Bright
J. Brown
W. Brown
W. Briers
J. Billinge
T. Bridge

J. Briers
H. Beard
E. F. Bluck
J. J. Bridgham
P. Berry
R. Cathcart
P. Cunningham
T. Connor
J. J. Clisham
W. Chorley
H. Callery
C. Cook
J. Conroy
P. J. Carolen
T. Clisham
F. Caldwell
Jos. Carter
H. Callery
W. B. Chew
H. Critchley
Thos. Colgan
Jos. Cunliffe
F. Cokayne
Saml. Clark
C. Conqueror
M. Carney
J. Carney
J. Coates
A. Cunningham
Harold Clark
Thos. Carrington
Fred Collier
H. Cowne
J. F. Clarke
Jno. J. Cook
O. Cooper
T. C. Cousins
Alec Clitheroe
N. Cheetham
Albert Crooks
C. O. Coates
F. Crilly
J. Callagan
G. Cox
J. Crawford
L. Chorley
A. Chamberlain

B. Carr
J. Cardwell
M. Cooney
J. Clarke
J. Coatsworth
J. Cooper
F. Crump
J. Cassons
J. Coleman
W. Clarke
P. Carr
P. Corrigan
T. Cosgrove
J. Critchley
W. Carson
J. Colville
W. Cliffe
J. Colquitt
J. Coleman
W. Curden
W. Caine
J. Conqueror
J. Carson
J. Cotton
J. W. Carns
T. Cunningham
J. Cowley
C. Chorley
T. Cropper
G. Chisnall
G. Carney
J. Collinson
C. Cole
J. Cullington
J. Chisnall
A. Cunliffe
B. Carter
J. Christopher
O. Cotton
J. Culley
B. C. Clapham
W. Cotterill
J. Cooper
E. Crockett
W. Cook
W. Critchley
F. A. Cook

J. Collins
J. R. Crooks
W. Cruss
J. Cook
H. Clarke
J. Casson
S. R. Cowell
C. J. Coulbourne
J. Conqueror
W. Clark
T. Cosgrove
B. Carr
T. Cropper
T. Cunningham
J. Crompton
P. Corrigan
J. Critchley
H. Corr
W. Colquitt
J. Caffrey
W. Crompton
W. Cardwell
J. Connaughton
E. Callaghan
M. Connaughton
J. Clitheroe
R. Corner
W. Clarke
W. Cain
W. Corden
G. Cog
J. Crawford
F. Grilly
J. Coatsworth
J. Clarke
W. Cowell
J. Downey
P. Devine
J. Dyer
L. Dalton
W. Daniels
R. Dickinson
P. Dorning
John Davies
Jas. Dolan
P. Dixon
Chas. Davies

W. H. Devlin	F. Dorning	Ernest Fazakerley	J. Fillingham
J. Duffy	J. Dwyer	Alf. Fenny	J. Foy
Jno. Dennett	F. Dorning	W. Foreshaw	W. Forbes
T. Downs	J. Didsbury	J. Foster	H. Fairclough
P. Downey	P. Dingsdale	Jos. Foster	W. Flood
F. Davies	J. Dinsdale	John Fitzgerald	M. Feegan
J. Devlin	P. Downey	Wm. Flynn	R. Frodsham
J. Duffy	F. Davies	M. Fagan	D. Flynn
H. Day	J. Dowlin	E. Finch	P. Fearnley
A. E. Dalzell	W. Dolan	G. Foster	T. Finch
W. Davies	W. Evans	R. Foster	G. Fairhurst
W Dingsdale	W. Edwards	W. Fillingham	B. Fairclough
J. Dingley	A. Eden	R. Fenney	A. Fairclough
B. Dennett	Arthur Entwistle	A. Foster	E. Finney
A. G. Dickin	A. E. Ellard	P. Fillingham	W. Foster
P. Downey	R. Eames	J. Frodsham	J. Fay
T. Dyas	W. Egerton	W. Finny	M. Fagan
L. Dinsdale	E. Eddowes	C. Friar	D. Fairclough
J. Dingsdale	T. Ellison	J. R. Forsyth	G. Foster
G. Dean	H. Eccleston	W. Fairclough	R. Finch
T. Dean	G. Edwards	J. Fay	R. Foster
S. Davies	T. Ellison	D. Fairclough	W. Fillingham
M. Dolan	E. Ellis	S. Flynn	W. Fillingham
J. Donnelly	A. Elliott	H. Foster	M. Grady
T. Dillon	A. Evres	W. Fillingham	E. Gleeson
W. Dunn	J. Eden	J. Finney	W. Glover
W. Dixon	M. Egan	T. Featherstone	R. W. Galworthy
W. Dickson	T. Ellison	H. Farrell	J. T. Greenough
J. Dixon	A. Edwards	G. Fairhurst	J. Graham
R. Dickinson	T. Edwards	T. Finch	T. Garner
J. T. Davies	C. Eden	H. Forber	J. Gibbon
G. W. Dyer	D. J. Evans	J. W. Fillingham	C. Glover
A. G. Dickens	S. Edridge	P. Featherstone	L. Gandy
P. Downey	R. Eames	G. Fripp	J. Gee
T. Dyer	W. Everton	T. R. Friar	J. Garrity
J. Davies	E. Ellis	B. Fairclough	J. Gallagher
J. Dingsdale	J. Eccleston	J. Finn	Geo. Gordon
B. Davies	J. Fenney	S. Forman	Arthur Goodwin
J. Dolan	E. Foster	E. B. Fazakerley	R. J. Green
W. Davies	T. Finney	J. Finney	A. P. Gee
J. Davies	W. Fenney	J. Fairclough	Jno. Gee
A. Derbyshire	W. Ford	J. Farrer	Chas. Green
J. Davies	S. Fairhurst	J. Frodsham	Jno. Grund
W. Darlington	J. Fairclough	E. Fiswick	Frank Grimson
J. Dancer	J. Fackey	W. Flood	Jos. Green
W. Davies	J. French	W. Foster	Ed. Garrity
P. Dempsey	Jno. Foster	C. Frodsham	Saml. Gerrard

Saml. Graham	H. Gaskell	W. H. Hornby	J. R. Holford
A. Gully	G. Greenall	A. Rimmer	J. W. Hardman
R. Greenough	H. Gerrard	F. Hartley	J. Henshaw
Walter Groves	J. Gaskell	J. Hampson	J. A. Hines
Samuel Gore	W. Gill	H. Hewitt	M. O. Hare
H. Gilbert	A. Gardner	F. Henton	W. J. Harrison
Thos. Goodwin	H. Gerrard	N. H. Howell	J. Haselden
Frank Gibbons	T. Greenall	S. Hollingsworth	J. Halton
John Greavey	S. Green	E. Hindley	J. Hull
J. Garrett	J. Garnett	Walter Halsall	M. E. Houghton
T. Gill	J. Garratt	Rowland Hesford	F. Howard
E. Goodier	F. Gilligan	R. S. Helsby	J. Henthorn
J. Greenough	E. Gittins	A. Heyes	J. Heart
W. Garner	E. S. Greenough	W. Howard	T. Halliwell
B. Glover	B. Glover	O. Hamilton	T. Hull
W. Glover	T. Grimes	Jos. Hatton	J. Higginson
P. Giliker	J. Gromley	Gilbert Hughes	F. Hackett
R. Glover	W. Gauchwin	Jas. Hewitt	T. Hankinson
T. Gaskell	E. Gregory	Jos. Heaton	W. Hewitt
J. Graham	J. Gannon	Jos. Harrison	H. Houghton
H. Gaskell	J. Greenough	John Hill	H. Hill
H. Gerrard	E. Goodier	H. C. Howell	J. Holding
J. Gaskell	T. Gill	W. A. Hunter	T. Hurst
W. Gearing	A. Gregson	C. A. Hill	J. Hitchmough
G. Graham	W. Grimes	J. Hunt	T. Hurst
T. Gilgan	H. Harrison	C. Hull	J. Holland
J. Garnett	J. Howden	J. Hall	W. Hurst
G. Greenall	Chas. Houghton	J. Halsall	J. Heyes
T. Garner	Thos. Hill	W. Howard	H. Hope
T. Gill	Rd. Hesketh	H. Hill	R. Hughes
J. Grimley	J. Hughes	P. Haycock	F. Harrison
J. Gore	J. Heaton	A. Holt	E. Harrison
J. Gregory	W. Hickton	W. Hill	B. Hobin
T. Gormley	D. Hardman	F. Heyes	R. J. Hughes
J. Greenall	A. Heyes	T. Howe	J. Hamilton
F. J. Glover	J. T. Halton	H. Hunter	R. Hunt
W. G. Green	J. Hughes	W. Hope	H. Hulton
T. Gauchwin	J. Harrison	M. Hagan	J. Hunt
W. B. Gibson	T. Hughes	A. Hughes	E. Harrison
E. Gee	W. Higginshan	J. Holdcroft	R. Hockenhall
G. Gordon	S. Howard	C. Hodgkinson	J. Harrison
P. Gaskell	A. Hughes	R. Houghton	E. Hughes
E. Glover	T. Hennessy	E. Howarth	S. Hunter
F. Gosling	J. Harris	W. Heyes	J. Hill
J. Green	T. Howarth	M. Helland	W. Halton
J. Gillespey	A. Hankey	T. Hayes	F. Hyde
T. Green	H. Halsall	W. Halton	P. Heyes

A. Howard	C. Hull	R. Jones	W. Kilgallon
M. Hunt	J. Hall	G. Jackson	J. Kilmurray
A. Hurst	M. Holland	F. Jones	G. Kilshaw
H. Heather	G. Hughes	F. W. Jarkes	A. Kay
F. Howitt	J. Henderson	P. Kinsey	J. H. Kellett
J. Hodgins	J. B. Ingham	W. Keene	T. Kay
H. Horsley	R. Innes	J. Kilmurray	G. Kerns
J. Hatton	O. H. Jones	H. Knowles	E. Kiernan
T. Howard	S. Jones	J. Kerrigan	P. Kilmurray
H. Hartley	Alf. Jones	A. Keefe	J. Knockton
J. Hobart	Jno. Johnson	F. Kerr	T. Kelly
P. Hackett	John Jones	J. Kay	J. Kay
C. H. Holmes	T. Jackson	J. Kerrigan	W. Keogh
R. Howard	G. Jackson	Ralph Kay	P. Kinsella
W. Hughes	H. Jennion	Thos. Kelly	W. Kehoe
D. Hayes	E. Jones	Peter Kenny	J. Kerr
W. Hewitt	A. Jervis	Bernard Kiernan	T. Knowles
T. Howe	J. Jennings	John Kinsella	T. H. Lewis
W. Hope	T. Johnson	J. Kerr	G. Lowe
S. Hunter	T. J. Jones	J. Kelly	A. Lydiate
H. Houghton	W. Jones	W. Kalroe	J. Langley
J. Henthorn	J. Johnson	J. Kay	R. Lewis
T. Halliwell	J. E. Jones	E. Kennedy	J. Lally
T. Hill	W. Jones	J. Kendrick	J. Lawrenson
F. Howard	T. Jones	P. Kilroy	W. Lynch
J. Higginson	J. Johnson	J. Kelly	Syd. Lambert
J. Heart	J. W. Jones	C. J. Kearns	Fred Lancaster
H. Hill	H. Jones	J. Kay	Chas. Latham
J. Holding	A. Jennings	P. Kelly	Jas. Lea
T. Hurst	T. Johnson	W. Kilgallon	Edgar Lea
T. Hurst	J. Jackson	W. Kerry	L. Lambert
J. Hitchmough	B. Johnson	P. Kinsella	W. Litherland
S. Harwood	S. Johnson	B. Kelly	D. Large
J. Hatton	T. W. Jones	J. W. Kirkham	H. J. Lyon
J. Hill	J. L. Jones	T. R. Kinsey	Arthur Lea
H. Hill	W. Jones	J. Knowles	Jas. Lynch
J. Howard	W. Jones	H. Kiernan	W. L. Lee
S. Harrison	H. Jones	H. King	J. Large
P. Halliwell	G. Johnson	J. Kennedy	A. Lowe
E. Heyes	R. Jones	W. Keogh	W. J. Lyon
J. Hand	E. Jones	J. Kay	J. T. E. Lea
J. Hodgins	T. Jones	T. Kelly	J. Lea
J. Holdcroft	T. Johnson	J. E. Killey	F. Leyland
C. Hodgkinson	H. Jennion	B. Kiernan	R. Linney
R. Houghton	J. Jones	P. Killey	J. W. Lynan
F. Howarth	D. Jones	J. Kay	A. Litherland
W. Heyes	A. Jones	P. Kelly	P. Lea

J. Lane	W. Leyland	M. Morton	J. Moss
E. Lockett	P. Leyland	H. McBryde	J. Martindale
W. Liptrot	E. Lawson	J. Martin	L. Martland
P. Livington	W. Leyland	J. Myers	T. Maguire
A. Ledwith	O. Lawrenson	C. Mather	H. McManus
J. Leyland	W. J. Lyon	J. Mason	M. McMenaney
J. Large	J. Ledwith	S. Mather	L. McCooey
H. Lythgoe	J. McManus	J. Martin	R. Melling
T. Lethbridge	J. T. Mather	J. Meadows	J. Maguire
G. T. Lowe	D. Mulcahy	A. Marsh	P. Malone
E. Lyon	J. McDonald	L. Melling	J. Melding
J. Lamb	W. J. Mustard	J. McComas	P. Marsh
T. Lamb	J. Murphy	L. Mulligan	J. Middlehurst
G. A. Leather	A. Molyenux	J. Maher	D. McClurg
J. Lea	J. McGrail	T. Mather	J. Marsh
T. Latham	J. Morrison	H. Maylin	J. Martin
J. Lyon	J. Millington	W. McCormack	T. Muldoon
H. Langton	J. McDonald	J. McColl	J. Middlehurst
J. Lloyd	R. Mather	J. Morris	J. McGrath
H. Lowes	J. Miskell	J. Mather	H. Marsh
G. Lees	J. Mapley	T. Metcalfe	J. Marsh
J. Leyland	W. Middlehurst	E. Mather	T. Mather
H. Leyland	W. Moulsdale	J. McCabe	G. Millsop
E. Leonard	W. Murray	C. McCompany	J. H. Moore
W. Langley	A. C. Morris	T. Morrison	W. McIntyre
J. Large	G. Marsh	J. Moran	H. Mannion
W. Lloyd	Jas. Maguire	R. Makin	J. F. Mees
H. Leach	Martin Morrison	M. McGann	M. Middlehurst
H. Leyland	Jas. Muldoon	A. McLoughlin	T. Mee
W. Liptrot	Peter Maloney	T. H. Marsh	M. Maher
P. Livingstone	Hy. Marsh	E. Morris	J. McLoughlin
A. Ledwith	Jas. Mortimer	L. Murphy	J. W. Makin
J. Leather	H. Marsh	G. McKie	J. McGanley
J. Large	Sam Martin	A. Mousdale	W. McGonnigle
J. Leyland	B. Moran	E. Mather	W. Mercer
T. Lethbridge	David McBryde	E. Morris	H. Molyneux
H. Lythgoe	W. Molyneux	J. Marsh	F. McCormack
J. J. Lewis	F. McHale	H. Molyneux	S. Martin
J. F. Loader	F. McHale	J. Mackery	P. McHale
W. Lawrenson	L. McGinty	J. Meadows	J. Middlehurst
S. Lea	John Middlehurst	J. Mather	J. Mather
W. Lacey	Rd. Morgan	J. Marsh	J. Mills
J. Langford	Jas. Miller	F. Murphy	J. Marsh
T. Leonard	Jos. Martin	J. Milne	J. J. Murray
O. Lally	Stanley Monks	J. Murphy	J. McEgan
W. Lunt	G. Morris	H. Mulroy	J. W. Moran
W. Liptrot	Jno. Muir	G. McDonald	T. Moores

E. Morris	J. Oates	W. Proudlove	C. Price
T. H. Marsh	Jno. Orrett	R. Pickering	... Plumpton
L. Murphy	E. J. C.	T. Price	J. Parker
D. Mackie	Coulbourne	J. Potter	W. Potter
J. Milno	M. O'Hara	A. Pye	J. Prescott
J. Murphy	T. O'Donnell	S. Pritchard	W. Peel
A. Moulsdale	A. J. Ormrod	J. Penketh	J. Prescott
H. Marsh	W. H. Ormrod	R. Puscell	W. H. Penketh
J. Mosley	H. Oldham	T. Prescott	E. Pritchard
J. Millington	T. Owen	H. Palmer	W. Parr
M. Maloney	S. Oakes	W. Pendleton	W. Proudlove
J. McManus	J. O'Brien	T. Pennington	W. E. Percival
J. Meadows	W. Owen	T. Peyton	T. Parr
H. Maylis	P. C. Owen	W. Pagett	H. Parr
J. Maher	P. Owens	W. Proudlove	J. Pierce
W. McCormick	R. Oldham	H. Parr	J. Price
A. Marsh	J. J. Ogie	T. Parr	G. Penketh
L. Melling	H. Oldham	W. Parr	F. Prescott
J. McColl	A. J. Ormrod	W. E. Percival	T. Pagett
J. McComas	W. H. Ormrod	E. Pritchard	A. Pickett
J. Mason	J. O'Niell	J. Price	W. Proudlove
S. Mather	W. Oakey	O. Pearce	J. Potter
J. Naylor	H. O'Reilly	E. Pickavance	T. Pounceby
W. Naylor	H. Owen	J. Preston	R. Purcell
F. Naylor	J. Pye.	J. T. Pennington	T. Prescott
Jos. Naylor	E. Pugh	J. Potter	J. Pickavance
J. Naylor	J. Pimblett	W. Pennington	J. Pearce
H. Naylor	H. Preston	J. Pearce	P. Pearce
Jno. Nuttall	W. Pollock	J. Preston	C. Preston
Chas. Newbury	A. Pearce	J. Palin	H. Pearson
Thos. Nicksen	S. Preston	W. Pennington	L. Rigby
Thos. Naylor	J. Potter	A. Prescott	T. Reynolds
E. Nelson	J. Price	T. Purcell	J. Richardson
T. Noone	John Pennington	F. W. Parkes	J. Rafter
P. Nicholson	David Pye	C. Preston	T. Robinson
G. Noah	Alf. Pennington	F. Purnell	H. Robinson
R. Naylor	Rd. Painter	W. Price	Arthur Rowe
W. Naylor	J. T. Pyke	J. Powell	Thomas Rigby
N. Naylor	Jos. Platt	J. Potter	S. J. Roberts
E. Newcombe	F. Pendlebury	H. Pennington	Jas. Reid
H. Naylor	E. G. Patterson	J. Powell	J. L. Reid
N. Naylor	J. Pemberton	P. Pickavance	P. F. Routley
J. Neary	G. T. Pennington	W. Prescott	Jas. Ryan
T. Noone	Jas. Prescott	J. Peel	J. Richards
P. Nicholson	Wm. Pye	P. Peel	Alf. Reid
O. Nicholson	John Pennington	C. Preston	Peter Rigby
J. Newson	G. Pilkington	J. Platt	Jas. Rothwell

Chas. Risley	J. Rigby	Wm. Swift	H. Sarsfield
P. S. Robertshaw	J. Rigby	Jas. Sudworth	C. Smith
H. O. Roberts	J. Roberts	J. Smith	K. Smith
Jno. Roberts	J. Ryan	G. Spencer	H. Stott
Jos. Rigby	J. Rigby	J. Seddon	B. Shenton
Thos. Ratcliffe	M. Ross	W. Smith	J. Stevenson
J. Ryan	W. Rowland	J. Smart	A. Sullivan
J. Rushton	J. Randles	J. Smith	J. Speakman
T. Roberts	I. Ramsdale	T. Sumner	T. Seddon
I. Ramsdale	H. Roberts	J. Simms	J. Simmons
T. Rigby	J. Ryan	J. Stanley	T. Smith
R. Roberts	T. Roberts	W. Smith	F. Sephton
C. W. Richardson	W. Roberts	J. Sudworth	A. Stubbs
H. Rawlinson	M. Ryan	S. Shuter	A. Schofield
G. Rogers	M. Robinson	J. Sumner	W. Sephton
W. Reynolds	W. Shadwell	F. Swift	J. Smith
J. A. Raw	Alf. Skerrett	P. Street	W. Smith
A. Rogers	J. Smith	C. Stanley	W. Spibey
G. Rothwell	H. Scott	J. Stanley	J. Seddon
W. Roberts	J. Smith	W. Simpson	G. Spencer
G. F. Rees	H. Stowell	C. Smith	A. Sharratt
J. Rishton	G. C. Slades	K. Smith	T. Starkey
C. Roberts	A. Schofield	H. Sarsfield	H. Swift
P. Roddy	T. Swift	S. Saxon	T. Swindells
J. Richardson	J. Simms	B. Shenton	W. Swift
H. Roberts	J. Simms	H. Stott	J. W Simcox
J. Randles	W. Shepherd	A. Sullivan	R. Simms
M. Rose	P. Simpson	J. Simmons	C. Sullivan
J. Rigby	Edward Smith	H. Scarisbrick	J. Tinsley
J. Rogerson	Jas. Smith	J. Swindells	T. Taylor
T. Radcliffe	W. F. Stott	D. Stanley	J. Taylor
T. Reid	Chas. South	J. Smith	J. P. Thompson
J. H. Rigby	Albert Steele	A. Stanworth	F. Tatlock
H. Rigby	John Sullivan	R. Simms	Jas. Taylor
J. Robinson	Wm. Seaton	J. Stevenson	G. Thorpe
J. Roberts	Arthur Scott	J. Speakman	W. Twist
P. Roberts	Thos. Smith	T. Seddon	Geo. Turton
J. Roughley	Jno. Seddon	T. Smith	Peter Thompson
H. Robinson	Howland Smith	C. Stewart	A. F. Trotter
T. Robinson	Jas. Stott	A. Seddon	G. Tunstall
W. Roberts	R. A. Sutton	T. Scott	Albert Topping
I. Rogers	Hy. Stowell	R. Slater	F. Turner
R. Rimmer	A. Smart	F. Sutton	V. Terry
W. Rigby	Geo. Stewart	N. Sowerbutts	P. Teeling
J. Rogerson	John Scott	A. Smart	P. Tonge
J. Rushton	Harold Scott	G. E. Swift	T. Tierney
C. Roberts	Geo. Stronge	S. Saxon	H. Thomas

W. Tickle	J. Turner	S. Woodward	J. Webster
H. Taylor	T. Unsworth	J. Wyatt	J. Waterworth
A. Taylor	H. Vince	J. Westhead	C. Walsh
A. Taylor	J. Vose	T. Webster	J. Wilson
T. Tipton	H. Wright	H. Webster	J. J. Welding
G. Talbot	H. Wislon	P. N. Williams	G. White
W. Thomas	W. Winstanley	J. Warburton	A. Winstanley
W. H. Tickle	J. Wilson	O. G. Wright	G. Waring
P. Tolan	W. Whitby	W. Webster	J. Wilkinson
W. Todd	A. West	V. Wilkinson	W. White
E. Taylor	J. Winstanley	G. Webster	J. Wayman
P. Tickle	E. Wilson	H. Wilkinson	J. Wilkinson
H. Thorp	P. Wainwright	J. Waterworth	A. Woods
W. H. Thomas	R. Woodhead	R. Wilson	H. H. Williams
T. Trayner	C. Williams	J. Webster	A. Woodward
A. Tyson	J. Webb	C. Walsh	W. Welsby
W. Tierney	A. Wills	J. J. Welding	T. Waterworth
J. Topping	J. Williams	G. White	S. Woodward
J. W. Tickle	J. Woodward	A. Winstanley	W. Woodward
P. Turner	G. Webster	J. Wilson	J. Wright
P. Travis	Ed. Westhead	J. A. Walker	S. Williams
C. Thelwell	Thos. Wilson	W. Wilson	J. Westhead
T. Thompson	Thos. Williams	T. Waterworth	S. Williams
J. Topping	Thos. Whalley	J. Williams	J. Wyatt
J. Topping	Chas. Woods	W. Winstanley	H. White
W. Thomas	Jas. Wilkinson	P. White	J. Wilkinson
W. H. Tickle	H. D. West	J. Wilton	J. Wills
G. Talbot	Frank White	W. Woodward	S. Wilkinson
W. H. Thomas	Chas. Woods	J. Wignall	W. Wildman
W. E. Trickett	Saml. Watkins	P. White	A. Watkins
P. Tonge	Fred. Waine	E. Warwick	P. Williams
T. Tierney	Chas. Wathen	E. Wilson	H. Williams
H. Thomas	Geo. Williams	L. Whittle	M. Welsh
J. T. Trotter	W. Williamson	T. Wilson	S. Woodward
J. Thompson	Peter Woods	P. S. Williams	J. Wills
W. Thomas	S. Williams	J. Williams	J. Wilson
E. Topping	J. Wright	W. Wood	J. Wilson
A. E. Thomas	S. Williams	W. Wright	A. Weldon
W. T. Tully	J. Wilson	A. Williams	J. Yates
G. Thompson	I. Wharton	J. A. Walker	D. Yates
H. Thomas	G. Wilkinson	B. Willetts	Thos. Yates
J. Telford	J. Webster	J. Webster	S. Yates
R. A. Taylor	W. Woodward	T. Whalley	W. Yates

Appendix 2: Personnel

The following list of men who served with the battalion is split into three sections; officers, men who enlisted with the battalion, and men who were posted to or transferred to the battalion from other battalions or regiments.

Names in bold indicate men who were with the battalion when it arrived in France on 6 November 1915. The battalion's War Diary records the battalion strength on arrival as 29 officers and 1,007 other ranks.

Where an entry has an asterisk (*) at the end of the line this indicates that the man re-enlisted with a different unit after being discharged from the Pals.

Where an entry has an exclamation mark (!) at the end of the line this indicates that the man re-enlisted with a different unit after being discharged from the Pals and that he died with that subsequent unit.

Where a man was posted to the Pals from a Territorial battalion of the South Lancashire Regiment his six digit service number is given. Those who enlisted prior to the Territorial renumbering in 1917 will have originally had a four digit number but this is not shown. The blocks of numbers allocated to the Territorial battalions of the South Lancashire Regiment are as follows:

4th Battalion	200001 - 240000
5th Battalion	240001 - 265000
14th Battalion	265001 - 290000

It is assumed that all those men without 'outcome' details survived and were discharged after the war.

Due to the loss of military records in a bombing raid in 1940, it is not expected that the following lists will ever be 100% complete.

Further details of the men may be found at http://www.sthelenspals.org.uk

Officers

Name	Rank	Coy.	Joined	Outcome	
Acton, John J	Lt.		15/12/17	rel.	24/05/19
Albiston, J	2/Lt.		02/11/18		
Anderson, Donald K	2/Lt.		06/10/18		
Arnold, Richard	Lt.		13/10/18		
Askew, George G	Capt.	C			
Bacon, Stanley C	2/Lt.		13/10/14		
Barrington-Ward, Victor M	Capt.	B	14/10/14	rel.	02/10/19
Baynes, John E	2/Lt.		12/02/17	rel.	13/05/19
Beal, George F	Maj.	C		rel.	28/01/20
Berry, Frederick	Capt.				
Bishop, Thomas N	Lt.		16/07/16		
Blackburne, John I	Lt.		06/10/18		
Bonnyman, Francis J	Maj.	A		rel.	25/04/22
Boshell, William D	2/Lt.		12/10/14	rel.	15/06/17
Boulton, Sydney E	Capt.				
Brackenbury, C	Lt.		16/07/16		
Bradley, Arnold	2/Lt.		02/06/15	rel.	24/10/16
Bretherton, William	Lt.	A	03/05/15	rel.	24/09/20
Brooke, Harry K	Capt.	D	09/11/14	rel.	28/03/19
Brown, H J	2/Lt.				
Buchan, W T	Lt.				
Buchanan, Robert B	Lt.		27/03/15		
Burn, Roddam W	Capt.	A	15/10/14	rel.	26/03/20
Bury, Ralph F	Maj.	A			
Carr, Robert	2/Lt.		06/10/18		
Champion, Alan T	Maj.	A	05/10/14	rel.	14/06/19
Champion, Charles C	Lt.-Col.		29/09/14	rel.	24/06/19
Champion, Eric O	2/Lt.	C	05/12/14	k.i.a.	10/06/17
Clench, Stanley T	Capt.	C	23/02/17	rel.	18/05/20
Cole, J R	Lt.	D	24/02/17	dis.	19/01/19
Coulson, Eric J	Lt.	B	16/07/16	rel.	24/04/18
Craig, Falconer	2/Lt.		24/04/15		
Culshaw, John G	Lt.	C	10/06/15	rel.	12/04/19
Dean, Albert G	Capt.		04/06/15	rel.	05/02/19
Diplock, Alfred B	Lt.		21/04/15		
Dixon, Charles J	Capt.	B	17/10/14	rel.	26/02/19
Dixon, S	Lt.				
Dixon, W H	Lt.				
Dixon-Nuttall, Frank	2/Lt.		06/02/18		
Douglas, Malcolm	Capt.		14/12/14	d.	17/11/18
Douglas, Richard M	2/Lt.				
Dunthorne, Robert G	Capt.	B	25/03/17	rel.	30/07/19
Earle, C E	Capt.				
Edwardes, Hubert W	2/Lt.		12/10/14	rel.	04/09/20
Ellis, W J	2/Lt.				
Evans, Frederick O	Maj.	C		rel.	16/01/19

Name	Rank	Coy.	Joined	Outcome	
Featherby, Charles R	Lt.		27/03/15	rel.	15/06/20
Fenn, Herbert F	Lt.-Col.		16/05/16	rel.	03/12/19
Fieldhouse, Herbert M	Capt.		10/12/17	rel.	08/11/18
Fletcher, John H	Lt.	A	29/09/14		
Fletcher, William G	2/Lt.		19/10/14	d.o.w.	14/10/16
Forester, Thomas	Capt.	C	14/01/15	rel.	26/06/19
Fox, R	Capt.				
Fry, David C	2/Lt.		19/10/14	rel.	16/11/19
Gardner, Albert	2/Lt.		13/02/16		
Garton, Reginald W	Lt.	B	23/02/15	k.i.a.	01/07/16
Gleave, G E	2/Lt.		09/01/17		
Goodwin, Henry A C	Lt.	A	03/09/14		
Gorman, H W	Lt.	A			
Griffith, T F	2/Lt.				
Griffiths, Charles P	Capt.	D	16/07/16		
Gwynn-Williams, R H	Maj.		06/05/15		
Harpur, Kenneth N	2/Lt.		25/11/17		
Harrington, Sir John L	Lt.-Col.		08/02/15	rel.	16/05/16
Harvey, Henry C	2/Lt.		14/12/17		
Hawker, Charles E	2/Lt.		14/12/17		
Hawkes, Alfred G	2/Lt.		27/11/15		
Hayes, Stanley R	2/Lt.		02/11/18		
Helman, A E	2/Lt.				
Henshaw, Lindley	Lt.	B	06/10/18		
Hitchen, J H	2/Lt.		12/10/14		
Hitchen, W G	2/Lt.		19/10/14		
Hodges, Harold A	Capt.	D		k.i.a.	24/03/18
Holman, A E	2/Lt.		14/12/17		
Holmes, John	2/Lt.		16/09/17		
Hopwood, Albert E	2/Lt.		01/04/15	dis.	04/05/16
Howes, R A	Lt.		04/01/17		
Huggins, Arthur M	Capt.		17/10/14	rel.	13/04/15
Hughes, Arthur E	2/Lt.		06/08/17		
Humphreys, Edward H	2/Lt.		14/06/15		
Hurley, Alan D	2/Lt.		25/11/17		
Hurst, Hal W	2/Lt.		13/10/14		
Hyman, Ezra H	2/Lt.			d.	01/11/18
Jolliffe, John H	Lt.	C	19/01/17		
Jones, Herbert	2/Lt.	C	06/10/18	d.o.w.	05/11/18
Kirkpatrick, D	2/Lt.		06/10/18		
Kirkpatrick, James	2/Lt.				
Knight, Allan	2/Lt.		06/08/17	k.i.a.	23/03/18
Kuny, S	M.O.				
Langford, John W	Lt.		23/12/14		
Langton, R	Lt.				
Lea, Albert	Lt.			dem.	07/11/19

Name	Rank	Coy.	Joined	Outcome	
Leake, Robert L	Lt.	B	24/02/17	rel.	16/04/19
Lean, A G	Lt.				
Lewis, Arthur W	Lt.	C	16/07/16	rel.	15/05/19
Lidgett, John C	Lt.		12/02/17	k.i.a.	23/03/18
Mallalieu, J P	Lt.		09/12/17		
Manning, Archibald R	Lt.	A	15/01/15		
Marshall, Oswald H	Lt.		06/10/18		
McEwan, W	Lt.		06/10/18		
McIntyre, J	2/Lt.				
McKenzie, B F	Lt.	D	10/01/17		
McLeod-Braggins, Samuel W	Lt.	A	16/07/16	rel.	05/02/19
Mercer, J E	2/Lt.	A	15/02/17		
Miller, Ralph W	2/Lt.		08/04/15	rel.	01/07/19
Moffat, H H	Lt.				
Myles, W A	Lt.		15/04/17		
Nash, Leonard A	2/Lt.	B	14/06/15	rel.	16/10/19
Newman, F C	2/Lt.		06/10/18		
Newsham, Thomas	2/Lt.		06/10/18		
O'Connor, Edward J	Lt.				
Owen, William J	Lt.	D	23/02/17	rel.	26/03/19
Parr, Edgar B	2/Lt.	B	19/10/14	d.o.w.	21/11/16
Parsons, Joshua	Lt.	A	06/09/15		
Pawle, Alfred G	Lt.-Col.		16/11/14	rel.	07/02/15
Payne, Joseph T	Capt.			rel.	26/05/19
Peck, Cedric E	Lt.		08/07/15	rel.	21/01/19
Peters, J J	2/Lt.		26/01/17		
Pethick, John E	Capt.	A	15/10/16	rel.	01/01/20
Potter, Tom	Maj.	D			
Potter, W E	Lt.		06/10/18		
Prance, Stanley	2/Lt.		06/10/18		
Radcliffe, Willoughby F	Capt.				
Rae, Harold	2/Lt.		25/11/17		
Ramsbottom, N S	Lt.		28/02/17		
Ratcliffe, D	Lt.				
Reece, Frederick B	2/Lt.		20/04/15	d.o.w.	20/04/18
Rice, Adolphus H	Q.M.		06/05/15	rel.	13/07/19
Ridsdale, William	Lt.	B	16/07/16	rel.	24/01/19
Robinson, M D	Capt.	C			
Rowley, Harold B	Capt.		11/01/15		
Ryden, L	Lt.		06/10/18		
Ryder, A H	2/Lt.		04/06/15		
Sagar, John R	2/Lt.		01/12/14		
Shaw, Richard J	2/Lt.		15/02/17	d.o.w.	26/06/17
Skerritt, A C	2/Lt.		06/10/18		
Smith, Alton E C	Capt.		05/10/14	rel.	13/01/17
Smith, Clarence	2/Lt.		01/11/18		

Name	Rank	Coy.	Joined	Outcome	
Smith, Graham E	2/Lt.		06/07/15	rel.	21/11/17
Stedman, Archibald G	Lt.		02/12/18		
Struthers, Robert J	Capt.	A	14/06/15	rel.	01/04/19
Symon, Carril H	Lt.		14/05/15	rel.	26/03/19
Taylor, J	Capt.		12/01/17		
Taylor, James	Capt.				
Taylor, S H	2/Lt.		06/10/18		
Thomas, Robert W	Col.		01/09/14	rel.	16/11/14
Thompson, William R	2/Lt.		29/09/14		
Thomson, Gerald	2/Lt.		25/11/17		
Tilford, George	Lt.		15/09/16	rel.	11/07/19
Tomkinson, Cecil R	Lt.		25/11/17		
Tompson, G	2/Lt.				
Unsworth, Cyril J	2/Lt.		29/08/15	d.o.w.	07/07/16
Walker, Alexander D	Lt.		10/01/15	rel.	10/05/19
Walker, George H	Lt.	A	14/06/15	k.i.a.	28/07/17
Warr, F O	2/Lt.				
Watson, Stanley K	2/Lt.	B	14/06/15		
Weatherley, A R	2/Lt.		19/01/17		
West, Harry D	Lt.	A			
Williams, R	Lt.				
Wood, A J	Lt.				
Woods, Stanley E	Lt.		19/12/14	rel.	09/02/19
Woolcock, Horace J	Lt.		05/04/15	rel.	22/06/19

Other Ranks (Enlisted)

Name	Rank	No.	Coy.	Joined	Outcome	
Abberley, Roger L	Sgt.	20293	A			
Abbott, Henry	L/Cpl.	20508	C		dis.	17/02/19
Abram, Robert J	Sgt.	21596				
Ackers, John	Pte.	21815		31/05/15	d.o.w.	09/09/17
Adams, John	Pte.	20259	A	04/09/14	dis.	02/12/14
Adamson, George	Pte.	20433	B	08/09/14	dis.	06/02/15
Adamson, Robert	Bglr	21065		14/09/14	dis.	24/12/14
Adamson, Robert	Pte.	21657		22/05/15	dis.	31/10/19
Aitken, John T	Sgt.	21168	D	18/11/14	k.i.a.	21/03/18
Aitken, Robert	Pte.	20943			dis.	05/03/19
Alcock, Edward	Pte.	20176	A			
Alcock, Henry	Pte.	20513	C	08/09/14	dis.	13/07/17
Allcock, Vernon	Pte.	20266		08/09/14	dis.	09/03/19
Allen, James	Pte.	21504	A	02/03/15	dis.	09/07/17
Allen, John	Cpl.	20599			dis.	20/01/19
Allen, Stephen	Pte.	21732	F	26/05/15	dis.	08/07/15
Allen, Thomas	Pte.	21405				
Allender, Bertrand J	L/Cpl.	20087		07/09/14	k.i.a.	01/07/16
Almond, Joseph	Pte.	21318	A	23/01/15	d.o.w.	24/06/17
Anders, Charles	Pte.	20314			dis.	27/03/19
Anders, Henry	Pte.	21824				
Anders, Thomas	Cpl.	20319			dis.	28/02/19
Appleton, Charles	Pte.	21668		22/05/15	dis.	02/08/16
Appleton, James	Bglr	21063		11/09/14	dis.	24/12/14 *
Appleton, John W	Pte.	20165		04/09/14	dis.	28/06/16
Appleton, William	Pte.	20304			dis.	19/07/19
Archbold, Henry	Pte.	20005		05/09/14	dis.	17/12/17
Archer, ...	Pte.	21586				
Archer, Arthur	Pte.	20758		08/09/14	dis.	24/10/14
Archer, Frederick	Pte.	20734	C			
Armstrong, James	Pte.	21658	A	22/05/15	dis.	05/02/19
Ashall, Albert	Sgt.	20505	C		dis.	03/02/19
Ashall, Arthur	Cpl.	20365	B		dis.	
Ashall, George	Pte.	20617	C		dis.	05/03/19
Ashby, Edward	Sgt.	21176	C	08/09/14	d.o.w.	01/08/17
Ashcroft, Harry B	Pte.	20229				
Ashcroft, Henry	Pte.	20254	A	08/09/14	dis.	04/10/18
Ashcroft, James	Pte.	20668		05/09/14	dis.	13/01/19
Ashcroft, John	Sgt.	20024			k.i.a.	02/10/18
Ashcroft, Ralph	Sgt.	21261			dis.	15/01/19
Ashcroft, Richard	A/Cpl.	21276			dis.	08/07/19
Ashley, Joseph	Pte.	21051		28/09/14	dis.	25/01/19
Ashley, Thomas	Pte	21868				
Ashton, Edmund	Pte.	21866	B	05/06/15	dis.	25/01/19
Ashton, Edward	Pte.	21123		12/10/14	dis.	21/06/15
Ashton, Herbert	Pte.	21423		04/02/15	dis.	07/07/15

Name	Rank	No.	Coy.	Joined	Outcome	
Ashton, James	Pte.	21284	C	20/01/15	dis.	24/04/15
Ashton, James	Pte.	21418		20/01/15	dis.	15/08/16
Ashton, John	Pte.	21600	A		dis.	28/03/19
Atherton, Adam	Pte.	21955	C	28/07/15	dis.	07/04/19
Atherton, Albert	L/Cpl.	21132	A			
Atherton, James	Pte.	21910		10/07/15	d.	09/05/17
Atherton, James	Pte.	21003	D		dis.	26/04/19
Atherton, Joseph	Pte.	20887	D	08/09/14	dis.	03/05/19
Atherton, Thomas	Cpl.	20865	D	08/09/14	dis.	17/01/19
Atherton, Thomas	Sgt.	20481		08/09/14	dis.	11/02/19
Atherton, William	L/Cpl.	20795	D	04/09/14	k.i.a.	23/03/18
Atkinson, James	Pte.	21872				
Atkinson, Richard	Pte.	20449			dis.	23/04/19
Bagnall, Sidney	Pte.				k.i.a.	03/05/17 !
Bagot, Patrick	Sgt.			24/09/14	dis.	22/09/16
Bailey, Richard	Pte.	20349		07/09/14	dis.	07/10/14 *
Baines, James H	Pte.	22033				
Baldwin, Frank	Pte.	21706		26/05/15	k.i.a.	08/10/16
Baldwin, Robert	Pte.	20790		08/09/14	dis.	25/08/17
Bamber, Albert	Pte.	20681			dis.	27/01/19
Bamber, Edward	Cpl.	20256	A		dis.	27/03/19
Bamber, James	Pte.	20605			dis.	16/03/19
Bamber, William	Pte.	21503				
Bamford, William	Pte.	21665		22/05/15	dis.	11/06/19
Banks, Henry	Pte.	20636		04/09/14	dis.	18/02/19
Barclay, Thomas S	Pte.	21097	A	30/09/14	k.i.a.	23/03/18
Barker, Henry P	Pte.	21466			dis.	17/01/19
Barnes, Horace	L/Cpl.	20102				
Barnes, John	Sgt.	20475			d.o.w.	12/10/18
Barnett, Robert	Pte.	21218	A		dis.	22/03/16
Barrett, Edward	Pte.	21757		27/05/15	dis.	28/06/15
Barrett, George	Pte.	21059	A	12/04/15	dis.	16/04/18
Barrow, George	Pte.	20424		04/09/14	dis.	25/10/14 *
Barrow, James	Pte.	20117	A	07/09/14	dis.	23/05/19
Bartley, John	Pte.	21114		07/09/14	dis.	02/05/17
Barton, Alfred M	W.O. II.	20778	C		dis.	07/05/19
Barton, James	Sgt.	21437			dis.	26/02/19
Barton, John	Pte.	20680		08/09/14	dis.	05/03/17
Basnett, James	Pte.	21573				
Bate, Frank	Pte.	21357			dis.	07/02/19
Bate, John	Pte.	21529			k.i.a.	13/10/18
Bate, Oswald	Cpl.	20298			dis.	30/01/19
Bate, Samuel	Pte.	20689				
Bate, Thomas	Pte.	20661	C		dis.	08/02/19
Batten, John	L/Cpl.	20099		07/09/14	d.o.w.	31/03/18
Battersby, William	Pte.	20468		04/09/14	dis.	16/12/14 *

Name	Rank	No.	Coy.	Joined	Outcome	
Baxter, Joseph	Pte.	20801				
Beard, John A	Pte.	20379		05/09/14	dis.	07/10/14 *
Beard, Joseph	Pte.	20523	C	07/09/14	d.o.w.	16/12/15
Beavis, Ernest A	Pte.	21137			dis.	28/01/19
Bebbington, James	Pte.			04/09/14	dis.	15/04/19
Beckett, Thomas	Pte.	21240	A	15/01/15	k.i.a.	01/07/16
Beddow, William	Pte.	21804		31/05/15	dis.	22/09/16
Bedson, Thomas	Pte.	21891	A		dis.	12/01/19
Beech, William	Pte.	20362	B		dis.	14/03/19
Beesley, Albert	Pte.	21887	A		dis.	28/03/19
Beesley, Edwin	L/Cpl.	20002	A	05/09/14	k.i.a.	27/09/18
Beesley, Thomas	Pte.	20316		05/09/14	d.	17/06/15
Begley, John J	Pte.	20972				
Bell, John W	Pte.	21358	C	25/01/15	dis.	01/01/19
Bellard, Peter	Pte.	21731				
Bellis, Joseph	Pte.	20698		07/09/14	dis.	01/10/14
Bennett, Henry	Pte.	20055	A	04/09/14	d.o.w.	10/07/17
Bennett, Peter	Pte.	21901		30/06/15	k.i.a.	02/09/18
Bentham, Henry	Pte.	21700			dis.	31/01/19
Benyon, James	Pte.	21461			dis.	15/01/19
Benyon, John	Pte.	21030			dis.	12/03/19
Berrey, Herbert	Sgt.	20779	D		dis.	27/02/19
Berry, B	Sgt.					
Berry, John	Pte.	21688		26/05/15	dis.	16/02/16
Bibby, Joseph	Pte.		A			
Bibby, William	Pte.	21431		08/02/15	dis.	11/08/15
Billington, Herbert	Pte.	20019			dis.	16/03/19
Birkett, Robert	Pte.	21954	C	28/07/15	d.	05/08/17
Birks, William J	L/Cpl.	20136	A	04/09/14	dis.	30/05/19
Bisby, George	Pte.	21660		22/05/15	dis.	28/09/16
Bishop, James	Cpl.	21456	C		dis.	17/02/19
Bithell, Thomas	Pte.	21968		04/08/15	dis.	24/04/19
Blackmore, John	Pte.	21735				
Blagg, Joseph	Pte.	20404			dis.	13/01/19
Blake, William G	L/Sjt.	20567	A	05/09/14	k.i.a.	23/03/18
Blakoe, John	Pte.	20510	C			
Blood, John	Pte.	20977			dis.	05/03/19
Bluck, Emanuel F	L/Cpl.	20825		05/09/14	dis.	31/08/17
Boardman, George M	C.Q.M.S.	20056	B		dis.	12/03/19
Boardman, Horace	Pte.	21659	A	22/05/15	d.o.w.	26/04/18
Boardman, James	Pte.	21389	E	01/02/15	dis.	03/05/15
Boardman, Walter H	Pte.	20852	D		dis.	08/08/19
Boden, John	R.S.M.	20313		05/09/14	dis.	02/10/16
Bolton, Henry	Pte.	21555	B	12/05/15	dis.	18/01/19
Booth, Richard	Pte.	20003	A	05/09/14	dis.	12/02/19
Booth, William N	Pte.	20639	C		dis.	19/01/19

Name	Rank	No.	Coy.	Joined	Outcome	
Bott, Thomas W	Pte.	20593		04/09/14	dis.	08/01/15 *
Bott, Wilfred	Pte.	20584		05/09/14	dis.	06/02/15
Bowden, Frederick	Pte.	21454	C	12/02/15	d.o.w.	23/07/16
Bowden, J	Sgt.					
Bowes, Arthur	Pte.	21644				
Boyes, Walter	Pte.	21482	B		dis.	27/01/19
Boylan, John	Pte.	21388		30/01/15	dis.	10/04/19
Bracken, Thomas	Cpl.	20342			dis.	19/02/19
Bracken, William	Pte.	20551			k.i.a.	20/09/18
Bradbury, Peter	Pte.	21292		21/01/15	dis.	05/02/15
Bradbury, Thomas H	A/Cpl.	20030	A	05/09/14	d.	29/05/18
Bradford, Richard T	Pte.	21430				
Bradshaw, John	Pte.	20979			dis.	12/12/19
Bradshaw, Robert	Pte.	21725	B	26/05/15	k.i.a.	18/11/16
Brady, William	Pte.	21907	B	12/07/15	d.o.w.	25/06/17
Brady, William	Pte.	21713		26/05/15	dis.	22/09/16
Brakeley, John	Pte.	21415		02/02/15	dis.	01/05/19
Bratby, James	Pte.	21733			dis.	27/09/19
Bray, Joseph	Pte.	21631		25/05/15	d.o.w.	15/10/18
Breese, John H	Pte.	21147		07/11/14	dis.	27/09/16
Brian, Edgar	Pte.	21687		25/05/15	dis.	10/03/16
Bridge, Edward	Pte.	21101	B			
Briers, George	Pte.	20838		08/09/14	dis.	10/08/18
Briers, James	Pte.	21055		12/04/15	dis.	22/05/15
Bright, Oliver	Pte.	20798		05/09/14	dis.	07/09/18
Brimelow, James	Pte.	20953		08/09/14	dis.	28/03/17
Briscoe, Robert	Pte.	20971		08/09/14	k.i.a.	21/03/18
Britton, ...	Sgt.					
Broderick, Thomas	L/Cpl.	20894				
Brogan, Josiah	Pte.	21920		14/07/15	dis.	22/07/15
Brookes, James	Pte.	21759		26/05/15	dis.	03/03/16
Brough, John J	Pte.	21943				
Brown, Daniel	Pte.	21353	E	26/01/15	dis.	10/03/16
Brown, Edward	Pte.	20058		05/09/14	dis.	16/12/14
Brown, Isaac	Pte.	21451		15/02/15	dis.	23/03/19
Brown, James	Pte.	21684				
Brown, John E	Pte.	20160	A	08/09/14	d.o.w.	18/05/18
Brown, John T	Pte.	20133	A	04/09/14	dis.	21/01/19
Brown, Samuel	Pte.	20973	D	05/09/14	dis.	21/02/19
Brown, William	Pte.	20820		05/09/14	dis.	08/02/15
Brown, William	Pte.	21256				
Brownbill, Harold	Pte.	20519			dis.	17/02/19
Bryan, William	Pte.	20057	A	04/09/14	k.i.a.	01/07/16
Buckley, Hugh	Pte.	20375				
Buckley, Thomas	Pte.	21058	C	07/09/14	dis.	28/10/14
Bullock, Albert	Pte.	20746	C	07/09/14	dis.	06/03/19

Name	Rank	No.	Coy.	Joined	Outcome	
Bullock, John W	Pte.	20169	A		dis.	09/03/19
Burdekin, Thomas	Pte.	20017		04/09/14	dis.	18/01/18
Burgess, James	Pte.	21847		02/06/15	d.o.w.	28/03/18
Burgess, William P	Pte.	21836	D	01/06/15	d.o.w.	12/06/17
Burke, Joseph	Pte.	21718	C			
Burke, Patrick	Pte.	21598		20/05/15	dis.	23/04/18
Burke, Thomas	Pte.	21811		31/05/15	dis.	13/01/19
Burns, Frank	Pte.	21788	B	28/05/15	d.	26/01/17
Burns, John P	Pte.	21153				
Burns, Thomas	Cpl.	21150		09/11/14	dis.	01/06/17
Burns, William	Pte.	20458			dis.	27/02/20
Burrill, Horatio	Bglr	21084		04/09/14	dis.	28/12/14
Burrill, John	Pte.	20556		05/09/14	dis.	10/01/17
Burrows, Charles	Pte.	21170	D	17/11/14	k.i.a.	29/06/17
Burrows, James	Pte.	20372	B	04/09/14	k.i.a.	27/03/18
Burrows, John	Pte.	21299		20/01/15	dis.	21/03/19
Burrows, William	Pte.	20410		08/09/14	dis.	25/04/15
Burton, James	Pte.	21369				
Burton, Joseph	Pte.					
Bushell, William	Pte.	21971		07/08/15	dis.	25/02/19
Butler, Joseph	Pte.	21158				
Butler, Joseph W	Pte.	20816			dis.	27/01/19
Byrne, Francis	Pte.	20596	C	04/09/14	dis.	24/10/14 *
Byrne, Martin	Pte.	21625		24/05/15	d.o.w.	26/06/17
Byrne, Thomas	Pte.	21112		05/10/14	dis.	14/12/18
Byron, Edwin	Pte.	20049		05/09/14	dis.	25/10/14 !
Byron, George	Pte.	21646		24/05/15	dis.	09/06/15
Byron, Henry	Pte.	21956		30/07/15	d.o.w.	24/06/17
Caffrey, Joseph	Pte.	20453		04/09/14	dis.	08/10/14 *
Cain, William	Pte.	20386	B	05/09/14	dis.	23/01/19
Caldwell, William	Pte.	21663	C	24/05/15	dis.	26/02/19
Callaghan, Henry	Pte.	21337	A		dis.	28/03/19
Callery, Henry	Pte.	21553		24/04/15	dis.	20/01/19
Callery, William	Pte.	20232	A	08/09/14	dis.	03/02/19
Campbell, William	Pte.	20824	D			
Cantlon, John J	Pte.	21196		28/12/14	dis.	03/05/18
Cardwell, Richard	Pte.	21595				
Carey, Thomas	Pte.	20479				
Carney, George	Pte.	20730		04/09/14	dis.	06/02/15 *
Carney, Michael	Pte.	20243		05/09/14	dis.	16/10/14
Carney, Thomas	Pte.	21708				
Carney, William	Pte.	21747				
Carr, James	Pte.	20935	D		dis.	15/01/19
Carroll, James	Pte.	21333		25/01/15	dis.	13/01/19
Carroll, Matthew	C.S.M.	21019	D	08/09/14	k.i.a.	27/03/18
Carroll, William	Pte.	21334	C	25/01/15	k.i.a.	23/03/18

Name	Rank	No.	Coy.	Joined	Outcome	
Carson, John	Pte.	21905		09/07/15	dis.	17/08/16
Carter, Cornelius	Pte.	21264	E	18/01/15	d.	03/02/15
Carter, George	Pte.	20208				
Carter, Joseph	Pte.	20308		04/09/14	dis.	26/05/16
Cartledge, William	Pte.	21332		23/01/15	dis.	08/02/15
Cartwright, Frederick	Pte.	21325	D	25/01/15	k.i.a.	20/12/15
Cartwright, Joseph	Cpl.	20564		08/09/14	dis.	24/09/17
Caslin, Thomas	Pte.	20484		08/09/14	dis.	26/03/18
Caudwell, Walter G	Pte.	21821		31/05/15	dis.	28/01/16
Cayton, Thomas L	Bglr	21075		17/09/14	dis.	24/12/14 *
Chadwick, Thomas E	Pte.	20485		08/09/14	dis.	28/02/19
Chamberlain, Alex.ʳ	Pte.	21001			dis.	22/04/19
Chisnall, Gilbert	Sgt.	20361	A	04/09/14	dis.	15/02/19
Chisnall, Harry	Pte.	21939		21/07/15	dis.	16/10/15
Chisnall, James	Pte.	20143			k.i.a.	28/03/18
Chisnall, Joseph	Pte.	20873			dis.	15/01/19
Chorley, James	Sgt.	20797	C		dis.	06/03/19
Chorley, Thomas	Pte.	21109			dis.	26/03/19
Chorley, William	Pte.	20312			k.i.a.	01/06/18
Chorley, William	Pte.	20810		08/09/14	dis.	02/10/14
Christopher, John	Pte.	20432		07/09/14	dis.	08/02/15 *
Clapham, Bertie C	Pte.	20622	C		dis.	
Clarey, Michael	Pte.	21599	F	19/05/15	dis.	28/12/18
Clark, James	Pte.	20735		04/09/14	dis.	06/02/15 !
Clark, James	Pte.	21485			k.i.a.	13/10/18
Clarke, Aaron	Pte.	21371			k.i.a.	05/08/18
Clarke, Ernest	Pte.	20635			dis.	13/04/19
Clarke, Harold G	A/Cpl.	20282			k.i.a.	13/10/18
Clarke, James	Pte.	20693		07/09/14	dis.	02/10/14
Clarke, Thomas	Pte.	21802		31/05/15	dis.	24/10/17
Clarke, William	Pte.	20686		04/09/14	dis.	08/01/15
Clarke, William	Bglr.	21082		08/09/14	dis.	24/12/14
Clarke, William	Pte.	21453	C	12/02/15	k.i.a.	23/03/18
Claydon, William H	Pte.	21728	A	26/05/15	dis.	21/02/19
Clayton, Joseph	Pte.	22089			dis.	22/10/19
Clayton, William	Cpl.	21976	C			
Clifft, William	Pte.	20320			dis.	16/04/19
Clitheroe, John G	Pte.	21122	B	12/10/14	dis.	07/06/15 *
Clitheroe, Joseph	Pte.	20810			dis.	17/02/19
Clough, William	Pte.	21997		23/08/15	dis.	22/08/19
Coates, Christopher O	C.S.M.		D			
Cole, Charles J	Pte.	20538	C		dis.	20/02/19
Cole, James	Pte.	21172	D	17/11/14	d.o.w.	24/09/18
Collie, William	Pte.	21591	B	19/05/15	dis.	06/03/19
Collier, Frederick	Sgt.	20016	A	04/09/14	d.o.w.	11/05/17
Colligan, J	Pte.	20462				

Name	Rank	No.	Coy.	Joined	Outcome	
Collins, Frederick	Pte.	21694		25/05/15	dis.	26/07/16
Collins, Hugh	Pte.	20156				
Collins, John	Pte.	21045			dis.	17/02/19
Colquitt, J	Pte.	21135	B			
Colville, John	Pte.	20574			d.	15/03/16
Connaughton, John	Pte.	20248	A	05/09/14	dis.	24/10/14 *
Connaughton, Mich.[1]	Pte.	20739	C	05/09/14	dis.	25/04/18
Connor, John	Pte.	21898		28/06/15	des.	23/10/15
Connor, Thomas	Pte.	20775	D			
Connor, Thomas	Pte.	21948		26/07/15	dis.	18/09/15
Conroy, John	Pte.	20197		04/09/14	dis.	15/10/14
Cooban, James	Pte.	21883	A	14/06/15	dis.	26/05/16
Cook, Frederick	Pte.	20094	A		dis.	08/03/19
Cook, John	Pte.	20592	C			
Cook, William	Pte.	20502	C		dis.	16/08/17
Cooney, James	Pte.	21452	A	15/02/15	d.o.w.	20/06/17
Cooney, Michael	Pte.	21892			d.o.w.	29/03/18
Cooper, James	Pte.	20497	C	04/09/14	dis.	03/03/19
Cooper, James	Pte.	20558	C	05/09/14	dis.	23/02/19
Cooper, Joseph	Pte.	21290	B		dis.	04/02/19
Cooper, Oliver C	Pte.	20113			dis.	21/02/19
Corden, Charles	Pte.	20216	A	07/09/14	dis.	23/05/19
Cordingley, William	Pte.	20488				
Corless, Gordon	Pte.	21520				
Corns, Joseph W	Pte.	21719		26/05/15	dis.	22/08/16
Cornwell, Samuel H	Pte.					
Corrigan, Michael	Pte.	21195	B		dis.	17/04/19
Corrigan, Peter	Pte.	20745		05/09/14	dis.	22/10/17
Corrigan, Robert	Pte.	21464			dis.	09/01/19
Costello, Thomas	Pte.	21267	A	18/01/15	dis.	17/03/16
Cotter, Garrett	Pte.	20343		08/09/14	dis.	16/04/19
Cotterill, William	L/Cpl.	20804	D	05/09/14	k.i.a.	01/07/16
Cottington, John	Cpl.	20431		07/09/14	dis.	09/09/17
Cotton, John	Pte.	20514		03/09/14	dis.	27/03/19
Cotton, Owen	Pte.	21025	D			
Coulbourne, Charles J	Pte.	20142		04/09/14	dis.	22/01/19
Cousins, Thomas C	Sgt.	21090				
Cowen, John	Pte.	21221		11/01/15	dis.	20/03/19
Cowley, George	Pte.	20108	A		dis.	
Cowley, James	Pte.	21427		08/02/15	dis.	03/08/19
Cowpe, Herbert	Pte.	20630			dis.	16/03/19
Cox, George	Pte.	20870			dis.	27/01/19
Cox, John	Pte.	20344				
Crane, Frank	Pte.	20988			dis.	11/03/19
Crawford, James	Pte.	20785	D		dis.	13/01/19
Creaghan, John	Pte.	21633	B	24/05/15	d.o.w.	05/10/16

Name	Rank	No.	Coy.	Joined	Outcome	
Cribbin, Michael	Pte.	21422		05/02/15		
Crick, Frederick	Pte.	20348	B	07/09/14	dis.	26/02/19
Crilly, Francis	Pte.	20910	D	05/09/14	dis.	06/02/15 !
Critchley, Frederick M	Pte.	21429		08/02/15	dis.	17/02/19
Critchley, Joseph	Pte.	20419		08/08/14	dis.	02/10/14
Critchley, Joseph	Pte.	21856		06/06/15	dis.	23/06/15
Critchley, Joseph	Pte.	21205	C	05/01/15	k.i.a.	23/03/18
Critchley, Peter	Pte.	21793		29/05/15	d.	21/12/15
Critchley, Samuel	Pte.	21410		02/02/15	dis.	24/03/15 *
Critchley, William	Pte.	20815	D		dis.	13/01/19
Crockett, Horace	Pte.	20472	B		dis.	16/03/19
Croft, Harry	Pte.	20896	D	08/09/14	dis.	20/01/19
Crompton, Joseph	Pte.	20451	B	04/09/14	dis.	23/12/19
Crompton, Percival	Pte.	20148	E	08/09/14	dis.	03/03/19
Crook, George T	Pte.	21392	C	01/02/15	k.i.a.	25/03/18
Crook, James	Pte.	21304	A	21/01/15	dis.	23/01/19
Crooks, Albert	Pte.			05/09/14	dis.	12/11/14 *
Crooks, John R	W.O. II.	20272			dis.	19/07/19
Cropper, Albert	Pte.	21458		16/02/15	dis.	31/03/19
Cropper, Joseph	Pte.	21457		16/02/15	dis.	26/02/19
Cropper, Thomas	Pte.	20707		04/09/14	dis.	06/02/15 *
Crosby, George	Pte.	21607				
Cross, William	Pte.	20670		05/09/14	dis.	02/10/14 *
Crump, Frederick	Pte.	20127			dis.	21/03/19
Cullen, John	Pte.	21489				
Cullen, William	Sgt.	21313	D	23/01/15	dis.	02/03/19
Culley, John	Pte.	21328			k.i.a.	09/10/17
Cunliffe, Amos	Pte.	20962	D	07/09/14	dis.	14/12/18
Cunliffe, David	Pte.	21329		23/01/15	d.o.w.	08/07/16
Cunliffe, William	Pte.	21539		17/03/15	dis.	27/09/16
Cunning, James	Pte.	21989				
Cunningham, Arthur	Pte.	20907	D	05/09/14	dis.	14/12/18
Cunningham, James	Pte.	21618				
Cunningham, Timothy	Pte.	20789	D	05/09/14	dis.	08/03/19
Curran, Charles	Pte.					
Curren, Frederick	Pte.	21225	B		dis.	19/02/19
Curtis, Alfred	Pte.	21301		23/01/15	dis.	30/03/15
Dagnall, John T	Pte.	21425	B	05/02/15	dis.	25/01/19
Dalton, Samuel L	Pte.	20290	D	04/09/14	d.	22/03/17
Dancer, John H	Pte.	20501		07/09/14	dis.	22/09/16
Davies, Bernard	Pte.	20521		07/09/14	k.i.a.	03/06/17
Davies, Ernest	Cpl.	21273		19/01/15	dis.	10/12/19
Davies, Job	Pte.	20638	C		dis.	27/01/19
Davies, John	Pte.	20524			dis.	06/03/19
Davies, John	Pte.	21839		01/06/15	dis.	04/08/16
Davies, John T	Cpl.	20765	D		dis.	06/04/19

Name	Rank	No.	Coy.	Joined	Outcome	
Davies, John W	Pte.	21863		05/06/15	dis.	17/12/19
Davies, Joseph	Pte.	20515			dis.	29/08/17
Davies, Robert	Cpl.	20001	A	05/09/14	k.i.a.	23/03/18
Davies, Samuel	Pte.	20791	D		dis.	13/01/19
Davies, Samuel J	Pte.	21704	B	26/05/15	dis.	28/06/18
Davies, William	Pte.	20124	A	04/09/14	dis.	09/03/19
Davies, William	Pte.	20525			dis.	08/03/19
Davies, William	Pte.	21352	D	25/01/15	k.i.a.	01/07/16
Dawson, James	Pte.	20866	D	08/09/14	dis.	29/10/18
Deacle, Henry	Pte.	21753	B	27/05/15	k.i.a.	28/03/18
Dean, George	Pte.	20549	B	04/09/14	d.o.w.	15/06/16
Deary, James	Pte.	21544		23/03/15	dis.	08/05/17
Delaney, Daniel	Pte.	21613		20/05/15	dis.	08/02/19
Dempsey, Peter	Pte.	20968		07/09/14	dis.	16/12/14
Dennett, Henry	Pte.	21409		03/02/15	dis.	23/05/18
Dennett, John	Sgt.	20027	A	05/09/14	rel.	16/01/19
Dennett, Lawrence	Pte.	21338			dis.	13/03/19
Derbyshire, Austin	Pte.	20954		07/09/14	dis.	15/01/19
Derbyshire, Thomas	Pte.	21990		17/08/15	dis.	16/09/15 *
Devine, Michael	Pte.					
Devine, Thomas	Pte.	20703	C		dis.	13/01/19
Devlin, William H	Pte.	20688			dis.	27/01/19
Dickinson, Robert	Sgt.	20115	A			
Didsbury, Frank	Pte.	21531		15/03/15	d.o.w.	11/01/18
Dillon, Thomas	L/Cpl.	21086	D	05/09/14	k.i.a.	31/07/17
Dingley, John	Pte.	20253	A	07/09/14	dis.	12/03/19
Dingsdale, James	Pte.	20782	C	04/09/14	dis.	03/05/19
Dingsdale, Peter	Pte.	20522	C	07/09/14	dis.	22/03/19
Dingsdale, Thomas	Pte.	21307	B	22/01/15	dis.	11/10/17
Dingsdale, William	L/Cpl.	20131	A		dis.	18/03/19
Ditchfield, William	Pte.	20809			dis.	09/03/19
Dixon, George	Pte.	21637		24/05/15	dis.	24/04/19
Dixon, James	Pte.	20911			dis.	06/01/19
Dixon, Moses	Pte.	20195		08/09/14	dis.	22/10/17
Dixon, William	Pte.	21014	D	05/09/14	dis.	22/03/20
Dockerty, Mathias	Pte.	21266		18/01/15	dis.	28/05/18
Dodd, Charles	Pte.	21268			dis.	27/01/19
Dodd, Thomas	Pte.	21678		25/05/15	dis.	21/03/19
Dodd, William	Pte.	21628		24/05/15	dis.	29/09/16
Dolan, John	Pte.	20607		07/09/14	dis.	27/09/16
Dolan, Michael	Pte.	20456	B		dis.	25/03/19
Dolan, Owen	Pte.	21255			dis.	28/03/19
Donnelly, James	Pte.	20426		08/09/14	dis.	12/11/14
Donnelly, Thomas	Pte.	21651		25/05/15	dis.	10/03/16
Donoghue, George	Pte.	21271			dis.	04/03/19
Donohue, John	Pte.	21740		26/05/15	dis.	27/11/16

Name	Rank	No.	Coy.	Joined	Outcome	
Donovan, Michael	Pte.	20429		08/09/14	dis.	07/01/19
Dorning, Fred	Pte.	20042	A	07/09/14	dis.	02/06/19
Douglas, Thomas	Pte.	21282			dis.	02/03/19
Douglas, William	Pte.					
Downey, James	Pte.	21676		25/05/15	dis.	25/09/17
Downey, Reginald	Pte.	21604	A			
Doyle, Thomas	Pte.	20807	D	07/09/14	dis.	03/05/19
Drinkwater, Arthur	Sgt.	20274	B		dis.	22/02/19
Duckworth, Ernest	Pte.	21237		15/01/15	dis	21/05/15
Duffy, Denis	Pte.			05/09/14	dis.	*
Duffy, John	L/Cpl.	20774	D		dis.	07/03/19
Duggan, Christopher	Pte.	21634		24/05/15	dis.	16/02/16
Dumphy, John	Pte.	20074		07/09/14		
Dunne, William	Pte.	21017				
Durkin, John	Pte.		A		dis.	__/11/15
Durkin, John	Pte.	21937		19/07/15		
Dutton, Joseph	Pte.	21152	A		dis.	11/03/19
Dyas, John	Pte.	21009		04/09/14	dis.	08/01/15 *
Dyas, Thomas	Pte.	20840		04/09/14	dis.	21/11/18
Dyer, George W	Pte.	20940		04/09/14	dis.	26/05/16
Dysart, William	Pte.	21627		24/05/15	dis.	06/06/17
Eames, Robert	Pte.	20932		04/09/14	dis.	02/10/14
Eaves, ...	C.S.M.		A			
Eaves, Thomas	Pte.	21179				
Eccleston, Herbert	Pte.					
Eccleston, Joseph	Pte.	20679	C	04/09/14	dis.	23/01/19
Eccleston, William	Pte.	21488		25/02/15	dis.	11/03/15 *
Edden, James	Pte.	21312		23/01/15	dis.	13/01/19
Edden, John	Pte.	21336			dis.	15/01/19
Eddowes, Peter	Pte.	20562			dis.	06/04/19
Eden, Albert	Pte.	20398		05/09/14	dis.	12/11/14
Eden, Charles	Pte.	20503		07/09/14	dis.	04/03/19
Eden, James	Pte.	21501		03/03/15	dis.	19/03/15 *
Eden, John	Pte.	20329	C		dis.	
Edgerton, John	Pte.	21995			d.o.w.	17/08/17
Edgerton, William	Pte.	20891			dis.	17/03/19
Edridge, Sydney	Pte.	20534				
Edwards, Albert	Pte.	20628	C	05/09/14	k.i.a.	01/07/16
Edwards, Goulding	Sgt.	20598	C	04/09/14	dis.	16/11/17
Edwards, I	Pte.		D			
Edwards, John	Pte.	21187	C	15/12/14	d.	27/01/15
Edwards, John M	Pte.	20948	D	05/09/14	d.o.w.	14/07/17
Edwards, Richard	Sgt.	20582	C	07/09/14	dis.	04/04/19
Edwards, Thomas	Pte.	20631	C		dis.	22/02/19
Edwards, William	Pte.	20588	C		dis.	31/03/19
Edwards, William	Pte.	20826		07/09/14	dis.	22/09/16

Name	Rank	No.	Coy.	Joined	Outcome	
Elliott, Henry	Pte.	20542	C	05/09/14	k.i.a.	23/03/18
Ellis, Edwin	Pte.	21004				
Ellis, John	Pte.	21008	B	08/09/14	dis.	05/07/18
Ellis, Joseph	Pte.	21569			dis.	24/01/19
Ellis, Michael	Pte.	20753		08/09/14	dis.	01/10/14
Ellison, Thomas	Pte.	20241	A		dis.	27/01/19
Ellison, Thomas	Pte.	20597	C		dis.	12/04/19
Entwistle, Arthur	Pte.	20270	A	05/09/14	dis.	23/02/19
Evans, Ellis	Pte.	21185		14/12/14	dis.	27/09/16
Evans, Emrys	Pte.	21972		09/08/15	dis.	29/09/16
Evans, Francis	C.S.M.		D			
Evans, H J	R.S.M.					
Evans, James	Pte.	20742			dis.	13/01/19
Evans, Joseph	Pte.	21744				
Evans, William	Pte.	20174			dis.	18/05/17
Fagan, James	Pte.	21277				
Fagan, Michael	Pte.	20723		05/09/14	dis.	12/06/15
Fagan, Michael	Pte.	20214				
Fairbank, Frederick	Pte.	21537				
Fairclough, Arthur	Pte.	20060	A	05/09/14	dis.	08/03/19
Fairclough, Benjamin	Pte.	20926		04/09/14	dis.	20/09/18
Fairclough, Hugh	Pte.	20088	A			
Fairclough, Robert	Pte.	20095	A	08/09/14	dis.	07/12/18
Fairclough, Walter H	Pte.	20924	D		dis.	13/01/19
Fairhurst, John	Pte.	20119	A		dis.	30/01/19
Fairhurst, Lambert	Pte.	20646	C	05/09/14	dis.	25/03/19
Fairhurst, Samuel	L/Cpl.	20285		04/09/14	dis.	12/05/19
Fairhurst, Thomas	Pte.	20902	D	07/09/14	dis.	20/01/19
Fairhurst, William	Pte.	21460		16/02/15	dis.	26/05/16
Fallon, John T	Pte.	21413	E	02/02/15	dis.	13/03/15
Farrar, Peter	Pte.	20743	C	08/09/14	dis.	01/12/14 *
Farrell, Charles	Pte.	21465		17/02/15	dis.	25/01/19
Farrell, James	Pte.	21298	B		dis.	12/02/19
Fawcett, Robert	Pte.	21326			dis.	09/05/19
Fazakerley, Edward B	Pte.	20034	A		dis.	16/03/19
Fazakerley, Ernest	Pte.	20371			dis.	13/03/19
Fearnley, Peter	Pte.	20732	C		dis.	03/03/19
Fearnley, Thomas	Pte.	21547				
Fegan, Michael	Pte.	20192		04/09/14	dis.	22/09/16
Fenney, Joseph	Pte.	21305				
Fenney, William	Pte.	21873		11/06/15	dis.	13/08/19
Fildes, Frederick	Sgt.	20530		08/09/14	dis.	20/07/17
Fildes, Joseph	Pte.	21906	A	09/07/15	dis.	12/08/16
Files, Ernest	Pte.	21931		16/07/15	dis.	24/07/18
Fillingham, Joseph	Pte.	20641	C	05/09/14	dis.	23/01/17
Fillingham, Peter	Pte.	20277			dis.	22/03/19

Name	Rank	No.	Coy.	Joined	Outcome	
Fillingham, William	Cpl.	20500			dis.	28/01/19
Finch, Herbert	Pte.	20759		05/09/14	dis.	28/09/18
Finch, Thomas	Pte.	20643	C	05/09/14	dis.	16/08/18
Findley, Thomas	Pte.	20879		08/09/14	dis.	28/03/19
Finn, Joseph	Pte.	20721			dis.	15/01/19
Finnesey, Alfred	Pte.	20273	E	30/03/15	dis.	14/05/15
Finney, Edward	Pte.	20918	D		dis.	26/03/19
Finney, John	Pte.	20931			dis.	21/02/19
Finney, John	Pte.	21835		01/06/15	dis.	22/03/16
Finney, John J	Sgt.	20334		05/09/14	k.i.a.	22/07/17
Finney, Joseph L	Pte.	21036				
Fishwick, Eli	Pte.	20812			dis.	02/02/19
Fitzgerald, Edward	Pte.	49033				
Fitzgerald, Philip	Pte.	21771				
Fitzhenry, John	Pte.	21622		24/05/15	dis.	19/08/16
Fitzpatrick, Thomas	Pte.	21126		15/10/14	dis.	22/01/19
Flanagan, James	L/Sjt.	20984	D	07/09/14	d.o.w.	14/05/18
Fleming, James	Pte.					
Fleming, John	Sgt.	20140	A		dis.	14/03/19
Fletcher, J	Sgt.		A			
Flood, William	Pte.	20464		07/09/14	dis.	04/04/19
Flynn, David	Pte.	20106	A	04/09/14	dis.	23/02/19
Forbes, William	Sgt.	20568	C		dis.	17/02/19
Ford, Michael	Pte.	21709		26/05/15	dis.	01/05/19
Ford, William	Cpl.	20766			dis.	30/01/19
Foreman, Stanley W	Pte.	20147	A	05/09/14	d.	20/06/16
Forrest, John	Cpl.	20430	B	08/09/14	dis.	25/02/19
Forshaw, Gilbert	Pte.	21834			dis.	27/03/19
Forshaw, William	Pte.	20091	A	05/09/14	d.o.w.	05/07/17
Forster, Robert	Pte.	20696	C	04/09/14	k.i.a.	22/12/17
Forsyth, Joseph R	Pte.	20843	D	08/09/14	dis.	27/01/19
Foster, Alfred	L/Cpl.	20869	D	04/09/14	k.i.a.	29/05/17
Foster, Arthur	Pte.	20268		08/09/14	dis.	01/02/19
Foster, Charles	Pte.	21889		16/06/15	dis.	24/03/16
Foster, Edward	Pte.	21946		22/07/15	dis.	05/07/17
Foster, Harry	Pte.	20107	A		dis.	07/03/19
Foster, John T	Pte.	21789	B	27/05/15	k.i.a.	21/03/18
Foster, Matthew	Pte.	21670		25/05/15	dis.	15/02/19
Foster, Robert	Pte.					
Foster, Thomas	Pte.	21034		05/09/14	dis.	02/10/14
Foster, Wilfred	Pte.	20764	D	04/09/14	dis.	14/01/19
Foster, William	Pte.	21173	D	17/11/14	k.i.a.	28/06/17
Foster, William	Pte.	21603	B	09/05/15	dis.	25/02/19
Foster, William	Pte.	21023		08/09/14	dis.	02/10/14
Foy, Joseph	Pte.	20602			k.i.a.	04/10/17
Friar, Albert	Pte.	20021			dis.	22/01/19

Name	Rank	No.	Coy.	Joined	Outcome	
Friend, Ernest	Pte.	21384			dis.	02/01/17
Frodsham, John	L/Cpl.	20089	A	07/09/14	k.i.a.	23/03/18
Frodsham, John	Pte.	20888		07/09/14	dis.	02/10/14
Frodsham, Richard	Pte.	20339			d.o.w.	19/10/18
Frost, Frederick J	Pte.	21583		15/05/15	d.	25/10/18
Furay, Thomas	Pte.	20969		04/09/14	dis.	19/02/19
Gallagher, George	Pte.	21404	C	02/02/15	d.o.w.	14/06/17
Gallagher, Joseph	Pte.	20223		05/09/14	dis.	08/02/19
Galsworthy, Robert W	Pte.	20000	A	05/09/14	dis.	19/02/19
Gannon, Thomas	Pte.	21401		01/02/15	dis.	22/11/17
Garbage, William	Pte.	20942	D		dis.	17/03/19
Garbutt, Frank	Pte.	21247		16/01/15	dis.	21/11/18
Gardner, Albert	L/Cpl.					
Garner, Joseph	L/Cpl.	20577	C	07/09/14	d.	10/07/18
Garner, Thomas	Pte.	20059		05/09/14	dis.	07/06/15 *
Garner, Walter	Pte.	20748				
Garrity, Edward	Pte.	20474			dis.	27/04/17
Garrity, Edward	Pte.	20589	C		dis.	21/03/19
Gaskell, George	Pte.	21984		15/08/15	dis.	09/10/15
Gaskell, Peter	Pte.	20340	B		dis.	02/06/18
Gaskell, William	Pte.	21680			des.	19/06/17
Gauchwin, Malachy	Pte.	21151	D			
Gauchwin, Thomas	Pte.	20452			dis.	08/04/19
Gauchwin, William	Pte.	21012			dis.	11/09/19
Gavin, Martin	Pte.	21953		28/07/15	dis.	30/06/18
Gear, Henry	L/Cpl.	20324			d.o.w.	06/11/18
Gearing, William	Pte.	20561	C		dis.	21/02/19
Gee, Arthur P	Cpl.	20011				
Gee, James	Sgt.	20029			dis.	15/07/19
Gee, William	Pte.	20529	C		dis.	22/02/19
George, Frederick S	Pte.	21820		31/05/15	dis.	06/03/19
Geraghty, Joseph	Pte.	21808			dis.	29/10/18
Gerrard, Harold	Pte.	20323			d.o.w.	02/11/18
Gerrard, Herbert	Pte.	20685	C	04/09/14	dis.	29/04/15 *
Gerrard, Samuel	Pte.	20757	C	04/09/14	dis.	01/12/14
Gerrity, John	Pte.	21199			dis.	20/03/19
Gibbons, William	Pte.	21862	D	05/06/15	d.o.w.	02/07/16
Gilgan, Thomas	Pte.	20295			dis.	28/02/19
Gilgannon, Michael	Pte.	21707				
Gill, Charles	Pte.	20777	D	07/09/14	k.i.a.	03/12/17
Gill, Thomas	Pte.	20729				
Gilleece, Walter	Pte.	21468				
Gilligan, F	Pte.					
Gittins, Edward	Pte.	20704				
Gittins, Thomas	Pte.	21765			dis.	09/04/19
Gleave, James	Bglr	21077	D	14/09/14	dis.	24/12/14 !

Name	Rank	No.	Coy.	Joined	Outcome	
Gleave, William	Pte.	21578		17/05/15	dis.	17/03/16
Glover, Bertie	Pte.	20434			dis.	13/01/23
Glover, Edward	Pte.	20315	A	04/09/14	k.i.a.	23/03/18
Glover, Frederick J	Pte.	20098		05/09/14	dis.	13/02/19
Glover, Henry	Pte.	21629		24/05/15	dis.	17/05/17
Glover, Robert	Pte.	20157			dis.	02/03/19
Glover, William	Cpl.	20271	A	04/09/14	dis.	09/03/19
Glynn, William	Pte.	20330	B		dis.	28/03/19
Glynn, William	Pte.	21705		26/05/15	dis.	22/01/19
Goodwin, Arthur G	L/Cpl.	20008	A	05/09/14	dis.	19/02/19
Gordon, George	Pte.	20116	A		dis.	31/03/19
Gore, James	L/Sjt.	20236	A		dis.	24/02/19
Gorman, Ernest J	Pte.	21848				
Gormley, James	Pte.	21845		03/06/15	dis.	12/07/17
Gormley, Thomas	Cpl.	20903	D	05/09/14	dis.	24/01/19
Gosling, Fred	L/Cpl.	20128	A		dis.	01/03/19
Grace, Cecil	Pte.	20215	A	08/09/14	dis.	24/06/19
Grady, Lawrence	Pte.	20919		05/09/14	dis.	14/04/16
Graham, Thomas	Pte	21936				
Grayson, Elias	Pte.	21362		26/01/15	dis.	19/06/15
Grayson, John	Pte.	20982			dis.	20/02/19
Greavey, John	Pte.	21020	D	08/09/14	dis.	05/02/15
Green, James	Pte.	21768	A	27/05/15	dis.	06/04/19
Green, James H	Sgt.	20069	A			
Green, John	Pte.	20874	D	04/09/14	dis.	29/07/18
Green, Joseph	Pte.	21548		31/03/15	des.	02/08/15
Green, Thomas	Pte.	21263	D		dis.	07/04/19
Green, William H	Pte.	21798			dis.	04/03/19
Greenall, George	Pte.	20853	D	04/09/14	k.i.a.	10/04/18
Greenall, Job	L/Cpl.	20109	C	05/09/14	dis.	24/03/19
Greenall, John	Pte.	21890			dis.	13/03/19
Greenall, Thomas	Pte.	20413	A	05/09/14	dis.	24/01/18
Greenall, William	Pte.	21846				
Greenall, William	Pte.	21223	B	11/01/15	dis.	05/02/15
Greenhall, Peter	Pte.	21347		25/01/15	dis.	07/11/16
Greenough, John	Pte.	20731				
Greenwood, Edward	Pte.	21021	D	08/09/14	dis.	06/02/15
Gregory, James	L/Cpl.	20104	A			
Gregson, Arthur	Sgt.	20408	B		dis.	20/03/19
Gregson, Joseph	Pte.	20198	A		dis.	05/03/19
Gresty, Frank	Bglr	21081		19/09/14	dis.	24/12/14 *
Griffiths, John	Pte.	21447			dis.	16/07/17
Griffiths, John B	L/Cpl.	20885	D		k.i.a.	27/03/18
Griffiths, John H	Pte.	21577		15/05/15	dis.	26/04/19
Griffiths, William	Pte.	21671		25/05/15	dis.	07/03/19
Grimes, Thomas	Sgt.	20699	C		dis.	10/03/19

Name	Rank	No.	Coy.	Joined	Outcome	
Grimes, Thomas	Pte.	21331	C	22/01/15	dis.	19/03/19
Grimes, William	Pte.	20799			dis.	30/01/19
Grimshaw, William E	Pte.	20835	C		dis.	13/01/19
Grounds, William	Pte.	21368		26/01/15	d.	30/10/18
Groves, John E	Pte.	21662		24/05/15	dis.	24/12/15
Groves, Walter	Pte.	20603	C		dis.	16/02/19
Groves, William	Pte.	20995	D	04/09/14	d.o.w.	24/12/15
Grumley, Peter	Pte.	21056		08/09/14	d.o.w.	23/04/18
Grundy, Fred	Pte.	21076	C	14/09/14	dis.	24/10/14
Grundy, James	Pte.	21182		08/09/14	dis.	25/09/14
Grundy, William	Pte.	21499				
Guest, Henry	Pte.	21167	B	16/11/14	dis.	10/04/15
Hackett, George W	Pte.	20986	D		dis.	08/08/19
Haddock, George W	Cpl.	21155				
Hadley, George C	Pte.	20134		04/09/14	dis.	10/10/18
Haggerty, ...	L/Sjt.					
Haggerty, James	Pte.	21666		11/05/15	dis.	25/04/18
Hall, Aaron	Pte.	21783			dis.	03/02/19
Hall, Albert J	L/Cpl.	20828	D	07/09/14	d.o.w.	31/07/17
Halliwell, Peter	Pte.	20675	B	07/09/14	k.i.a.	21/03/18
Halsall, Daniel	Pte.	21585	A	17/05/15	dis.	13/05/19
Halsall, John	Pte.	20489		04/09/14	d.	03/12/17
Halsall, John	Pte.	21653		26/05/15	dis.	31/03/16
Halsall, Walter	Pte.	20355	B	04/09/14	dis.	02/04/19
Halton, Joseph T	Sgt.	20719	C		dis.	23/03/19
Hamilton, James A	Pte.	20939		07/09/14	dis.	26/12/18
Hamilton, Joseph	Pte.	20656			dis.	04/12/19
Hampson, John	Pte.	20141	A		dis.	26/03/20
Hand, John W	Cpl.	20672	C	08/09/14	dis.	27/01/19
Hankinson, David	Pte.	21402	C			
Hankinson, Joseph	Pte.	21841	F	02/06/15	dis.	14/06/15 *
Hankinson, Thomas	Pte.	20217	A	08/09/14	k.i.a.	08/06/17
Hankinson, Thomas	Pte.	21308	D	22/01/15	dis.	10/03/16
Hanley, William	Pte.	21526	C	11/03/15	k.i.a.	11/07/16
Hannon, Joseph	Pte.	20618		07/09/14	des.	06/01/15
Hannon, Lawrence	Pte.	21679		25/05/15	d.o.w.	28/03/18
Hardman, Joseph W	Pte.	20206	A	05/09/14	dis.	27/03/18
Harker, Gilbert	A/Cpl.	20677			dis.	09/01/19
Harris, John	Pte.	21556		12/05/15	dis.	13/03/19
Harrison, Arthur	Pte.	21100			dis.	27/01/19
Harrison, Edgar	L/Cpl.	20006	A	05/09/14	dis.	21/02/19
Harrison, Edward	Pte.	21372		27/01/15	dis.	22/03/20
Harrison, Frederick	Pte.	20036			dis.	10/04/19
Harrison, George	Pte.					
Harrison, Gilbert	Pte.					
Harrison, James	Pte.	20363	B	05/09/14	dis.	02/03/19

Name	Rank	No.	Coy.	Joined	Outcome	
Harrison, James	Pte.	21842		02/06/15	dis.	14/06/15 *
Harrison, John	Pte.	21814		31/05/15	dis.	03/12/15
Harrison, Joseph	C.S.M.	20581	C	08/09/14	dis.	30/01/19
Harrison, Joseph	Pte.	20744	E	04/09/14	dis.	29/04/15
Harrison, Peter	C.S.M.					
Harrison, Richard	Pte.	21552				
Harrison, Thomas	Pte.	21294	C	23/01/15	dis.	08/02/15
Harrison, W	Pte.	21580				
Harrison, William J	Pte.	20309		04/09/14	dis.	03/07/18
Hart, Harold	Pte.	21893	A	14/06/15	dis.	07/01/19
Hart, William	Pte.	21293	C		dis.	27/01/19
Hartley, Frank	Pte.	20161	A	04/09/14	k.i.a.	22/10/16
Hartley, Herbert	Cpl.	20173			dis.	28/03/19
Hatton, James	Pte.	20164			dis.	28/03/19
Hatton, William	Pte.	20647			d.o.w.	14/10/18
Havey, ...	Pte.	21215				
Hayes, Dennis	Pte.	20520				
Hayes, Matthew	Pte.	21957		30/07/15	dis.	27/03/18
Heather, Henry	Pte.	21016	D		dis.	26/02/19
Heaton, John	Pte.	21060		05/09/14	dis.	05/02/15
Helsby, John R	Pte.	21800			dis.	22/03/19
Helsby, Richard S	Sgt.	20483		04/09/14	dis.	04/03/18
Helsby, Samuel	Pte.	21198		04/09/14	dis.	03/02/17
Helsby, William	Pte.	21441	B	11/02/15	k.i.a.	21/10/16
Henderson, David	Pte.	21545		23/03/15	dis.	31/03/20
Henderson, John	Pte.	21016	C		dis.	27/01/19
Hennessey, Owen	Pte.					
Hennessey, Thomas	Pte.	20454			dis.	01/07/19
Henry, William	Pte.	21302	A	21/01/15	dis.	27/04/15
Henshall, John	Pte.	20207	A			
Henton, ...	Pte.					
Herringshaw, William	Pte.	20642			dis.	16/02/19
Hesketh, Richard	Pte.	20037	A	04/09/14	dis.	17/12/17
Heslip, James	Pte.	21755	D	27/05/15	d.o.w.	03/08/17
Hewitt, James	Pte.	21763		27/05/15	dis.	03/12/15 *
Hewitt, William	Pte.	21226		11/01/15	dis.	13/10/17
Heyes, Alfred	Pte.	20284	B		dis.	05/02/19
Heyes, Elias	Pte.	20637				
Heyes, Frederick	Pte.	20545	C		dis.	23/03/19
Heyes, Roger	Pte.	21041		05/09/14	dis.	28/03/19
Higgins, John	Pte.	21246		16/01/15	dis.	08/02/15
Higgins, Thomas	Pte.	21949		27/07/15	dis.	08/08/19
Hignett, Joseph W	Sgt.	20180	A		dis.	17/02/19
Hill, Alfred	Pte.	21782		27/05/15	dis.	31/05/18
Hill, Edward	Pte.	20967	C	06/04/15	k.i.a.	26/06/16
Hill, Edward	Pte.	21693				

Name	Rank	No.	Coy.	Joined	Outcome	
Hill, Henry	Sgt.	20219			dis.	19/01/19
Hill, Herbert	Pte.	20172	A		dis.	07/04/19
Hill, James	Pte.	21351	C	25/01/15	dis.	20/01/19
Hill, John	Pte.	20126				
Hill, John	Pte.	20715	C	05/09/14	d.	14/03/18
Hill, John	Pte.	20996		07/09/14	dis.	15/04/16
Hill, Robert	Pte.	21623	A			
Hill, William	Pte.	20614		04/09/14	dis.	24/04/18
Hill, William	Pte.	21228			dis.	03/04/19
Hilton, James	Pte.	20585	C	05/09/14	dis.	15/01/15
Hindley, James	Pte.	21535		16/03/15	dis.	30/03/19
Hindley, Louis	Pte.	20105			dis.	08/03/19
Hine, James A	Cpl.	20937	D	04/09/14	dis.	11/04/19
Hinton, Charles	Pte.	21838		01/06/15	dis.	22/03/20
Hobart, John J	Pte.	20615			k.i.a.	13/10/18
Hodgins, James	Pte.	20168	A	05/09/14	k.i.a.	01/07/16
Hogan, Peter	Pte.	21902				
Hogan, Thomas	Pte.	21476		23/02/15	dis.	14/04/16
Hogg, Robert	Pte.	21579	A	17/05/15	dis.	31/03/19
Hoggins, William	Pte.	21511		08/03/15	dis.	03/05/19
Holden, John	Sgt.	21897		28/06/15	d.	03/05/16
Holland, Henry	Pte.	20655	C		dis.	13/01/19
Holland, John	Pte.	21797				
Holland, Lawrence	Pte.	20338	C	08/09/14	d.	10/10/15
Hollingsworth, Saml	Pte.	20013			dis.	05/03/19
Holmes, Arthur	Pte.					
Holmes, Charles H	Cpl.	20053	A	04/09/14	dis.	04/09/17
Holmes, James	Pte.					
Holmes, Richard	Pte.	21885		15/06/15	dis.	03/07/17
Holmes, William	Pte.	20819	D	08/09/14	dis.	11/06/15
Holt, ...	Sgt.					
Hood, George	Pte.	20958	D	08/09/14	d.o.w.	14/02/16
Hooligan, Patrick	Pte.	21260	E	18/01/15	dis.	13/03/15
Hopkins, Patrick	Pte.	20728		04/09/14	dis.	12/11/14
Horsley, H	Pte.					
Horton, Charles	Pte.	20151		04/09/14	dis.	12/10/14 *
Horton, Henry	Pte.	21239				
Houghton, Frank	Pte.	21216	B	09/01/15	dis.	15/11/15
Houghton, George	Pte.	20394			dis.	22/02/19
Houghton, Harry	Pte.	20717	C		dis.	27/01/19
Houghton, John	Sgt.	20634		08/09/14	dis.	03/02/19
Houghton, Matthew E	Pte.	20359			k.i.a.	28/03/18
Houghton, Peter	Pte.	20663	C	08/09/14	d.o.w.	27/07/16
Houghton, Thomas	Pte.	21378	A	18/01/15	k.i.a.	01/07/16
Howard, Albert	Pte.	20335	B		dis.	19/03/19
Howard, Robert	Pte.	20486	B	08/09/14	d.o.w.	01/03/16

Name	Rank	No.	Coy.	Joined	Outcome	
Howard, Thomas	Pte.	20676		04/09/14	dis.	08/10/14
Howarth, Albert	Pte.	21230	A	14/01/15	des.	04/06/15
Howden, James T	Pte.	20110	A		d.	26/10/18
Howe, Thomas	Pte.	20872		07/09/14	dis.	22/07/17
Howitt, Frank	Pte.	20260		05/09/14	dis.	24/10/14 *
Hoy, Andrew	Pte.	21674		25/05/15	dis.	09/06/15 *
Hudson, William	Pte.	20555		07/09/14	dis.	12/11/14
Hughes, Albert E	Pte.	21253	B	18/01/15	dis.	29/05/15
Hughes, David	L/Cpl.	20892	D	08/09/14	k.i.a.	23/03/18
Hughes, Harry	Pte.	20921			dis.	27/01/19
Hughes, Henry J	Pte.	20178			dis.	23/02/19
Hughes, James	Pte.	21375				
Hughes, John	Pte.	20153	A	04/09/14	k.i.a.	23/03/18
Hughes, John	Cpl.	20570			dis.	17/03/19
Hughes, John	Bglr	21091		17/09/14	dis.	24/12/14
Hughes, William	Pte.	20854			dis.	13/01/19
Hull, Thomas	Pte.	21202			dis.	12/02/19
Humphreys, John	L/Cpl.	20469	B	07/09/14	dis.	02/08/19
Hundley, Henry	Pte.	20957	D		dis.	21/03/19
Hundley, James	Pte.	20959	D	08/09/14	dis.	08/01/15
Hunt, Richard	Pte.		D			
Hunt, Robert	Pte.	21007		05/09/14	dis.	30/07/19
Hunt, William	Pte.	21521			dis.	12/03/19
Hunter, John	Pte.	21742				
Hunter, William	Pte.	21554		26/04/15	dis.	19/03/19
Hunter, Wilson	Pte.	21483	E	24/02/15	dis.	24/04/15
Hunwick, Edward N	Sgt.	20079	A		k.i.a.	30/08/18
Hurst, Alfred	Pte.	20578	C	05/09/14	dis.	05/11/18
Hurst, James	Pte.	20864		07/09/14	dis.	03/05/19
Hurst, Walter	Pte.	21912		12/07/15	dis.	26/05/16
Hurst, Walter	Pte.	21116		02/10/14	dis.	28/01/15
Hurst, William	Pte.	20066			dis.	23/04/19
Hurst, William	L/Cpl.	21209			dis.	
Hutton, Henry	Pte.	20667	C		dis.	06/03/19
Hutton, J	Pte.		C			
Hutton, William	Pte.	21777		24/05/15	dis.	05/05/16
Hyland, John	Pte.	21781			dis.	28/01/19
Hynes, Thomas	Pte.	21245	A	16/01/15	k.i.a.	21/10/16
Ingham, John B	Pte.	20871		04/09/14	dis.	07/03/19
Inglis, J	Pte.					
Innes, Robert	Pte.	20125	A		dis.	25/02/19
Ireland, John	Pte.	21516		03/03/15	dis.	10/03/16
Irwin, William	Pte.	21772		26/05/15	dis.	31/03/16
Jackson, George	Pte.	20960		05/09/14	dis.	15/01/15 *
Jackson, George T	Pte.	21876				
Jackson, Herbert	Pte.	21214	A	14/01/15	dis.	13/03/15

Name	Rank	No.	Coy.	Joined	Outcome	
Jackson, John	Pte.	20392			dis.	14/02/19
Jackson, John	Pte.	21417			dis.	09/05/19
Jackson, John W	Pte.	20893		08/09/14	dis.	02/10/14 *
Jackson, Robert	Pte.	21175	B	23/11/14	k.i.a.	03/07/16
Jackson, Robert	Pte.	21608				
Jackson, Thomas	Sgt.	20070	A	05/09/14	k.i.a.	01/07/16
Jackson, Thomas	Pte.	21593	A	18/05/15	dis.	24/05/18
James, William	Pte.	21730		26/05/15	dis.	09/06/15
Jameson, Joseph	Pte.	21382			dis.	29/01/19
Jennings, Albert	Pte.	20436		07/09/14	dis.	02/10/14
Jervis, Abraham	Pte.	20442			d.	17/11/18
Johnson, Arthur W	Pte.	21103	B		dis.	11/03/19
Johnson, Francis	Pte.	21397		01/02/15	dis.	07/04/19
Johnson, George	Pte.	21169		17/11/14	dis.	05/01/15
Johnson, Harold	Pte.	21398		02/02/15	dis.	02/11/17
Johnson, Hugh	L/Cpl.	20884	D		dis.	27/01/19
Johnson, James	Pte.	21602	A	19/05/15	dis.	13/01/19
Johnson, James	Pte.	21449		15/02/15	dis.	07/03/16
Johnson, John	Pte.	21766		27/05/15	dis.	19/06/16
Johnson, Joseph	Pte.	20560	C			
Johnson, Peter	Pte.	20246		04/09/14	dis.	25/10/14
Johnson, Peter	Pte.	21462				
Johnson, Richard	Pte.					
Johnson, Samuel	Pte.	20621		04/09/14	dis.	25/07/19
Johnson, Thomas	Pte.	20900		07/09/14	dis.	04/11/19
Jones, Alfred	Pte.	21047		05/09/14	dis.	12/11/14 *
Jones, Charles	Pte.	21557			dis.	26/02/19
Jones, David	Pte.	20738	C		dis.	07/03/19
Jones, Edward	Pte.	20645	C		dis.	27/01/19
Jones, Edward	Pte.	20713	C		dis.	07/03/19
Jones, Frederick	Pte.	21376	C		dis.	25/03/19
Jones, Hugh	Pte.	21024	D	07/09/14	k.i.a.	28/03/18
Jones, James	Pte.	21289	C	20/01/15	dis.	26/02/19
Jones, John	Pte.	20130		05/09/14	k.i.a.	21/08/18
Jones, John	Pte.	20989	D	08/09/14	d.o.w.	25/03/18
Jones, John T	Pte.	21859		07/06/15	dis.	07/04/16
Jones, Joseph E	Pte.	21991				
Jones, Moses	Pte.		E			
Jones, Owen	Pte.	21487		23/02/15	dis.	14/06/15
Jones, Richard	Pte.	20858	D	04/09/14	dis.	
Jones, Robert	Pte.	20083		07/09/14	dis.	16/12/14 *
Jones, Robert	Pte.	21549				
Jones, Sidney	Pte.	20082	A		dis.	27/09/16
Jones, Thomas	Pte.	21612	A		dis.	17/03/19
Jones, Thomas	Pte.	21636		24/05/15	dis.	14/03/16
Jones, Thomas	Pte.	21918		12/07/15	dis.	09/10/15

Name	Rank	No.	Coy.	Joined	Outcome	
Jones, Thomas W	Pte.	20054				
Jones, Trevor	Sgt.	20848		04/09/14	dis.	21/08/19
Jones, William	Pte.	20233			dis.	22/02/19
Jordan, Frank	Pte.	21233	A	15/01/15	dis.	26/07/19
Judges, George	Pte.	21518				
Kane, Edward	Pte.	21717		23/05/15	dis.	23/10/18
Kavanagh, George	Pte.	20527			dis.	17/02/19
Kay, ...	Pte.	20876				
Kay, James	Pte.	20416			d.o.w.	11/04/18
Kay, James	Bglr	21066	D	11/09/14	dis.	28/12/14 *
Kay, John	Pte.	20423			dis.	22/02/19
Kay, John Henry	Pte.	20690		07/09/14	dis.	02/10/14
Kay, Ralph	Pte.	20200	A	04/09/14	k.i.a.	10/07/16
Kay, Thomas	Pte.	21699		25/05/15	dis.	25/04/18
Kearns, John	Pte.	20600		07/09/14	dis.	02/10/14 *
Keefe, John T	Pte.	20470		07/09/14	dis.	02/01/19
Keeffe, Andrew	Pte.	20623			dis.	06/03/19
Keegan, James	Pte.	20166		08/09/14	dis.	08/01/16
Keenan, John	Pte.	21142	B	10/11/14	des.	06/12/14
Keegan, Thomas	Pte.	20155		08/09/14	dis.	30/06/15
Keery, James	Pte.	21274				
Kellett, John E	Pte.	20286		07/09/14	dis.	12/11/18
Kelly, John	Pte.	21566		16/05/15	des.	08/06/15
Kelly, John	Bglr	21068	A	08/09/14	dis.	24/10/14
Kelly, Patrick	Pte.	21779	C	27/05/15	k.i.a.	01/07/16
Kelly, Thomas	Pte.	20158	A	08/09/14	k.i.a.	08/07/17
Kelly, Thomas	Pte.	20629	C	05/09/14	k.i.a.	01/07/16
Kelly, William	Cpl.	20409			dis.	26/04/19
Kelly, William	Pte.	21493	B	01/03/15	dis.	28/03/19
Kennedy, Edward	Pte.	20987	D	04/09/14	dis.	06/02/15 *
Kennedy, James	Pte.	20851		05/09/14	dis.	17/12/15
Kenny, John	Pte.					
Kenny, Peter	Pte.	20302		04/09/14	dis.	01/08/16
Kenny, William	Pte.	20381	B	04/09/14	k.i.a.	01/10/16
Kenwright, John	Pte.	21110	B		dis.	12/03/19
Keogh, William	Pte.	20999	D	05/09/14	d.o.w.	29/06/16
Keogh, William	Pte.	20726		05/09/14	dis.	07/06/15 *
Kerr, Frank	Pte.	21703				
Kettle, Hugh	L/Cpl.	21455	C		dis.	31/01/19
Kiernan, Bartholomew	Pte.	21050	B	05/09/14	dis.	12/11/14
Kiernan, Bernard	Pte.	20103	A		dis.	
Kiernan, Edward	Pte.	21052		07/09/14	dis.	08/02/15
Kilmurray, Hugh	Pte.	20466		08/09/14	dis.	12/11/14
Kilmurray, Joseph	Pte.	20331	B			
Kilroy, Henry	Pte.	20471			k.i.a.	13/10/18
Kilshaw, George	Pte.	20526				

Name	Rank	No.	Coy.	Joined	Outcome	
Kilshaw, William	Pte.	21354	A	25/01/15	dis.	29/04/18
Kilshaw, William	Pte.	21527	C		dis.	23/07/19
Kinder, Isaac	Pte.	21148		07/11/14	dis.	06/08/18
Kinder, Richard	Cpl.	21243			d.	23/03/18
King, Bernard	Pte.	21049		07/09/14	dis.	15/10/14
Kinsey, Thomas R	Pte.	20121	B	08/09/14	k.i.a.	01/07/16
Kirkham, James W	Pte.	20014	A			
Knockton, John	Pte.	20917	A		dis.	27/01/19
Knowles, James	Pte.					
Knowles, John	Pte.	21162				
Knowles, John	Pte.	21070		19/11/14	dis.	05/12/14
Knowles, Sheridan	Pte.	22321				
Knowles, Thomas	Q.M.S.	20857			dis.	13/01/19
Kyte, George	Pte.	21826		31/05/15	dis.	16/02/16
Lacey, George W	Pte.	20387			dis.	27/01/19
Lacy, William	Pte.	20111			dis.	04/03/19
Lally, George	Pte.	20983			dis.	15/05/19
Lambert, Louis	Pte.	20949	D	04/09/14	d.o.w.	21/12/15
Lancaster, John W	L/Cpl.	21250	A	15/01/15	dis.	15/03/19
Lane, John	Pte.	20209				
Lane, Louis	Pte.	20167	A			
Langford, John	Pte.					
Langley, Henry	Pte.	21278		19/01/15	dis.	29/11/19
Langley, William	Pte.	20875	D		dis.	
Langton, Henry	Pte.	20262	A	05/09/14	dis.	24/02/19
Large, James	L/Cpl.	20028	A	07/09/14	d.o.w.	09/09/16
Large, Joseph	Sgt.	20831	D	08/09/14	dis.	23/01/19
Large, Thomas	Pte.	21330	C	23/01/15	dis.	08/06/15
Larkin, John E	Pte.	21584		17/05/15	dis.	29/01/19
Lathom, Thomas	Pte.	20261			dis.	21/03/19
Lawrenson, Herbert	Pte.	20068	A		dis.	25/02/19
Lawrenson, John	Pte.	20761		08/09/14	dis.	18/01/19
Lawrenson, Oswald	Pte.	20062	A		dis.	03/04/19
Lawrenson, William	Pte.	20235			dis.	14/01/19
Lawrenson, William	Pte.	21421		01/03/15	dis.	30/03/15
Lawson, Edward	Pte.	20422		07/09/14	dis.	03/03/17
Lea, Arthur	Pte.	20321		04/09/14	dis.	07/10/14 *
Lea, Charles	Pte.	21210	C	05/01/15	dis.	31/10/16
Lea, John	Pte.	20664			dis.	27/01/19
Lea, John	Pte.	20441		04/09/14	dis.	21/11/19
Lea, Stephen	Pte.	20366				
Leach, James	Pte.	21610		18/05/15	dis.	23/12/19
Leadbetter, John	Pte.	21626				
Leadbetter, Samuel	Pte.	21391		01/02/15	d.	28/03/18
Leadley, Frank S	Pte.	21370		26/01/15	dis.	28/01/15
Ledwith, Andrew	Sgt.	21002	D	04/09/14	dis.	25/01/19

Name	Rank	No.	Coy.	Joined	Outcome	
Ledwith, John	C.S.M.	21039		04/09/14	dis.	28/01/19
Lee, Henry	Pte.	20659	C			
Lee, James	Pte.	21477		23/02/15	dis.	
Lee, James	Pte.	20269			dis.	28/01/19
Lee, John	Pte.	21581		18/05/15	dis.	24/01/18
Lee, John	Pte.	21624		24/05/15	des.	28/09/17
Lee, John W	Pte.	21414	B	03/02/15	dis.	03/01/19
Lee, Joseph	Pte.	21715		25/05/15	dis.	11/03/19
Lees, George	Pte.	20930	C		d.o.w.	04/04/18
Leigh, James	Pte.					
Lenneham, ...	Pte.					
Lenton, Harry	L/Cpl.	21474	B	22/02/15	k.i.a.	21/03/18
Lenton, Thomas	Cpl.	21532	D	15/03/15	dis.	06/03/19
Leonard, Frederick	Pte.	21832		01/06/15	dis.	28/09/19
Lethbridge, Thomas	L/Cpl.	20709	C	05/09/14	d.o.w.	23/06/17
Lewis, Hugh	Pte.	21615	C	16/03/16	k.i.a.	22/04/18
Leyland, Harry	Pte.	21470	B	21/02/15	dis.	13/03/15
Leyland, Henry	Pte.	20867	D	05/09/14	dis.	29/01/19
Leyland, John	Pte.	20880			k.i.a.	25/10/18
Leyland, Peter	Pte.	20796	D	07/09/14	k.i.a.	30/09/18
Leyland, Peter	Pte.	21042		08/09/14	dis.	22/12/14 *
Leyland, W	L/Sjt.					
Leyland, Walter	Pte.	20391		07/09/14	dis.	22/09/16
Leyland, William	Pte.	20565	C		dis.	17/03/19
Leyland, William	Cpl.	20881	C	07/09/14	dis.	14/03/19
Lilly, John W	Pte.	21428			dis.	18/01/19
Lindop, Ernest	Pte.	20052				
Lingard, John	Pte.	20496		08/09/14	dis.	25/10/16
Liptrot, William	Pte.	21119	B	04/09/14	dis.	01/12/14 *
Liptrot, William	Pte.	20955	D	07/09/14	dis.	25/01/19
Litherland, William	Pte.	20358			dis.	11/02/19
Littler, Henry	Pte.	20863			dis.	27/01/19
Littler, Isaac	Pte.	21217	A	09/01/15	dis.	14/06/15 *
Littler, Thomas	Pte.	21212	D	08/01/15	dis.	14/12/18
Littler, William	Pte.	21211			dis.	08/01/19
Llewellyn, William J	Cpl.	21320			dis.	02/04/19
Lloyd, James	Pte.	20855	D	05/09/14	d.o.w.	07/06/17
Lloyd, Thomas A	Pte.	21115	B		dis.	05/03/19
Lloyd, William	Pte.	20317		04/09/14	dis.	08/01/15 *
Loader, John E	C.S.M.	20084	C			
Longworth, George	Pte.	21983				
Longworth, William	Pte.	21977	B	10/08/15	dis.	11/02/19
Lowe, Albert	Pte.	20925	D		dis.	29/03/19
Lowe, George	Pte.	21259			dis.	27/01/19
Lowe, George T	Pte.	20586	C	04/09/14	dis.	06/07/18
Lowe, James	Pte.	20347	B		dis.	05/03/19

Name	Rank	No.	Coy.	Joined	Outcome	
Lowery, Thomas S	Pte.	21667		22/05/15	dis.	21/02/19
Lunt, Joseph	Pte.	21322	A	25/01/15	dis.	31/05/15
Lunt, William	Pte.	20998		07/09/14	dis.	02/10/14
Lynam, John W	Pte.	20837			dis.	05/02/19
Lynch, James	Pte.	20905	D		dis.	16/03/19
Lynch, Patrick	Pte.	20762	D		dis.	14/07/18
Lynch, Thomas	Pte.	21436		11/02/15	dis.	05/02/19
Lyon, Harry J	Pte.	20031	A			
Lyon, John	Pte.	21567				
Lyon, Samuel	Pte.	21069		11/09/14	dis.	28/12/14
Lyon, Thomas	Pte.	21878		12/06/15	dis.	02/01/19
Lyon, Thomas	Pte.	21958		03/08/15	dis.	03/08/19
MacDonald, George	Pte.	20823			dis.	13/03/19
Maguire, Thomas	Pte.	20992		07/09/14	dis.	02/10/14
Maher, James	Pte.	20492		07/09/14	dis.	15/10/14 *
Maher, Michael	Pte.	20352			k.i.a.	13/10/18
Makin, John	Pte.	21411	D	02/02/15	dis.	27/01/19
Makin, John W	Pte.	20287		05/09/14	dis.	29/11/17
Makin, Robert H	Pte.	20993	D	04/09/14	k.i.a.	30/06/17
Makinson, Patrick	Pte.	21154	B	09/11/14	k.i.a.	27/05/17
Malone, Augustine	Pte.	21980	A	10/08/15	dis.	18/02/19
Malone, Philip	Pte.	20895		07/09/14	dis.	07/10/14
Maloney, Michael	Pte.	20861			dis.	20/02/19
Maloney, Peter	Pte.	20132	A	04/09/14	k.i.a.	30/07/16
Mangan, Charles	Pte.	21297		21/01/15	dis.	04/02/19
Marsden, Thomas	A/Cpl.	21238				
Marsh, A M	R.I.M.S.					
Marsh, Albert J	Pte.	21979				
Marsh, Alexander M	Q.M.S.	21062		18/09/14	dis.	13/09/16
Marsh, Frederick	Bglr.	21079	D	17/09/14	dis.	28/12/14 *
Marsh, James	Pte.	20015			dis.	04/03/19
Marsh, James	Pte.	20258	A		dis.	15/02/19
Marsh, James	Pte.	20516		04/09/14	dis.	07/06/15
Marsh, James R	Pte.	20303	B		dis.	
Marsh, John	Pte.	20403		05/09/14	dis.	25/02/16
Marsh, John	Pte.	20457	B	07/09/14	dis.	12/11/14 *
Marsh, Peter	L/Sjt.	20351	B		dis.	25/02/19
Marsh, Peter	Pte.	20425		08/09/14	dis.	30/12/18
Marsh, Thomas H	Pte.	20856	D	04/09/14	dis.	01/12/14
Marsh, Walter	Pte.	21854	D	05/06/15	dis.	23/10/18
Martin, John	Pte.	21072		13/04/15	dis.	25/09/17
Martin, Johnson	Pte.	21000	D		dis.	05/04/19
Martin, Samuel	Pte.	20421	B		d.	28/10/18
Martin, Samuel	L/Sjt.	20345	B	04/09/14	k.i.a.	21/10/16
Martindale, James	Pte.	20697		07/09/14	dis.	14/05/18
Mascall, John J	Pte.	20781			dis.	08/03/19

Name	Rank	No.	Coy.	Joined	Outcome	
Mason, John	Pte.	21144	B	04/11/14	k.i.a.	28/01/16
Mason, Walter	Pte.					
Mather, Arthur	Sgt.	21207	C	05/01/15	dis.	26/09/17
Mather, Charles	Pte.	20187	A			
Mather, Edward	Pte.	20097	A			
Mather, Fred	Pte.	21994		24/08/15	dis.	03/12/15
Mather, James	Pte.	20805		08/09/14	dis.	15/01/15
Mather, John	Pte.	20048	A	04/09/14	dis.	08/04/19
Mather, John	Pte.	20191		04/09/14	dis.	25/05/18
Mather, John W	Pte.	21028				
Mather, Joseph	Pte.	20700	C			
Mather, Thomas	Pte.	20877	D	04/09/14	dis.	22/06/17
Mather, Thomas	Pte.	20909	D	05/09/14	d.o.w.	28/03/18
Mather, William	Pte.	20073	A	08/09/14	dis.	15/04/19
Matthews, W	S/Sgt.					
May, John	Pte.	21605		20/05/15	des.	05/09/15
Maylin, Henry	Pte.	20904	D	05/09/14	k.i.a.	28/04/18
McBryde, David	L/Cpl.	20281	A		dis.	20/03/19
McCabe, John	Cpl.	21053			dis.	13/03/19
McCabe, William	Pte.	21497		02/03/15	dis.	20/04/15 *
McCann, William	Pte.	21669			dis.	19/04/20
McClurg, James	Pte.	20841			dis.	13/02/19
McComas, Isaac	Cpl.	20382	B	04/09/14	dis.	18/02/19
McConnell, William	Pte.	20333	B	04/09/14	k.i.a.	27/03/18
McCooey, Lawrence	Pte.	21010		07/09/14	dis.	25/04/17
McCormick, John	Pte.	21928		14/07/15	k.i.a.	02/11/18
McCormick, Michael	Pte.	21743		26/05/15	dis.	05/03/19
McDermott, Edward	Pte.	21502	A	03/03/15	k.i.a.	12/04/18
McDonald, James	Pte.	21367	A	26/01/15	k.i.a.	01/07/16
McDonald, John	Pte.	20546			dis.	23/02/19
McDonald, Joseph	Pte.	20507	C		dis.	01/03/19
McDonald, Richard	Pte.	20847	D	07/09/14	dis.	30/01/19
McEntee, John	Pte.	20390		05/09/14	dis.	07/10/14
McEwen, James	Pte.	20878			dis.	26/03/19
McGauley, John	Pte.	20583		04/09/14	dis.	06/02/15
McGhee, Martin	Pte.	21475	D		dis.	31/03/19
McGowan, Patrick	L/Cpl.	21435	C	14/02/15	des.	02/05/17
McGrath, John	Pte.	20364			dis.	17/01/19
McGunnigle, William	Pte.	20283	B	04/09/14	dis.	26/02/19
McHale, Francis	Cpl.	20767			dis.	14/01/19
McInerney, Simon	Cpl.	21438	E	11/02/15	dis.	20/03/19
McIntyre, William	Pte.	20740		05/09/14	dis.	12/11/14
McKeegan, James	Pte.					
McKeegan, Thomas	Pte.					
McKie, George	Pte.	20682		05/09/14	d.o.w.	16/04/18
McLeod, Angus	Pte.	20146			dis.	17/01/19

Name	Rank	No.	Coy.	Joined	Outcome	
McLoughlin, Edward	Pte.	20439	B	04/09/14	dis.	04/04/19
McLoughlin, James	Pte.	20883	D	05/09/14	d.o.w.	29/06/17
McManus, Bernard	Pte.	20741	C	07/09/14	dis.	12/11/14 *
McManus, John	Pte.	20788			dis.	13/01/19
McManus, Thomas	Pte.	21399		01/02/15	dis.	29/10/19
McMenamy, Michael	Pte.	20445	A	07/09/14	dis.	01/04/19
McNamee, Francis	Pte.	21360		25/01/15	dis.	01/08/19
McNichol, James	Pte.	21750	B	26/05/15	k.i.a.	10/03/18
Meadows, Henry	Pte.	21819		31/05/15	dis.	28/03/19
Meadows, James	Pte.	20756	C	05/09/14	dis.	14/01/19
Meadows, Jonathan	Pte.	20541	C		dis.	22/02/19
Meakin, Albert E	Pte.	20183			dis.	19/11/19
Meaney, ...	Pte.					
Meara, Thomas	L/Cpl.	21149	C	09/11/14	dis.	25/01/19
Mees, Joseph T	Pte.	21141		05/09/14	dis.	13/07/17
Melding, James	Pte.	20836		07/09/14	dis.	01/11/18
Melia, James	Pte.	21722	F	26/05/15	dis.	09/06/15
Melling, Richard	Pte.	20963	D	07/09/14	d.	22/10/17
Mellor, Arnold	Pte.	22336				
Mercer, Charles	Pte.	21966		06/08/15	dis.	07/04/19
Mercer, John	Pte.	20238		21/09/14	dis.	02/10/14
Mercer, William	Pte.	21775		27/05/15	dis.	22/09/15
Middlehurst, Charles	Pte.					
Middlehurst, James	Pte.	20026		05/09/14	dis.	04/03/19
Middlehurst, James	Pte.	20318		07/09/14	dis.	25/03/19
Middlehurst, John	Pte.	21242	E	16/01/15	dis.	13/03/15
Middlehurst, John J	Pte.	20418		05/09/14	dis.	05/04/19
Middlehurst, Moses	Pte.	20438	B		dis.	29/01/19
Middlehurst, Thomas	Pte.	20450		08/09/14	dis.	25/05/15 *
Middlehurst, Wm A	Pte.	20212			dis.	20/02/19
Miller, Ambrose	Pte.	21589				
Miller, Benjamin	Pte.	21450		15/02/15	dis.	26/06/15
Miller, William H	Pte.	21791	C			
Milligan, Albert M	L/Cpl.	20289	B	08/09/14	dis.	24/01/19
Milligan, George	Pte.		D			
Milligan, William J	C.S.M.					
Millington, Charles	Pte.	21366	A	26/01/15	dis.	25/01/19
Mills, Alfred H	Pte.	21442		11/02/15	dis.	15/02/19
Mills, John W	Pte.	20145	A	04/09/14	d.o.w.	10/03/16
Mills, Peter T	L/Cpl.	20620	C	08/09/14	k.i.a.	23/12/16
Millsop, George	Pte.	21013	D	05/09/14	dis.	03/12/19
Milne, John	Sgt.	20573			dis.	27/01/19
Mitchell, William	Pte.	21400			dis.	13/01/19
Molyneux, Albert	Pte.	20150	A		dis.	12/02/19
Molyneux, Harry	Pte.	21295	C		dis.	17/02/19
Molyneux, Herbert	Sgt.	20332			dis.	02/04/19

Name	Rank	No.	Coy.	Joined	Outcome	
Molyneux, Joseph	Pte.	20590	C	08/09/14	d.o.w.	05/08/16
Molyneux, Richard	Pte.					
Molyneux, Thomas	Pte.	21163		28/09/14	dis.	02/07/15 *
Molyneux, W	Pte.		B			
Molyneux, William	Pte.	21311			k.i.a.	15/08/18
Montgomery, John	Pte.	20240	A	04/09/14	dis.	15/01/15 *
Montgomery, Thomas	Pte.	21803	A	26/05/15	k.i.a.	01/07/16
Mooney, Edward	Pte.	21027				
Mooney, Thomas	Pte.	22121				
Moore, James	Pte.	20252		08/09/14	dis.	08/01/15
Moore, James	Cpl.	20832		07/09/14	dis.	05/03/17
Moore, Joseph H	Sgt.	20750		05/09/14	dis.	12/02/18
Moran, James	Pte.	21754	F	27/05/15	dis.	11/02/19
Morris, Alfred C	Pte.	20182	A	05/09/14	dis.	21/01/19
Morris, Edward	Pte.	20480	D	07/09/14	dis.	01/12/14
Morris, Edward	Pte.	21655		22/05/15	dis.	27/06/19
Morrison, Joseph	Pte.	21726	C	26/05/15	dis.	05/03/19
Mortimer, James	Pte.	20612	C	04/09/14	dis.	18/02/19
Morton, William	Pte.	20540		08/09/14	dis.	15/10/14
Moulton, Henry	Pte.	21032		08/09/14	dis.	15/03/16
Mulaghton, Lawrence	Pte.	20245				
Mulcahy, Sidney	Pte.	21734		26/05/15		
Muldoon, James	Pte.	20776		04/09/14	dis.	15/01/15
Mulhearne, John	Pte.	21864		07/06/15	dis.	11/09/17
Mullen, James	Pte.	21473	A	22/02/15	k.i.a.	01/07/16
Mullen, Walter	Pte.	21538	D	17/03/15	k.i.a.	08/07/16
Mulvey, James	Pte.	21590		19/05/15	dis.	26/02/19
Murphy, James	Pte.	21654		25/05/15	des.	25/06/16
Murphy, John	Pte.	20446	B	05/09/14	dis.	14/04/19
Murphy, Lawrence	Pte.	20806			dis.	13/01/19
Murphy, Peter J	Pte.	21287			dis.	08/03/19
Murray, Clement	Pte.	21951		26/07/15	dis.	03/12/15
Mustard, William J	L/Cpl.	20531	C	04/09/14	d.o.w.	02/07/16
Myers, Isaac	Pte.					
Myers, John	Sgt.	20763	D	04/09/14	dis.	24/09/18
Myers, Thomas	Pte.	20210	A	08/09/14	d.o.w.	20/02/16
Nash, George	Pte.	20928			dis.	05/05/19
Naylor, Albert	Sgt.	21840				
Naylor, Frederick	Cpl.	21094		08/09/14	dis.	28/03/19
Naylor, Harry	Sgt.	20032			dis.	17/02/19
Naylor, Hugh	Pte.	20275		03/09/14	dis.	29/03/19
Naylor, Joseph	Pte.	20265			dis.	19/03/19
Naylor, Richard	Pte.	20076		04/09/14	dis.	26/07/17
Naylor, Thomas	Pte.	20336	B	07/09/14	k.i.a.	15/08/16
Naylor, Thomas	Pte.	20491	B	08/09/14	dis.	12/02/19
Naylor, William	Pte.	21092	A	05/09/14	dis.	05/06/19

Name	Rank	No.	Coy.	Joined	Outcome	
Needham, Charles	Pte.	21463		15/02/15	dis.	19/06/15
Newcombe, Edward	Pte.	20802	D	05/09/14	dis.	20/02/19
Newman, John	Pte.	21561		15/05/15	dis.	19/06/15
Newton, John	Pte.	20991		07/09/14	dis.	07/06/15
Newton, Thomas	Pte.	21649			k.i.a.	13/10/18
Newton, William	Pte.	21784		27/05/15	dis.	16/02/16
Nichol, Robert	Pte.					
Nicholls, John	Pte.	21748		26/05/15	dis.	11/04/19
Nicholson, Oswald	Pte.	20710		07/09/14	dis.	14/01/19
Nickson, Thomas	Pte.	20278		04/09/14	dis.	02/04/18
Nicoll, Robert C	Pte.	21203	C	02/01/15	dis.	20/09/16
Nolan, John	Pte.	21365	A			
Noon, Thomas	Pte.	20829			dis.	05/01/19
Norbury, Charles	C.S.M.	21037	D	05/09/14	k.i.a.	28/07/16
Norbury, John	Pte.	20337		08/09/14	dis.	07/10/14
Norris, Thomas	Pte.	21638		24/04/15	dis.	10/03/16
Oakes, William	Pte.	21054	B	05/09/14	k.i.a.	01/07/16
Oakley, W	Pte.					
Oates, John	Sgt.	21849			dis.	28/03/19
Oates, Peter	Pte.	20490			dis.	20/03/19
O'Brien, James	Sgt.	20204	A	04/09/14	dis.	14/08/17
O'Brien, John	Pte.	20845		07/09/14	dis.	16/12/14
O'Connor, Christopher	Pte.	21508		04/03/15	dis.	25/01/19
O'Donnell, Thomas	Pte.	21011		05/09/14	dis.	07/06/18
O'Garra, William P	Pte	21572		17/05/15	dis.	16/05/19
Ollerhead, Richard	Pte.	21099			dis.	13/01/19
Ollerton, George	Pte.	20780		04/09/14	dis.	29/04/15 *
O'Neill, James	Pte.	20733	B			
O'Neill, John	Pte.	21769		27/05/15	dis.	21/09/18
O'Neill, Joseph	Pte.	21506		03/03/15	dis.	04/08/16
O'Neill, Patrick	Pte.	21809				
O'Reilly, Henry	Pte.	20047	A	04/09/14	k.i.a.	26/04/17
Orford, John	Pte.	21262	A	18/01/15	dis.	22/02/16
Orford, Joseph	Pte.	20842			dis.	27/04/19
Ormesher, John	Pte.	21884				
Ovens, Francis	Pte.	21316	A		k.i.a.	01/07/16
Ovens, James	Pte.	21236		16/01/15	dis.	19/05/16
Ovens, John	Pte.	21317			dis.	11/02/19
Ovens, Peter	Pte.	20420		04/09/14	dis.	16/12/14
Owen, Frank C	Pte.	20039		07/09/14	dis.	22/04/19
Owen, George	Pte.	20768	D		dis.	
Owen, George	Pte.	21682		24/05/15	d.o.w.	11/07/16
Owen, Harry	Pte.	20771	D		dis.	27/01/19
Owen, James	Sgt.	20718	C	05/09/14	dis.	15/01/19
Owen, John	Pte.	20706		08/09/14	dis.	13/06/15
Owen, John T	Pte.	21309	D	23/01/15	dis.	28/08/17

Name	Rank	No.	Coy.	Joined	Outcome	
Owen, Richard	Pte.	20202	A	05/09/14	dis.	22/08/19
Owen, Thomas	Cpl.	20100			dis.	13/02/19
Owen, William	A/W.O.II.	20350			dis.	18/03/19
Owens, William	Pte.	21778				
Paget, Thomas	Pte.	20149	A	05/09/14	dis.	14/09/16
Paget, William	Pte.					
Painter, Richard	L/Cpl.	20092		07/09/14	dis.	20/09/16
Painter, William	Pte.		A			
Palin, James	Pte.	20310	B	05/09/14	dis.	22/03/20
Pape, Harry	L/Cpl.	21445			dis.	20/02/19
Parker, Henry	C.Q.M.S.	20494		21/09/14	dis.	15/01/15
Parker, John J	Sgt.	20566	C	05/09/14	k.i.a.	10/06/17
Parkinson, John	Pte.	21645		24/05/15	dis.	16/09/15
Parr, George	Pte.	20415		08/09/14	k.i.a.	01/07/16
Parr, J	L/Sjt.					
Parr, James	Pte.	20118	A	08/09/14	d.o.w.	24/07/16
Parr, William	Pte.	20952		03/09/14	dis.	03/05/19
Parry, Richard	Sgt.	20649		08/09/14	dis.	15/09/17
Partridge, Rowland G	Pte.	21235		15/01/15	dis.	12/03/15
Patterson, Edward G	Pte.		B			
Payne, John T	R.S.M.	21091				
Pearce, Albert	Pte.	20974	D		dis.	05/03/19
Pearce, George	Pte.	20787	D		dis.	27/01/19
Pearce, Thomas	Pte.		C			
Peel, John	Pte.	20653		07/09/14	dis.	06/02/15
Peel, Peter	L/Cpl.	20665			dis.	27/03/19
Peel, William	Pte.	20652	C		dis.	21/01/19
Peel, William	Pte.	21738	C	26/05/15	dis.	26/11/20
Peers, Alfred	Pte.	21249	C	18/01/15	dis.	08/03/19
Pemberton, John	Pte.	20306	B	04/09/14	dis.	12/01/19
Pendlebury, Frederick	Cpl.	20043	A		d.o.w.	29/03/18
Pendleton, John W	Pte.	21188	C	15/12/14	k.i.a.	30/05/18
Pendleton, William	Pte.	20300	B		dis.	23/02/19
Penketh, Ernest	Pte.	21673		25/05/15	k.i.a.	27/08/18
Penketh, George	Pte.	20123			dis.	12/05/19
Penketh, William H	Pte.	20651		04/09/14	dis.	29/04/15
Pennington, Alfred	Pte.	20020		05/09/14	dis.	23/01/15
Pennington, Edward	Pte.	21319		23/01/15	dis.	27/01/19
Pennington, Edward O	Pte.	21851		11/06/15	dis.	23/05/19
Pennington, George T	Pte.	20399				
Pennington, Henry	Pte.	20046		05/09/14	dis.	25/10/14 *
Pennington, J	L/Sjt.					
Pennington, James	Pte.	20576	C		dis.	24/03/19
Pennington, James	Pte.	21379			dis.	19/04/17
Pennington, John	Pte.	20644				
Pennington, John	Pte.	21852			dis.	30/01/19

Name	Rank	No.	Coy.	Joined	Outcome	
Pennington, John	Pte.	21306		22/01/15	dis.	28/01/15
Pennington, John T	Pte.	20038	A	05/09/14	dis.	26/08/18
Pennington, Thomas	Pte.	20154	A	03/09/14	dis.	23/02/19
Pennington, William	Pte.	20830			dis.	12/03/19
Pepper, Edward	Pte.	21234				
Percival, James	Pte.	21479			dis.	30/01/19
Perry, William	Pte.	21303		21/01/15	dis.	21/06/15
Phelan, Patrick	Pte.					
Pickavance, George	Pte.	20437		07/09/14	dis.	06/02/15 *
Pickavance, James	Pte.	20396			dis.	05/03/19
Pickavance, John	Pte.	20889	D		dis.	22/01/19
Pickavance, John	Pte.	21346	C		dis.	06/03/19
Pickavance, Joseph	Pte.	21083	D		dis.	11/04/19
Pickavance, Peter	Pte.	20862		05/09/14	dis.	14/01/19
Pickavance, Richard	Pte.	21829		01/06/15	dis.	10/09/17
Pickering, James	Pte.	20384			dis.	13/02/19
Pickett, Alfred	Pte.	20803	D	04/09/14	dis.	18/03/18
Pickles, Edward	Sgt.	20736	B	07/09/14	k.i.a.	02/07/16
Pierce, William	Pte.	21139	B	28/10/14	des.	27/11/14
Piggott, Ralph	Pte.	20085	A	07/09/14	dis.	16/03/19
Piggott, William	Pte.	21776		27/05/15	dis.	06/08/19
Pike, James	Pte.	21944				
Pike, Joseph	L/Cpl.	20985	D	05/09/14	d.o.w.	09/07/16
Pilkington, George	Pte.	20849			k.i.a.	13/10/18
Pilkington, J	Pte.	21080	D			
Pilkington, R	Pte.		D			
Pilkington, Vincent	Pte.	20144	A		dis.	20/02/19
Pilling, Joseph F	Pte.	20897	D		dis.	29/01/19
Plant, Walter	Pte.	21344	B	25/01/15	dis.	04/01/19
Platt, Henry	Cpl.	21871			dis.	29/10/18
Platt, James	Cpl.	20035	A		dis.	18/01/19
Platt, Peter	Pte.	21127	B	15/10/14	dis.	04/04/18
Platt, William	Sgt.	21157	A	09/11/14	dis.	25/01/19
Plumpton, Job	Pte.	20139		07/09/14	dis.	02/07/15
Pope, Isaac	Pte.	21184	B		dis.	30/01/19
Porter, Frank	Pte.	21118		03/10/14	dis.	24/10/14
Potter, Henry M	Pte.	20580	C		dis.	16/03/19
Potter, James	Pte.	20417			dis.	27/01/19
Potter, James	Pte.	21895		21/06/15	dis.	06/10/15
Potter, John	Pte.	20965	D	08/09/14	d.o.w.	30/05/17
Potter, John T	L/Sjt.	20368	B		dis.	05/03/19
Potter, Thomas	Pte.	21560			dis.	16/03/19
Pounceby, Thomas	Pte.	21038		07/09/14	dis.	13/09/15
Pounceby, William	Pte.	20086	A		dis.	13/02/19
Pountain, Edward	Pte.	21224				
Powell, Charles	Pte.	20067		04/09/14	dis.	06/02/15 *

Name	Rank	No.	Coy.	Joined	Outcome	
Powell, John	Pte.	20669				
Prescott, Frank	Pte.	21120	B			
Prescott, James	Pte.	20499	C	04/09/14	dis.	13/03/15 *
Prescott, James	C.S.M.	21040	A	07/09/14	dis.	05/04/18
Prescott, James	Pte.	21046			dis.	07/03/19
Prescott, James	Pte.	20377	B	04/09/14	dis.	01/03/19
Prescott, Samuel	Pte.	21327				
Prescott, William	Pte.	20610			dis.	15/07/19
Preston, Charles	Pte.	20096				
Preston, Frank	Sgt.	20276	B	05/09/14	dis.	24/02/19
Preston, Harry	Cpl.	20402		04/09/14	d.o.w.	02/07/16
Preston, Job	Pte.	21727		26/05/15	dis.	27/11/16
Preston, John	Pte.	21018			dis.	04/07/19
Preston, Samuel	Pte.	20587		04/09/14	dis.	12/11/14
Price, John	Pte.	20539	C	05/09/14	d.o.w.	26/06/17
Price, John	Pte.	21412				
Price, Joseph	Pte.	21426			dis.	16/01/19
Price, Thomas	Pte.	20654		08/09/15	dis.	12/03/18
Price, Thomas	Cpl.	20793	D		dis.	11/03/19
Pritchard, Sydney	Pte.	20859		04/09/14	dis.	15/01/19
Proudlove, William	Pte.		D			
Purcell, William	Pte.	21801				
Purnell, Frank	Pte.	20619		05/09/14	dis.	02/10/15
Pye, Isaac	Pte.	21433	E	09/02/15	dis.	04/05/19
Pye, John J	Pte.	21630	F	25/05/15	d.	29/03/18
Pye, William	Pte.	20264	A	07/09/14	dis.	24/07/18
Pye, William	Pte.	20532	C	04/09/14	d.o.w.	03/04/18
Pyke, James T	Pte.	20012	A		dis.	22/03/19
Qualter, Michael	Pte.	21710		26/05/15	d.	15/10/18
Quirk, Frank	Pte.	21711	F	26/05/15	dis.	09/06/15 *
Radley, Joseph	Pte.	21799		29/05/15	dis.	03/01/16
Ralph, George	Pte.	21164	B	13/11/14	dis.	25/01/19
Ralphs, Richard	Pte.	21869		08/06/15	dis.	19/03/19
Randles, Albert	Pte.	21350		25/01/15	dis.	05/04/19
Randles, Henry	Pte.	21407		02/02/15	dis.	14/12/17
Randles, William	Pte.	21558		12/05/15	dis.	28/09/16
Ratcliffe, Joseph	Pte.	21104	B	02/10/14	k.i.a.	28/03/18
Raven, ...	C.S.M.					
Raw, John A	Pte.	20506	C	04/09/14	dis.	14/02/19
Rawlinson, Edward	Pte.	21816				
Reath, James	Pte.	21857		03/06/15	dis.	01/03/19
Reece, William H	Pte.	21505			dis.	27/01/19
Rees, George E	L/Cpl.	20129			dis.	20/02/19
Reid, James	Pte.	20727		04/09/14	dis.	24/10/14
Reid, John	Pte.	20360	B	04/09/14	dis.	13/11/14
Reid, John	Pte.	21533		18/03/15	dis.	22/09/16

Name	Rank	No.	Coy.	Joined	Outcome	
Reid, John M	Pte.	21165	D	13/11/14	dis.	24/10/18
Reynolds, Albert	A/Cpl.	21870	B	10/06/15	dis.	24/07/17
Reynolds, William	Pte.	20498			k.i.a.	13/10/18
Richardson, John	Pte.	21272		18/01/15	dis.	19/06/15
Richardson, Joseph	Pte.	20572	A	05/09/14	k.i.a.	23/06/16
Richardson, William	Pte.	21519			dis.	12/01/19
Rigby, Edward	Pte.	21472	C	16/03/16	k.i.a.	28/03/18
Rigby, James	Pte.	21355		26/01/15	dis.	10/09/17
Rigby, John	Pte.	21125	C	15/10/14	dis.	14/12/18
Rigby, John	Pte.	21675		25/05/15	dis.	03/02/19
Rigby, Joseph	Pte.	20401			dis.	11/05/19
Rigby, Thomas	Pte.	20923	D	04/09/14	dis.	07/03/19
Rigby, William	Pte.	21048	B	07/09/14	dis.	04/08/16
Rigby, William	Pte.	21695	C		dis.	27/01/19
Riley, Patrick	Pte.	20850		08/09/14	dis.	03/04/19
Rimmer, Arthur	Pte.	20267		04/09/14	dis.	13/03/19
Rimmer, John	Q.M.S.					
Roberts, Arthur	L/Cpl.	20712			dis.	18/01/19
Roberts, Benjamin	Pte.	21341	D	25/01/15	dis.	21/01/18
Roberts, Henry	Pte.	21469	B		dis.	07/03/19
Roberts, John	C/Sgt.	21160	C		dis.	19/02/19
Roberts, John	Pte.	21406	A	03/02/15	dis.	10/03/16
Roberts, John W	Pte.	21647			dis.	07/03/19
Roberts, Joseph	Pte.	20571	C	05/09/14	dis.	25/04/18
Roberts, Patrick	Pte.	20611	C			
Roberts, Peter	Pte.	21559			dis.	28/03/19
Roberts, Samuel	Pte.	20687	C			
Roberts, Thomas	Pte.	20569	C	05/09/14	d.o.w.	04/06/17
Roberts, William	Sgt.	20328	B		dis.	07/02/19
Roberts, William	C.S.M.	20547		05/09/14	dis.	19/12/17
Roberts, William	Pte.	20601	C	07/09/14	dis.	12/11/14 *
Robertshaw, Percy S	Sgt.	20044	A	05/09/14	rel.	24/03/19
Robinson, Bennett	Pte.	21342		25/01/15	dis.	28/06/18
Robinson, Francis E	Pte.	21941				
Robinson, James	Pte.	20976	D		dis.	27/01/19
Robinson, John J	Pte.	21396	A	01/02/15	d.	18/01/19
Robinson, John V	Pte.	21965				
Robinson, Robert	Pte.	20650		04/09/14	d.o.w.	08/08/17
Robinson, Samuel	Pte.	21940		19/07/15	dis.	30/10/18
Robinson, Thomas	Pte.	21823	A	01/02/15	dis.	14/12/18
Robinson, Thomas	Pte.	20230				
Roche, William	Pte.	21448		15/02/15	dis.	01/02/19
Rochford, Patrick	Pte.	21925		15/07/15	dis.	19/04/17
Roe, John G	Pte.	21507		04/03/15	dis.	28/03/19
Rogers, Leonard	L/Cpl.	20414			dis.	19/07/19
Rogerson, James	Pte.	20194	A		dis.	14/08/18

Name	Rank	No.	Coy.	Joined	Outcome	
Rogerson, John	Pte.	20196	A	05/09/14	dis.	30/03/19
Roney, Albert E	L/Cpl.	20786	D	07/09/14	d.o.w.	10/07/16
Roney, Daniel	Pte.	20794			k.i.a.	13/10/18
Rooney, John	Pte.	21774		27/05/15	dis.	04/03/19
Rose, Walter	Pte.	21643	F	25/05/15	dis.	09/06/15
Ross, Martin	Pte.			04/09/14	dis.	22/05/18
Rotherham, Harry	Pte.	20912			dis.	17/02/19
Rothwell, George	Pte.	20301	B		dis.	08/03/19
Rothwell, Thomas	Pte.	21183		07/12/14	dis.	05/02/19
Roughley, Edward	Pte.	21231			dis.	02/02/19
Roughley, Henry	Pte.	21491	B	26/02/15	d.	19/02/17
Roughley, Henry	Pte.	20660		08/09/14	dis.	08/01/15
Roughsedge, William	Sgt.	20898			dis.	18/01/19
Routley, Percy F	C/Sgt.	20064	A		dis.	13/03/19
Rowland, Joseph	Cpl.	21751		25/05/15	dis.	08/10/17
Rowland, William	Pte.	20927		05/09/14	dis.	08/02/15 *
Rowlands, William	Pte.	20257		07/09/14	dis.	04/10/17
Roy, George W	Pte.	21145	B	06/11/14	k.i.a.	02/08/17
Royden, William	W.O. II.	21107				
Ruddick, Christopher	Pte.	21973		07/08/15		
Ryan, Miles	Pte.	20997		04/09/14	dis.	02/10/14
Ryan, Thomas	Pte.	21923		13/07/15	dis.	13/12/18
Ryder, A H	Pte.					
Ryder, James	Pte.	21480	A		dis.	18/02/19
Rylance, John T	Pte.	20666				
Sams, Frederick	Pte.	20678	C		dis.	22/01/19
Sanders, George	Pte.	21275	E	19/01/15	dis.	08/02/15
Sanders, Herbert	Pte.	22047	C			
Sanderson, George	Pte.	21494	D	27/02/15	k.i.a.	16/07/17
Sandford, Henry	Sgt.	20818	D		dis.	30/01/19
Sandford, Richard	Pte.	20941			dis.	27/01/19
Sandford, Richard	Pte.	21795				
Saunders, Harry	Pte.	20476	B	08/09/14	dis.	12/11/14
Saunders, Hugh	Pte.	21817	A		dis.	28/02/19
Saunders, James P	Sgt.	21121	C			
Saunders, Thomas	Pte.	21745	D	26/05/15	dis.	20/01/19
Savage, Lawrence	Pte.	20908	D	08/09/14	dis.	18/03/19
Saxon, Martin	Cpl.	21420			dis.	02/04/19
Saxon, Robert	Pte.	21363	A		dis.	06/03/19
Saxon, William	Pte.	21364	C	21/01/15	dis.	20/04/15
Scarisbrick, Harry	Pte.	20370		05/09/14	dis.	10/03/16
Schofield, Alfred	Pte.	21026				
Scott, Arthur	Pte.	20354			d.o.w.	07/06/18
Scott, Edward	Pte.	21478				
Scott, Harry	Pte.	20065	A	04/09/14	dis.	12/03/19
Scott, J	C.Q.M.S.					

Name	Rank	No.	Coy.	Joined	Outcome	
Scott, John	Pte.	20341	B	11/09/14	dis.	24/02/19
Scott, Thomas	Pte.	20868		04/09/14	dis.	27/06/18
Seaton, William	Pte.	21043			dis.	23/02/19
Seddon, Adam	Pte.	21035		05/09/14	dis.	28/02/19
Seddon, Joseph	Cpl.	21178			dis.	14/01/19
Seddon, Thomas	Pte.	21220	A	11/01/15	dis.	13/03/15 *
Sefton, George	Pte.					
Sephton, Frederick	Pte.	20405			dis.	24/02/19
Sephton, George	Pte.	20821	D		dis.	14/01/19
Sephton, William H	Pte.	20406			d.o.w.	14/10/18
Seward, Arthur	Cpl.	21861				
Shacklady, Arthur	Bglr	21073	D	11/09/14	dis.	24/10/14 !
Sharkey, Thomas	Pte.	20249		04/09/14	dis.	07/10/14 *
Sharp, Peter	Pte.	21542				
Sharratt, Alfred	Sgt.	20552	B	03/09/14	dis.	28/01/19
Sharratt, John H	Sgt.	20311	B	08/09/14	dis.	22/02/19
Shaw, Archibald	Pte.	20040	A	07/09/14	dis.	27/11/17
Shaw, John	Cpl.	20640	C	07/09/14	k.i.a.	25/06/17
Sheen, John	Sgt.	20711	C	04/09/14	dis.	31/01/19
Sheffield, James	Pte.	21648	D	24/05/15	dis.	03/01/19
Sherratt, Henry	Pte.	21408		02/02/15	dis.	05/08/19
Sherwood, Arthur H	Pte.	21720	B			
Shingler, Thomas	Pte.	21343			dis.	13/01/19
Shuker, Samuel	Pte.	20400	B	04/09/14	dis.	02/05/18
Simms, Joseph	Pte.	20478	B			
Simms, Joseph	Pte.	21124	B	12/10/14	dis.	24/10/14 *
Simms, Joseph	Pte.	20373		04/09/14	dis.	24/10/14 *
Simms, Richard	Pte.	20901			dis.	14/01/19
Simpson, John	Pte.	21825		01/06/15	d.o.w.	21/12/17
Singleton, Thomas	Pte.	20702		04/09/14	dis.	23/01/19
Skelhorn, John	Pte.	21909	A	12/07/15	k.i.a.	01/07/16
Slater, Robert	C/Sgt.	20292	A	04/09/14	d.	17/07/18
Slater, William H	Pte.	21594	A			
Smart, Austin	Pte.	20353	B		dis.	12/03/19
Smart, Thomas	Pte.	22048			k.i.a.	13/10/18
Smart, William	Sgt.	20093	A	07/09/14	dis.	15/03/19
Smethurst, Moses	Pte.	21985				
Smith, Albert	Pte.	21576	A	17/05/15	dis.	12/12/17
Smith, Alexander	Pte.	20922		05/09/14	dis.	22/12/14
Smith, Archie	Pte.	21764		27/05/15	dis.	08/03/18
Smith, Arthur V	Pte.	21530	B	15/03/15	dis.	31/05/15 *
Smith, Charles G	Pte.					*
Smith, George	Pte.	20563				
Smith, George W	Cpl.	21191	C		dis.	17/03/19
Smith, Herbert	Pte.	21540		22/03/15	dis.	25/08/15
Smith, Isaac	Pte.	22417				

Name	Rank	No.	Coy.	Joined	Outcome	
Smith, J H	Pte.					
Smith, James	Pte.	21712				
Smith, John	Pte.	20112		04/09/14	dis.	22/10/14
Smith, John	Pte.	21790		28/05/15	dis.	08/07/15
Smith, Jonathan	Pte.	21692				
Smith, Martin	Pte.	21614	C	22/05/15	dis.	29/07/16
Smith, Michael	Pte.	21340				
Smith, Richard	Pte.	20760			dis.	10/01/19
Smith, Roland	L/Cpl.	20009			dis.	17/02/19
Smith, Sidney	Pte.	21204			dis.	27/01/19
Smith, Thomas	Pte.		C			
Smith, Thomas	Pte.	21310	A		dis.	23/01/15
Smith, Thomas K	Pte.	20914		04/09/14	dis.	29/01/20
Smith, William E	Pte.	20199	A	05/09/14	dis.	18/02/19
Smith, William E	Pte.	21986				
Southern, Robert	L/Cpl.	21570		16/05/15	dis.	24/07/16 *
Southern, William	L/Cpl.	20833		07/09/14	dis.	15/01/19
Sowerbutts, Nathaniel	Pte.	20135	A	07/09/14	k.i.a.	10/06/17
Sparks, George	Pte.	21686		25/05/15	dis.	23/03/20
Sparks, Josiah	Pte.	21403		02/02/15	k.i.a.	24/03/18 *
Speakman, Joseph S	L/Cpl.	20482		05/09/14	dis.	13/01/19
Speakman, William	Pte.	20827			dis.	14/01/19
Spencer, F	Sgt.		A			
Spencer, Robert	Sgt.	20933	D	08/09/14	dis.	22/11/17
Spencer, Samuel	C.S.M.	21057		08/09/14	dis.	04/12/15
Spencer, Thomas	Sgt.					
Springthorpe, William	Pte.	21617		21/05/15	k.i.a.	14/02/17
Stanley, Charles	Pte.	21921	A		dis.	
Stanley, James	Pte.	20994			dis.	31/03/19
Stanley, John	Pte.	21481	D	23/02/15	d.o.w.	21/12/18
Stanton, William	Pte.	21156		23/11/14	d.o.w.	03/07/16
Starkey, William	Pte.	21959		03/08/15		
Stephens, Arthur	Pte.	21697			dis.	28/04/19
Stott, James	C.Q.M.S.	21078			k.i.a.	11/10/18
Stott, William	Bglr	21093		17/09/14	dis.	24/12/14 !
Stowell, Henry	Pte.	20185			k.i.a.	13/10/18
Street, Peter	Pte.	20299	B		dis.	28/04/19
Stretch, Albert	Pte.	21383	E	29/01/15	dis.	19/06/15
Strettle, William	Pte.	21993		21/08/15	dis.	19/11/15
Strong, Oliver	Pte.	21874		10/06/15	dis.	09/10/15
Stronge, George	Pte.	21130		04/09/14	dis.	05/02/15
Stuart, Charles	Pte.	20435	B		dis.	15/03/19
Stubbs, Arthur	Pte.	20356	B	05/09/14	k.i.a.	22/06/16
Sudworth, James	Pte.	20906				
Sudworth, John	Pte.	20694	C	04/09/14	dis.	06/05/19
Sullivan, Charles	Pte.	20751	C	04/09/14	dis.	01/12/14 *

Name	Rank	No.	Coy.	Joined	Outcome	
Sumner, Thomas	Pte.	20374	B	08/09/14	dis.	07/03/19
Sutton, Francis	Cpl.	20041	A	05/09/14	d.o.w.	05/07/17
Sutton, Robert A	Sgt.	20294	B	07/09/14	d.o.w.	28/10/16
Sweeney, Joseph	Pte.					*
Sweeney, Michael	Pte.	20632		04/09/14	dis.	07/03/19
Swift, Henry	Cpl.	20754		07/09/14	dis.	30/12/18
Swift, John	Pte.	20684	C		dis.	27/01/19
Swift, Thomas	Pte.	20465			dis.	27/01/19
Swift, Wilfred J	L/Cpl.	21419	D		dis.	31/03/19
Swift, William	Pte.	20455		04/09/14	d.o.w.	18/04/18
Swift, William	Pte.	20920	B	07/09/14	dis.	11/09/18
Swindells, James	Pte.	20225			dis.	03/07/19
Taggart, John H	Sgt.	20517			dis.	13/02/19
Tatlock, Ernest	Cpl.	21206	A		dis.	28/01/19
Tatlock, Fred	Pte.	20081		05/09/14	dis.	16/12/14
Taylor, Daniel	Pte.	20078	A	08/09/14	dis.	04/05/19
Taylor, Edwin	Pte.	20297		04/09/14	dis.	06/02/15
Taylor, Henry	Pte.	21005	D	04/09/14	k.i.a.	19/12/15
Taylor, James	L/Cpl.	20383		04/09/14	dis.	21/11/18
Taylor, James	Sgt.	20813	D		dis.	03/02/19
Taylor, John	Pte.	21200		30/12/14	dis.	14/06/18
Taylor, Thomas	Pte.	21006	D		dis.	27/01/19
Taylor, Thomas	Pte.	21495		02/03/15	dis.	20/04/15
Taylor, William	Pte.	21373	B		dis.	13/01/19
Telford, John	Pte.	20783			dis.	27/01/19
Thelwell, Cornelius	Pte.	20518			dis.	20/03/19
Thelwell, Frederick	Pte.	21265	E	18/01/15	k.i.a.	24/04/17
Thomas, Albert E	Pte.	21467		18/02/15		
Thomas, D	C.Q.M.S.		C			
Thomas, Edward O	Pte.	21510			dis.	27/01/19
Thomas, Hugh	Pte.	20648	C	04/09/14	k.i.a.	20/11/17
Thomas, Hugh	Sgt.	21536	C		dis.	27/01/19
Thomas, William	Pte.	20163	A		dis.	29/01/19
Thompson, George	Pte.					
Thompson, John	Pte.	21432	B	09/02/15	dis.	15/02/19
Thompson, John	Pte.	20792	D			
Thompson, John	Pte.	20915		07/09/14	dis.	25/10/17
Thompson, Thomas	Pte.	20428	A	04/09/14	dis.	03/03/19
Thomson, George	Pte.	20239		04/09/14	dis.	07/01/19
Thornber, ...	Sgt.					
Thornburn, William J	Sgt.	20769		07/09/14	dis.	29/10/18
Thorpe, George	Cpl.	20075	A	04/09/14	dis.	04/03/19
Thorpe, Herbert	Pte.	20591	C		dis.	22/04/19
Tickle, Albert	Pte.	21696		21/05/15	d.o.w.	14/08/16
Tickle, Ernest	Sgt.	20033			k.i.a.	13/07/18
Tickle, John W	Pte.	20913	D			

Name	Rank	No.	Coy.	Joined	Outcome	
Tickle, Peter	Pte.	20007			dis.	30/03/19
Tickle, William H	Pte.	20784	D			
Tierney, Austin	Cpl.	21796		29/05/15	dis.	18/02/19
Tierney, Walter	Pte.	20159	A	05/09/14	d.o.w.	19/12/16
Tildsley, Albert	Pte.	21229	A	13/01/15	dis.	16/01/15
Timlin, Thomas	Pte.	21656		21/05/15	dis.	07/10/18
Timmons, James	Pte.	20448				
Tipton, Thomas	L/Cpl.	20467	B	04/09/14	k.i.a.	21/10/16
Tobin, Edward	Pte.	21190				
Todd, Joseph	Pte.	21601	D	18/05/15	dis.	15/10/17
Todd, William	Cpl.	20860			dis.	17/03/19
Tolan, Patrick	Pte.	20389		04/09/14	dis.	18/03/19
Topping, Alfred	Pte.	20966			k.i.a.	19/09/18
Topping, Henry	Pte.	21111				
Topping, John	Pte.	21390		01/02/15	dis.	26/07/17
Topping, Joseph	Sgt.	20511		04/09/14	k.i.a.	23/03/18
Travis, Peter	Pte.	20724		04/09/14	dis.	22/01/19
Traynor, Thomas	Pte.	20822				
Trickett, William E	Pte.	20077	A		dis.	09/03/19
Trotter, John T	Pte.	20606		04/09/14	k.i.a.	09/07/16
Tucker, Ernest	Pte.	21349			dis.	13/01/19
Tulip, Lancelot	Pte.	21134		19/10/14	dis.	16/11/18
Tully, Thomas	L/Cpl.	21031	D	04/09/14	dis.	20/05/19
Turner, Frank	Pte.	20193	A		k.i.a.	25/10/18
Turner, John J	L/Cpl.	21541	D	22/03/15	dis.	03/06/19
Turner, Richard	Pte.	20228	A			
Twiner, ...	Pte.					
Twist, Francis J	Pte.	20045		08/09/14	dis.	25/11/14
Tye, Andrew	Pte.	21254			dis.	14/01/19
Tyrer, Paul E	Pte.	21286	B		dis.	27/01/19
Unsworth, Thomas	Pte.	20594	D	04/09/14	dis.	26/02/19
Unsworth, William	Pte.	21691			dis.	03/03/19
Unsworth, William	Pte.	21528		11/03/15	dis.	30/03/15
Valentine, Frederick	Pte.	21844			dis.	16/03/19
Veasey, Thomas	Pte.	21192			dis.	06/03/19
Vose, John	L/Sjt.	20504	C		dis.	13/02/19
Wade, Arthur	Pte.	21780		28/05/15	dis.	07/09/17
Wade, John	Cpl.	21619	B	23/05/16	k.i.a.	29/04/18
Wade, Rowland	Pte.	21860		03/06/15	dis.	24/12/18
Walker, James	Pte.	20393	B	04/09/14	dis.	15/01/19
Walker, William	Pte.	21128	C	16/10/14	dis.	16/12/14
Wall, Lawrence	Pte.	21434		10/02/15	dis.	13/03/15
Walsh, Charles	Sgt.	20817	D		dis.	27/01/19
Walsh, D	Sgt.					
Walsh, Edward	Pte.	20604		07/09/14	dis.	22/05/19
Walsh, James	Pte.	21911		12/07/15	dis.	03/10/15

Name	Rank	No.	Coy.	Joined	Outcome	
Walsh, Patrick	Pte.	21609	F	16/05/15		
Walsh, Peter	Pte.	21917			dis.	19/03/19
Walsh, William	Pte.	21729			dis.	03/01/19
Warburton, John W	Pte.	21908				
Waring, George	A/Cpl.	20022	A		dis.	07/03/19
Waring, Joseph	L/Cpl.	21219	C	11/01/15	k.i.a.	18/09/18
Waring, Joseph	Pte.	21424	E	11/02/15	dis.	03/05/19
Waring, Robert	Pte.	20025	A			
Waring, Samuel	Pte.	21113		02/10/14	dis.	27/09/16
Waring, Thomas	Pte.	21281	A	19/01/15	dis.	08/03/19
Waring, Thomas	Pte.	21922				
Wassell, Frederick	Pte.	20673			dis.	11/03/19
Waterworth, James	Pte.	20808				
Wathen, Charles	Cpl.	20061	A		dis.	19/03/19
Watkins, Alfred	Pte.	20280	B		dis.	04/03/19
Watkins, Henry	Pte.	21117		06/10/14	dis.	05/03/19
Watkins, Samuel	L/Sjt.	20071				
Watkinson, Samuel	Pte.	21213	C	08/01/15	k.i.a.	12/06/17
Wayman, John	Pte.	20990		05/09/14	dis.	31/03/16
Webster, Charles	Pte.	20189	A	04/09/14	k.i.a.	10/07/16
Webster, Edward	Pte.	20369			dis.	04/03/19
Webster, George	Pte.	20579	C		dis.	19/02/19
Webster, Harold	Pte.	20288			dis.	20/03/19
Webster, Henry	Pte.	21514	A		dis.	27/01/19
Webster, Herbert	L/Cpl.	20205	A		dis.	24/02/19
Webster, James	Pte.	20175	A	07/09/14	dis.	01/03/19
Webster, James	Pte.	21716	D	25/05/15	dis.	03/03/19
Webster, Job	Pte.	20970	D	08/09/14	d.o.w.	19/06/18
Webster, John W	Pte.	21587	B	18/05/15	dis.	19/09/18
Webster, Thomas	Pte.	21131		04/09/14	d.o.w.	08/04/18
Webster, William	Pte.	20536			dis.	12/03/19
Weldon, Alfred	Pte.	20691	C		dis.	29/01/19
Welsh, Michael	Pte.	20964		07/09/14	dis.	02/02/15
West, Harold	Sgt.	20072	A	08/09/14	d.o.w.	09/12/16
Whalley, John	Pte.		C			
Whalley, Joseph	Pte.	20559	C	04/09/14	dis.	25/12/19
Whalley, Thomas	Pte.	20463		07/09/14	dis.	01/10/14
Whalley, Thomas	Pte.	20325		04/09/14	dis.	24/10/14
Whelan, Isaac	Pte.	22039		03/09/15	k.i.a.	27/03/18
Whitaker, Henry	Pte.	21575				
White, Edward	Pte.					
White, Edward J	Pte.	21927		17/07/15	dis.	29/01/16
White, George	Pte.	20839				
White, Herbert	Pte.	20770	D		dis.	04/03/19
White, James	Pte.	21810				
White, Patrick	Pte.	20800		05/09/14	dis.	02/10/14

Name	Rank	No.	Coy.	Joined	Outcome	
White, William	Pte.	21568				
Whitehouse, Arthur	Pte.	21335			dis.	27/01/19
Whittaker, Richard	Pte.	21251		18/01/15	dis.	25/01/19
Whittle, Joseph	Pte.	21850				
Whittle, Levi	Pte.	20557	C			
Whittle, Nathaniel	Pte.	21361		26/01/15	dis.	19/06/15
Whittle, Robert	Pte.	21186				
Wignall, James	Pte.	21880		14/06/15	k.i.a.	16/07/17
Wilcock, George	Pte.	21339		25/01/15	dis.	25/01/20
Wilcock, Thomas J	Pte.	21650	A	24/05/15	dis.	06/02/19
Wilde, Harold	Sgt.	20978	D	08/09/14	d.o.w.	23/10/18
Wilde, James	Pte.	21550	B	19/04/15	k.i.a.	14/04/18
Wilding, John J	Pte.	20844				
Wildman, William	Pte.	20811		04/09/14	dis.	02/10/14
Wilkinson, George	Pte.	20772				
Wilkinson, Herbert	Sgt.	20882	D	04/09/14	d.o.w.	04/12/17
Wilkinson, James	Pte.	20554				
Wilkinson, James	Pte.	20773				
Wilkinson, James	Pte.	20461		04/09/14	dis.	12/10/14
Wilkinson, Joseph	Pte.	20322			k.i.a.	28/03/18
Wilkinson, Vincent	Pte.	20201	A	04/09/14	dis.	11/03/19
Willetts, Benjamin	Pte.	21741	A	26/05/15	k.i.a.	12/06/17
Willetts, John	Pte.	20749	D		dis.	06/02/19
Williams, Arthur	Pte.	21085		12/09/14	dis.	09/03/19
Williams, David	Pte.	20671	C	08/09/14	dis.	26/01/19
Williams, Frank	Pte.	20625		08/09/14	dis.	26/05/16
Williams, J	Pte.	20929				
Williams, John	C.S.M.	20221	A			
Williams, John W	Sgt.	20203	A	05/09/14	d.	01/11/18
Williams, Llewellyn	Pte.	21512		06/03/15	dis.	25/01/19
Williams, Robert C	L/Sjt.	20186		08/09/14	dis.	31/01/18
Williams, Thomas	Pte.	21524		10/03/15	dis.	01/02/18
Wills, Joseph	Pte.	20544	C	04/09/14	dis.	27/09/18
Wilmore, Edward	Pte.	21244	D		dis.	03/04/19
Wilshaw, William E	Pte.	21606			dis.	05/03/19
Wilson, Ernest	Pte.	20222			dis.	06/08/19
Wilson, Edward	Pte.	20624				
Wilson, James	Pte.	20181			dis.	07/03/19
Wilson, Job	Sgt.	20378	D	08/09/14	d.	07/09/17
Wilson, John	L/Cpl.	20346			dis.	15/01/19
Wilson, Joseph	Pte.	20250		07/09/14	dis.	07/10/14
Wilson, Thomas	Pte.	21812		31/05/15	dis.	03/12/15
Wilson, Thomas	Pte.	21194		05/09/14	d.	15/09/14
Wilson, William	Pte.	20380			dis.	19/03/19
Wilton, Harry	Pte.	21571				
Wilton, Joseph	Pte.	20714			dis.	18/01/19

Name	Rank	No.	Coy.	Joined	Outcome	
Wilton, Thomas	Pte.	21377		27/01/15	dis.	04/12/18
Winnard, John	Pte.	21964	D	03/08/15	dis.	07/09/18
Winstanley, Albert E	Pte.	21915				
Winstanley, Austin	Pte.	20886	D		dis.	08/03/19
Winstanley, Austin	Pte.	20944	D		dis.	23/05/19
Winstanley, Ernest	Pte.	21947		26/07/15	dis.	25/01/19
Winstanley, John	Pte.	20211	A		dis.	06/04/19
Winstanley, Thomas	Pte.	21314	C		dis.	27/01/19
Winterbottom, T	Pte.					
Wiseman, John	Pte.					
Woodhead, Edgar	Sgt.	20220	C	05/09/14	rel.	20/06/19
Woods, Albert	Pte.	20296			dis.	31/03/19
Woods, Charles	Pte.	20023			dis.	27/09/16
Woods, Charles A	Pte.	20051	A	05/09/14	dis.	17/01/18
Woods, John	Pte.	20376	B	07/09/14	k.i.a.	02/12/17
Woods, John	Pte.	20487		05/09/14	dis.	08/03/19
Woods, Peter	Pte.	20752		04/09/14	dis.	06/02/15 *
Woods, Samuel	Pte.	21252	D	18/01/15	k.i.a.	14/06/17
Woods, William	Pte.	21632			dis.	15/01/19
Woodward, James	Pte.	21393		01/02/15	dis.	15/09/18
Woodward, John L	Pte.	20101	A	07/09/14	dis.	20/02/19
Woodward, Samuel	Bglr	21067		08/09/14	dis.	24/12/14
Worthington, James	Pte.	21813				
Wright, Joseph	Cpl.	20916			dis.	27/01/19
Wright, Osborne G	L/Cpl.	20120	A		k.i.a.	25/04/18
Wright, William	Pte.	20090				
Wylie, Thomas	Pte.	21664		24/05/15	k.i.a.	28/03/18
Yates, David	L/Cpl.	20411			dis.	15/03/19
Yates, Thomas	Sgt.	20509		04/09/14	dis.	03/02/19
Yates, Thomas	Pte.	21201	C			
Yates, William	Pte.	20575	D		dis.	16/03/19
Yorke, Edward	Pte.	20367		05/09/14	dis.	29/05/15 *

Other Ranks (Posted)

Name	Rank	No.	Coy.	Joined	Outcome	
Abbott, William H	L/Cpl.	205280			dis.	14/11/18
Abraham, Robert	Cpl.	13161			dis.	19/02/19
Adams, Harry O	Sgt.	22578		06/06/16	dis.	20/04/19
Adams, James	Pte.	203062				
Adams, John	Sgt.	240594			dis.	27/03/19
Adamson, Horace B	Pte.	31742				
Adamson, Peter	Pte.	240813				
Adderley, Richard	Pte.	46359				
Albinson, John	Pte.	31746				
Albiston, Thomas	Pte.	46325				
Allan, Alexander	Pte.	37500				
Alldred, Arthur	Pte.	46127				
Allen, John J	Pte.	37473				
Allen, Philip	Pte.	49228				
Allen, Ralph	Pte.	61665				
Allen, Walter	Pte.	49128				
Allison, Harold	Pte.	46318				
Allman, Charles	Pte.	34376				
Allsup, George J	Pte.	49026				
Almond, Peter	Pte.	28629				
Ames, Thomas	Pte.	46393				
Anders, James	Pte.	46149				
Anderson, Gilbert B	Pte.	49163				
Anderton, Richard	Pte.	32596			dis.	20/09/18
Andrews, Reginald T	Pte.	49314			k.i.a.	04/11/18
Anker, Ernest	Pte.	31818				
Antrobus, John	Pte.	39277				
Ardern, William E	Pte.	45120	C	29/12/17	dis.	07/03/19
Arnold, Charles	Pte.	22226				
Arnold, William	Pte.	40566				
Ashby, George A	Pte.	235104				
Ashley, Edwin J	Pte.	36460		29/03/17	dis.	23/02/19
Ashman, Albert E	Pte.	10213		16/11/17	k.i.a.	23/03/18
Ashton, Frank	Pte.	49164				
Ashton, Henry	Pte.	201597				
Astbury, Thomas	Pte.	14309			dis.	27/09/18
Atherton, Thomas	Pte.	46581				
Atkin, George V	Pte.	17084	B	01/07/17	k.i.a.	15/12/17
Atkin, Victor	Pte.	14164			dis.	14/03/19
Atkins, William	Pte.	14123			dis.	17/02/19
Atkinson, Joseph	Pte.	46086				
Atkinson, Robert	Pte.	14753			dis.	02/02/19
Atkinson, Robert I	Pte.	46523				
Atkinson, William	Pte.	31145				
Austin, Edward	Sgt.	48985				
Backhouse, Burrows	Pte.	37474				

Name	Rank	No.	Coy.	Joined	Outcome	
Bacon, George C	A/Cpl.	235119				
Bacon, William	Pte.	22158		03/09/16	dis.	05/02/19
Bagnall, George	Pte.	34300				
Bailey, Albert	Pte.	31248	A	14/04/17	k.i.a.	26/04/17
Bailey, Benjamin	Pte.	15505			dis.	02/04/19
Bailey, Harold	Pte.	70125				
Bailey, James H	Pte.	32642				
Bainbridge, George B	Pte.	49213				
Baker, William	Pte.	32583				
Baldock, Hedley C	Pte.	49130		13/09/18	dis.	23/09/19
Baldwin, Harold R	Pte.	49260				
Ball, Abraham	A/Cpl.	11942		30/09/18	dis.	09/03/19
Balls, Charles A	Pte.	24639				
Balmer, William	Pte.	241515			d.o.w.	27/09/18
Balmforth, William	Pte.	28415				
Banks, John W	Sgt.	203488			dis.	01/04/19
Barber, James H	A/Cpl.	22308				
Barber, Joe	Pte.	34338				
Barber, Percy	Pte.	49165				
Barbour, Andrew	Pte.	37467			k.i.a.	13/10/18
Bardsley, Aaron	Pte.	22334				
Bardsley, Elijah	Pte.	22351				
Barham, Arthur	Pte.	15456				
Barker, Ernest	Pte.	40023				
Barker, George W	Pte.	43072				
Barker, Robert A	Cpl.	22528			dis.	08/08/18
Barlow, John E	Pte.	29682		29/03/17	d.o.w.	28/06/17
Barnes, James	Pte.	26516			dis.	22/10/19
Barnes, Thomas	Pte.	49298				
Barnes, William	Pte.	31741				
Barr, James	Pte.	39334				
Barrett, Edwin	Pte.	40634				
Barrett, Joseph	Pte.	238066			dis.	21/02/19
Barrington, Thomas A	L/Cpl.	48987			dis.	13/02/19
Barrow, Fred	Pte.	31752				
Barrow, William	Pte.	240395		31/07/18	dis.	21/01/19
Bartlam, Frank	Pte.	49032				
Barton, Fred	Pte.	45121	B	29/12/17	dis.	01/10/19
Barton, John A	Pte.	14342			dis.	09/03/19
Barton, William	Pte.	46346				
Bate, Robert	Pte.	49581			dis.	26/05/19
Bateson, Percy	Pte.	13910			dis.	01/03/19
Bayliss, Thomas W	Pte.	49262				
Bean, Robert	Pte.	49166				
Bean, Robert D	Pte.	49109				
Beardow, Arthur	Pte.	49030				

Name	Rank	No.	Coy.	Joined	Outcome	
Beardsley, Arthur L	Sgt.	49133				
Beeley, William	Pte.	22342				
Bell, Albert E	Pte.	201226			dis.	13/02/19
Bell, John	Pte.	203145				
Bell, Robert H	Pte.	49098				
Bell, William	Pte.	32196				
Benbow, William	Pte.	45379			dis.	22/02/19
Bending, William E	Pte.	204858				
Bennett, Frederick W	Pte.	32192	A	22/02/17	dis.	02/03/19
Bennett, James	Pte.	6558				
Bennett, John	Pte.	18397			dis.	13/01/19
Bennett, John	Pte.	22319				
Bennett, Wilfred	Pte.	24039				
Bennett, William	Pte.	60139				
Benstead, William A	Pte.	204850		03/03/18	dis.	05/03/19
Bentley, Edward J	Pte.	45109				
Bentley, John	Pte.	46097				
Bergan, Harry	Pte.	37501				
Berresford, Harold	Pte.	45791				
Berry, Victor V	Pte.	49261				
Beswick, Ebenezer	Pte.	40842			d.	30/10/18
Bevan, Ernest S	Pte.	49230				
Biddle, Francis V	Pte.	29996				
Biddle, Henry J	Pte.	49285			dis.	10/07/19
Bigg, Walter	Pte.	37504				
Biggins, Frederick V	Pte.	49281				
Bignell, Samuel	Pte.	37458				
Bigwood, Frank	Pte.	37472			k.i.a.	13/10/18
Binks, Arthur	Pte.	46522				
Birch, Albert B	Pte.	37565				
Bird, Arthur	Pte.	204869				
Bird, William E	Pte.	49284				
Birtwistle, William	Pte.	43339				
Bishop, Henry	Pte.	49300				
Blackshaw, Joseph	A/Cpl.	34435				
Blackstone, Woolf	Pte.	36480				
Blair, William	Pte.	32035				
Bleasdale, James	Pte.	43976			dis.	31/08/18
Bloom, Joseph	Pte.	49222				
Bloy, Thomas	Pte.	46368				
Boardman, Harold	Pte.	46099				
Boardman, John	Pte.	16525		29/07/18	d.o.w.	05/11/18
Boddy, William	Pte.	203645	D	05/02/18	dis.	21/05/19
Boffey, John	Pte.	46109				
Bolderson, Henry	Pte.	48986				
Bolton, Herbert M	Pte.	204921				

Name	Rank	No.	Coy.	Joined	Outcome	
Bonney, Edward J	Pte.	32597				
Boon, Richard	Pte.	27679				
Boore, James E	Pte.	32641		29/12/17	k.i.a.	23/03/18
Boothman, Fred	Pte.	266271				
Bough, Lewis H	Pte.	49027				
Bowen, Harold M	Pte.	22554		25/05/16	d.	30/08/16
Boyer, Herbert L	C.S.M.	240010	B	12/01/18	k.i.a.	29/03/18
Bradshaw, Alfred	Pte.	201025		19/01/18	dis.	05/02/19
Bradshaw, David	Pte.	31739			dis.	16/04/19
Bradshaw, James W	Pte.	235047				
Bradshaw, Percy	Pte.	13042		06/10/18	dis.	21/01/19
Braithwaite, James	Pte.	43665				
Brakell, John	Pte.	240957		31/07/18	dis.	31/01/19
Brannan, Thomas	Pte.	43977				
Brassett, Albert J	Pte.	32321				
Brayshaw, Edgar	Pte.	49209		11/09/18	dis.	19/11/19
Breen, Thomas	Pte.	22298			dis.	07/01/19
Brennan, Frederick T	Pte.	49129			dis.	02/03/19
Brennan, Percy V	Pte.	49157				
Brennan, Thomas	A/Cpl.	3041			dis.	20/02/19
Brett, Arthur W	Pte.	21903			dis.	07/02/19
Briant, George	Cpl.	204916			dis.	02/04/19
Bridge, John	Pte.	22282	A	05/08/16	dis.	13/01/19
Bridgeham, Peter	Pte.	204259				
Brierley, Thomas H	Pte.	31749				
Brighton, Frederick	Pte.	49028				
Brimelow, William	Pte.	46120				
Brindley, Thomas	Pte.	43314				
Brittle, John D	Pte.	31210				
Broadbent, Albert	Pte.	31024			k.i.a.	13/10/18
Broadhurst, Harry	Pte.	203227				
Bromley, John W	Pte.	22350				
Brookes, William A	Pte.	31319				
Brooks, Charles G	Pte.	46344				
Brooks, George E	Pte.	37482			d.o.w.	07/11/18
Brooks, John T	Pte.	50325				
Brotherhood, William	Pte.	6323		24/10/16	d.	01/11/16
Brotheridge, Henry	Pte.	49288				
Brown, David	Pte.	22355				
Brown, Ernest	Pte.	49212				
Brown, George E	Pte.	204859		02/02/18	dis.	14/07/19
Brown, John	Cpl.	240047				
Brown, John	Pte.	15213				
Brown, John	Pte.	31822				
Brown, Norman	Pte.	36702				
Brown, Reginald	Pte.	22224			dis.	26/07/17

Name	Rank	No.	Coy.	Joined	Outcome	
Brown, Thomas	Pte.	203182			dis.	19/12/18
Brown, William	Pte.	203091			dis.	28/02/19
Brown, William	Pte.	34242			dis.	27/01/19
Brown, William C	Pte.	49018				
Brown, William E	Pte.	200315			dis.	24/02/19
Brown, William H	Pte.	37505				
Brown, William J	Pte.	19646				
Brownridge, Albert E	Pte.	49229			dis.	09/08/19
Buck, James	Pte.	43582		28/10/18	dis.	30/07/19
Buckle, Joseph	Pte.	49029				
Burch, Alfred L	Pte.	49299				
Burgess, Harry	Pte.	46333				
Burgess, James B	Pte.	22356				
Burgoyne, Fred	Pte.	49177				
Burke, John	Pte.	39344				
Burke, John	Pte.	202453				
Burns, John	Pte.	200923				
Burrows, Thomas A	Pte.	46144				
Butcher, Ernest S	Cpl.	58002				
Butler, Fred	Pte.	203181			dis.	15/03/18
Butler, Thomas H	Pte.	43933				
Button, Horace V	Sgt.	204861				
Buttrey, John	Pte.	200148			dis.	13/03/19
Bye, Herbert G	Pte.	204870				
Byrn, Alfred H	Sgt.	34025				
Caddick, James	Pte.	19401	C	14/04/17	d.o.w.	30/07/17
Cadwallader, Matthew T	Pte.	235405			d.o.w.	16/05/18
Caffary, John E	Pte.	204889			dis.	15/01/19
Cain, Ernest	Pte.	22152				
Cain, Lawrence	Pte.	45739				
Caine, James R	Pte.	49131				
Callen, Alfred	Pte.	49263				
Callery, Henry	Pte.	12404				
Callon, John	Pte.	19752				
Camm, Hugh	Pte.	28984				
Canning, George	Pte.	22206				
Capon, Ernest A	Pte.	49232				
Carley, Lawrence	Pte.	34288			dis.	10/02/19
Carlisle, Thomas H	Pte.	19895				
Carpenter, George J	Pte.	58003				
Carr, Septimus C	Pte.	44888				
Carroll, Thomas W	Pte.	17583				
Carroll, William	Pte.	241092		31/07/18	dis.	29/01/19
Carter, Walter	Pte.	49132				
Cartwright, Harry	S/Sgt.	204925			dis.	02/04/19
Cartwright, Joseph	Pte.	46525				

Name	Rank	No.	Coy.	Joined	Outcome	
Case, Joseph	Pte.	46380				
Casewell, Rowland C	Pte.	204991				
Catlow, John	Pte.	44440				
Cattanach, Hayden T	Pte.	58004				
Chadwick, James	Pte.	240805		01/10/18	dis.	28/03/19
Chadwick, Robert	Pte.	204903				
Chadwick, Wilfred	Pte.	238085			dis.	14/04/19
Challenor, George	Pte.	241107				
Chamberlain, Charles	Pte.	32627	C	29/12/17	k.i.a.	23/03/18
Chasey, Edward D	Pte.	49167				
Chatfield, Amos A	Pte.	49102				
Cheetham, Ernest	Pte.	43869				
Chesworth, William	Pte.	28973			dis.	13/09/19
Christie, William	Pte.	49111				
Christmas, Frederick J	Pte.	49257				
Clare, Peter	Pte.	200480			dis.	09/03/19
Clark, Charles E	Cpl.	204911				
Clark, Clarence	Pte.	39224				
Clark, Percy	Pte.	34302				
Clarke, Albert H	Pte.	46524				
Clarke, Edward	Pte.	16334			dis.	26/11/17
Clarke, Frederick	Pte.	204872				
Clarke, Harry	Pte.	241267			dis.	02/02/19
Clarke, Wilfred	Pte.	49456			k.i.a.	13/10/18
Clayton, Frank	Pte.	22009			dis.	16/04/19
Cleal, Alfred	Pte.	16721				
Cleary, James W	Pte.	49100				
Climie, George	Pte.	204917			dis.	08/05/19
Coates, William H	Cpl.	49141				
Collier, George	Pte.	204890		22/07/18	dis.	14/07/19
Collier, James R	Pte.	46163				
Collier, Richard	L/Cpl.	2854				
Collins, Charles H	Pte.	46156				
Collins, Dick	Pte.	204918				
Collins, Ernest	Pte.	36630				
Collins, Harry	Pte.	238049				
Collins, Joseph	Pte.	22357	D	05/08/16	d.o.w.	28/03/18
Collins, Richard	Pte.					
Collis, Frank H	Cpl.	49134				
Connor, Ernest	Pte.	45122				
Conroy, Arthur	Pte.	36013				
Conway, Martin	Pte.	31748				
Cook, James A	Pte.	49233		18/09/18	dis.	07/03/19
Cook, James W	Pte.	34445				
Cook, John	Pte.	34480				
Cooke, Arthur	Pte.	22315	A	03/09/16	k.i.a.	09/04/18

Name	Rank	No.	Coy.	Joined	Outcome	
Coombes, John	Pte.	39481			k.i.a.	31/07/17
Cooper, Albert	Pte.	49155				
Cooper, Alfred	Pte.	46342				
Cooper, Alfred S	Pte.	204871	A	22/07/18	dis.	04/06/19
Cooper, James	Pte.	58001				
Cooper, James A	Pte.	18008			dis.	13/01/19
Cooper, Peter	Pte.	19415				
Cope, Thomas J	Pte.	49197				
Corbett, John E	Pte.	203184			k.i.a.	31/07/17
Corfield, Harry	Pte.	22580			dis.	25/02/19
Corns, Joseph	Pte.	46096				
Couch, Alwyne	Pte.	49101				
Courtneidge, William E	Pte.	49034				
Cowan, Frank	Pte.	37475				
Coward, Robert	Pte.	43340				
Cowburn, William	Pte.	49045		22/07/18	dis.	01/02/19
Crabtree, Edwin	Pte.	203140				
Crane, Thomas A	Pte.	22024				
Crates, Arthur	Pte.	49069				
Critchlow, James	Pte.	14731			dis.	17/03/19
Croad, Herbert	Pte.	44259				
Croasdale, John	Pte.	29624				
Crofts, Edgar S	Pte.	28841				
Crompton, Percy	Pte.	46057				
Cronshaw, Aaron	Pte.	34342	A	12/05/18	dis.	18/03/19
Crook, Joseph	Pte.	46083				
Croxford, Arthur A	Cpl.	49231				
Culshaw, Joseph	Pte.	10530			k.i.a.	30/11/17
Culshaw, William	A/Sgt.	240336		16/05/18	dis.	18/01/19
Cummins, William	Pte.	26140				
Curl, Arthur T	Pte.	49214				
Curtis, Thomas E	Pte.	49103				
Dakin, Norman L	Pte.	22361	C	12/08/16	k.i.a.	23/03/18
Dally, Arthur L	Pte.	32628			d.	20/07/18
Dalton, James	Pte.	202418		03/10/18	dis.	06/02/19
Danify, George E	Pte.	49182				
Darby, Joseph	Pte.	43346			dis.	21/01/19
Darbyshire, George O	Pte.	46072				
Darnes, Arthur	Pte.	49193				
Davidson, George D	Pte.	49113				
Davies, A	Pte.					
Davies, David	Pte.	266118				
Davies, Edwin	Pte.	29951		29/03/17	k.i.a.	23/06/17
Davies, John	Pte.	46304				
Davies, John	Pte.	65161				
Davies, Joseph	Pte.	241528				

Name	Rank	No.	Coy.	Joined	Outcome	
Davies, Joseph H	Pte.	17528			dis.	16/11/18
Davies, Maurice E	Pte.	34030				
Davies, Richard	Pte.	45123			dis.	04/06/18
Davies, Richard	Pte.	266415				
Davies, Thomas	Pte.	48834				
Davies, Thomas	Pte.	241364			dis.	19/02/19
Davies, Walter D	Pte.	31738			dis.	15/01/18
Davies, William	L/Cpl.	22008	C	30/08/15	dis.	07/03/19
Davies, William	Pte.	22276	D			
Davies, William C	Pte.	235386				
Dawber, Thomas	Pte.	37459			dis.	14/08/19
Dawson, Arthur	Pte.	46064				
Dawson, Charles W	Pte.	200413			dis.	25/08/19
Dean, Frederick	Pte.	204908				
Delaney, Harold	Pte.	49206				
Dennon, Arthur	Pte.	46171				
Denton, Peter J	Pte.	200617			dis.	08/03/19
Derbyshire, John	Pte.	22198				
Derbyshire, Thomas	Pte.	22183		24/07/16	d.o.w.	23/05/18
Dewes, James A	Pte.	241678	D	30/01/18	dis.	16/04/19
Dickinson, John T	Pte.	49087				
Diggle, Wilfred	C/Sgt.	22579			dis.	
Dingley, Charles H	Cpl.	49112				
Dixon, James	Pte.	22290				
Dodd, John C	Pte.	32230				
Doherty, Thomas	A/Cpl.	46371				
Doubleday, Thomas	Pte.	49024	B	02/08/18	dis.	10/03/19
Douglass, Alfred	Pte.	49307			dis.	21/02/19
Downs, Clifford H	Pte.	49114				
Downs, Thomas P	Pte.	46068				
Doyle, John	Pte.	46104				
Doyle, Thomas	Pte.	49066				
Dring, William	Pte.	31218			k.i.a.	13/10/18
Drinkwater, Louis	Pte.	46188				
Driscoll, Edward	W.O. II.	5215	B	05/08/17	dis.	07/03/19
Ducker, Bernard	Pte.	49038		22/09/18	dis.	24/02/19
Duckett, Richard	Pte.	48787			dis.	28/03/19
Duffy, Daniel J	Pte.	14121	C		dis.	27/03/19
Duffy, John	Pte.	240843			dis.	28/03/19
Duffy, Lawrence	Pte.	46360				
Dunkerley, Tom	Pte.	203141			k.i.a.	13/10/18
Dunn, Martin	Pte.	22581			dis.	19/03/19
Easton, Arthur E	Pte.	204909				
Eaton, Charles W	Pte.	46063				
Eaton, Herbert	Pte.	46192				
Edwards, John	Pte.	31859				

Name	Rank	No.	Coy.	Joined	Outcome	
Edwards, Joseph W	Pte.	46353				
Edwards, Thomas	Cpl.	15060			dis.	31/03/19
Edwards, William	Pte.	202542				
Eglinton, John	Pte.	46349				
Elliott, Percival W	Pte.	34530			k.i.a.	21/08/18
Ellis, Alfred J	Pte.	49301				
Ellison, John F	Pte.	29952				
Elson, Daniel	Pte.	17707	B	14/04/17	d.	03/06/18
Emery, Wilfred	L/Cpl.	22004				
Emmett, John W	Pte.	37460			dis.	16/08/19
Entwistle, John	Pte.	44272				
Evans, Arthur	Pte.	45124				
Evans, Arthur	Pte.	46167				
Evans, Benjamin	Pte.	49234				
Evans, Frank	Pte.	31737				
Evans, Frederick	Pte.	204929			dis.	26/08/19
Evans, John R	Pte.	46584				
Evans, Joseph	Pte.	15123				
Evans, William	Pte.	12779	A	16/06/17	dis.	19/03/19
Everitt, William C	Pte.	32772				
Fairclough, Alfred	Pte.	240848			dis.	28/02/19
Fairclough, Thomas	Pte.	46169				
Fallon, Edward	Pte.	46132				
Fallon, Michael	Pte.	29865		31/07/18	dis.	08/07/20
Fancy, Sidney A	Pte.	49235				
Farley, George A	Pte.	49135				
Farnworth, Albert	Pte.	44199				
Farr, Albert S	Sgt.	204851				
Farrant, Edwin G	Pte.	58008				
Farrimond, Joseph	Pte.	46362				
Fearn, Sidney	Pte.	1872			dis.	11/02/20
Feasey, James E	Pte.	46323				
Fell, William D	Pte.	242893		19/01/18	dis.	13/02/19
Fenlon, Thomas	Pte.	10342	D			
Fenn, John W	Pte.	49198				
Fenney, John	Pte.	240908		07/08/18	dis.	15/07/19
Fernott, Frederick	Pte.	10231		22/06/18	dis.	14/07/20
Ferns, George	Pte.	266311				
Field, Albert	Pte.	204930				
Fielding, Foster A	Pte.	49040			dis.	27/03/19
Finney, James T	Pte.	46386				
Finney, Peter	Pte.	40043				
Fisher, John	Pte.	240874	C	16/03/18	dis.	23/02/19
Fitzhenry, James	Pte.	31736			dis.	09/07/17
Fleming, William J	Cpl.	34297		12/05/18	dis.	01/10/19
Fletcher, James	Cpl.	8309				

Name	Rank	No.	Coy.	Joined	Outcome	
Flint, Osric	Pte.	31375				
Flood, Joseph	Pte.	12927		17/04/17	d.	17/07/18
Foden, George	Pte.	22018			dis.	20/04/17
Foden, Herbert	Pte.	46162				
Forber, William	Pte.	203110				
Ford, Thomas G	Pte.	32066				
Forrest, Alexander	Pte.	46168				
Forty, John E	Pte.	202926				
Foskett, Sidney H	Pte.	49199				
Foster, Henry	Pte.	49142			d.	25/11/18
Foulds, Harry	Pte.	46348				
Fox, Richard	Pte.	265673				
Fox, William S	Pte.	10905			dis.	23/02/19
Francis, John	Pte.	204995			dis.	28/03/19
Franklin Walter, W	Pte.	37465				
Fryer, George	Pte.	44002				
Gaffney, William	Pte.	46337				
Gallacher, William	Pte.	204888				
Gallagher, Edward	Pte.	12965			dis.	24/03/19
Gallagher, James	Cpl.	238039			dis.	29/01/19
Gallimore, Arthur	Pte.	46154				
Garfield, William	Pte.	203019	C	06/03/18	dis.	19/03/19
Garner, John	Pte.	34520		20/05/18	dis.	24/04/19
Garratt, Henry	Pte.	16180		14/04/17	k.i.a.	18/06/17
Gartside, John	Pte.	17630			dis.	03/03/19
Gavaghan, Thomas	Pte.	241021		31/07/18	dis.	29/03/19
Geary, William	Pte.	49091			dis.	03/03/16
Geoghegan, William	Pte.	43912				
Gibbons, Thomas P	Pte.	32669				
Gibbs, Albert E	Pte.	70143				
Gidden, George	Pte.	49215				
Giles, John	Pte.	46131				
Gill, John	Pte.	203592				
Glassey, James	Pte.	19631				
Glenister, John S	Cpl.	204864				
Glover, Arthur	Pte.	49236				
Glover, Bert	Pte.	241948		01/10/18	dis.	06/10/19
Goddard, Thomas	Pte.	32629			d.o.w.	09/04/18
Godfrey, Henry	Cpl.	49104				
Goldberg, Louis	Pte.	34415			dis.	10/10/19
Goligy, Peter	Pte.	26622				
Goodridge, Gordon E	Pte.	49168				
Goodwin, Bernard J	Pte.	49211				
Goolding, Richard R	Pte.	49039				
Gorwood, William J	Pte.	18221			dis.	21/03/19
Gosling, Charles	Pte.	202543				

Name	Rank	No.	Coy.	Joined	Outcome	
Goulder, Leonard	Cpl.	8572				
Goulding, Herbert	Pte.	31798				
Gowans, William	Pte.	204887			dis.	21/01/19
Grace, Edward	Pte.	240658		31/07/18	dis.	06/04/19
Graham, James	Pte.	49041				
Gray, Daniel	Pte.	37469				
Green, John W	Pte.	49185				
Green, Wilfred H	Sgt.	204899				
Greenough, Edward	Pte.	241151			k.i.a.	04/11/18
Greenwood, Ernest	Pte.	36627				
Greenwood, Joseph W	Pte.	204157				
Greenwood, Thomas	Pte.	240141			dis.	08/08/19
Gregson, Alfred S	Pte.	46369				
Grice, John	Pte.	46049				
Griffin, Richard	Pte.	266123			dis.	09/08/18
Grime, Norman	Pte.	18461				
Grimes, Thomas	Pte.	5704			dis.	19/03/19
Guy, Walter	Pte.	49037			dis.	15/03/19
Haddock, William	Pte.	6705		02/05/17	k.i.a.	13/06/17
Hagger, Henry	Pte.	204919			d.o.w.	02/11/18
Hall, Henry	Pte.	46129				
Halliwell, Christopher	Pte.	43904				
Halliwell, John	Pte.	240649				
Hallworth, David	Pte.	44213				
Hallworth, Roland	Pte.	46093				
Halmshaw, James R	Pte.	266342	C	29/12/17	k.i.a.	23/03/18
Hamer, Richard	Pte.	26292				
Hames, William B	Pte.	31199				
Hammett, Albert	Pte.	49216				
Hammond, John	Pte.	32631				
Hampson, Harvey	Pte.	34313				
Hampson, James H	Pte.	16814			dis.	03/03/20
Hampson, John T	Pte.	36421		29/03/17	dis.	13/12/19
Hancock, Charles J	Sgt.	204863				
Handforth, Thomas	Pte.	28744	A	29/03/17	k.i.a.	23/03/18
Hanley, Lawrence	Pte.	34005		01/07/17	d.o.w.	20/09/18
Hanmer, Joseph	Pte.	11800			dis.	27/03/19
Hanson, Frank	Pte.	203151			k.i.a.	13/10/18
Harden, Joseph	Pte.	34354				
Harding, Herbert E	Pte.	16242				
Hardy, Albert E	Pte.	48992				
Harford, Thomas	Sgt.	4991		06/08/18	dis.	12/04/19
Hargreaves, Harold	Pte.	34312				
Harper, Ben A	Pte.	202451				
Harper, George	Pte.	39433			k.i.a.	09/12/17
Harper, William J	Pte.	49217				

Name	Rank	No.	Coy.	Joined	Outcome	
Harris, Alfred L	Pte.	45136			dis.	15/09/18
Harris, George A	Pte.	16089			dis.	12/03/19
Harrison, Charles	Pte.	46383				
Harrop, Joseph	Pte.	15385			dis.	21/03/19
Hart, Ernest W	Pte.	49043				
Hartley, John R	Pte.	34476		12/05/18	dis.	13/11/20
Harvey, William	Pte.	22017			k.i.a.	13/10/18
Harwood, Harry	Pte.	29644				
Haslam, Joseph	Pte.	265722		29/12/17	dis.	28/12/19
Haspey, Ernest	Pte.	27943				
Hastie, James L	Sgt.	201438				
Hatton, William	Pte.	31417			dis.	09/01/19
Hawkes, Frederick B	W.O. II.	204894				
Hawkes, Frederick G	Pte.	204865				
Haworth, William	Pte.	29625				
Haydock, John	Pte.	18588				
Hayter, Charles H	Pte.	266344				
Hazeldine, Samuel	Pte.	266127				
Hazzard, Albert S	Cpl.	31474				
Hedges, George	Pte.	58011				
Heeley, William	Pte.	31164				
Hegarty, Matthew	Pte.	241612		29/03/17	dis.	31/12/17
Helsby, Albert	Pte.	49666				
Helsby, Joseph	Pte.	203836				
Heneghan, Patrick J	Pte.	46056				
Henry, Edward	Pte.	45541				
Henson, Edwin	Pte.	49044				
Heppinstall, William	Pte.	46622				
Herbert, Arthur J	Pte.	49290				
Herford, Joseph H	Pte.	46330			dis.	16/09/19
Hermon, Alfred W	W.O. II.	70175				
Heseltine, Thomas	Pte.	43172				
Hesford, Herbert	Pte.	49151				
Hetherington, Lawrence	Pte.	43564			dis.	24/02/19
Heyes, James	L/Cpl.	22279	A	26/05/16	k.i.a.	26/06/17
Heyes, Thomas	Pte.	265493		31/07/18	dis.	29/01/19
Hibbitt, Frank	Pte.	48963				
Hicks, George	Pte.	37393				
Higginbotham, George	Pte.	22316				
Higgins, Archibald H	Pte.	49097				
Higgins, Martin	Pte.	15872	D	24/11/17	dis.	17/04/19
Highcock, James	Pte.	46598				
Higson, Isaac	Pte.	266393				
Hill, Frederick	Pte.	46070				
Hill, George	Pte.	15381			k.i.a.	28/06/17
Hill, Henry L	Pte.	204893				

Name	Rank	No.	Coy.	Joined	Outcome	
Hill, Jonathan B	Pte.	37498				
Hill, Samuel	Pte.	18072			dis.	25/02/19
Hill, Thomas	Pte.	49115			dis.	03/02/19
Hills, William R	Pte.	22014			dis.	01/04/19
Hilton, Alfred	Pte.	46375				
Hilton, Jeffrey	Pte.	46311				
Hindes, Francis T	Pte.	49225				
Hindley, Ernest	Pte.	46142				
Hiscock, Charles	Pte.	32787				
Hitchcock, John	Pte.	34505				
Hitchcock, Percy W	Pte.	204922				
Hobbs, Edward F	Pte.	204853		03/08/18	dis.	24/03/19
Hobson, Eric	Pte.	204905				
Hobson, Tom	Pte.	49218				
Hodge, William C	Pte.	32670			dis.	08/03/19
Hodgson, Harold W	Pte.	49158				
Hogarth, Frederick	Pte.	48989			dis.	29/01/19
Holden, James	Pte.	266570				
Holland, Charles S	Pte.	31794				
Holland, James H	Pte.	34352		12/05/18	dis.	04/03/19
Holland, John	Pte.	46045				
Hollinhurst, Walter	Pte.	46121				
Holmes, Frank	Pte.	46366				
Holtom, Sydney	Pte.	46174				
Holyoake, Percy	Pte.	31167				
Honeyball, Frederick W	Cpl.	13109		02/07/17	dis.	24/02/19
Honeyball, George A	Pte.	32630			dis.	01/10/18
Hope, Fred	Pte.	28966				
Hope, Samuel H	Pte.	49291				
Hordern, Frank	Pte.	31169				
Horlock, George A	Pte.	200910				
Horrocks, Fred	Pte.	36369				
Horsnall, James	Pte.	266346	C	29/12/17	d.	28/08/18
Houghton, Arthur	Pte.	242317		20/07/18	dis.	04/03/19
Houghton, Arthur F	Pte.	22277			k.i.a.	13/10/18
Houghton, John	Cpl.	16444			dis.	27/04/19
Howard, Alfred	Pte.	46066				
Howarth, Albert	Pte.	22006			d.o.w.	26/07/16
Howarth, Jonas T	Pte.	238064				
Howarth, Samuel	Pte.	46180				
Howells, William T	Pte.	13805			dis.	19/11/18
Hudson, George H	Pte.	46053				
Hudson, John	Pte.	37485				
Hughes, Albert	Pte.	31873	A	01/07/17	dis.	15/10/19
Hughes, Emrys	Pte.	46150				
Hughes, Isaac	Pte.	266129				

Name	Rank	No.	Coy.	Joined	Outcome	
Hull, John J	Pte.	44071				
Hulse, Edward	Pte.	204884				
Humphrys, Walter E	Pte.	47121				
Hunt, Harry	Pte.	238042		25/05/15	dis.	31/12/18
Hyams, Joseph	Pte.	49116		13/09/18	dis.	19/03/19
Ince, Ernest	Pte.	15884	C		dis.	18/03/19
Ions, John	Pte.	204895				
Irwin, Algernon H	Pte.	49238				
Jackson, Alexander	Pte.	49136				
Jackson, James H	Pte.	49200				
Jackson, James H	Pte.	34317				
Jackson, Samuel	Pte.	45080				
Jacobs, Benjamin	Pte.	32671			d.o.w.	24/03/18
James, Albert E	Pte.	29919		04/10/18	dis.	10/09/19
James, Frederick M	Pte.	266209				
James, James M	Pte.	45040				
Jameson, James	Pte.	46390				
Jameson, Thomas H	Pte.	28464				
Janson, Charles O	Pte.	49264		10/09/18	dis.	23/02/19
Jeffreys, George	Pte.	49090				
Jenkins, Arthur O	Pte.	48970			dis.	04/03/19
Jenkins, George	Pte.	34218				
Jenner, Charles	Pte.	49292				
Jinks, Walter C	Pte.	242464		01/10/18	dis.	02/03/19
Johnson, Alfred	Pte.	201918				
Johnson, Everard	Pte.	31745				
Johnson, Harry	Pte.	241635		29/03/17	dis.	01/03/18
Johnson, Harry V	Pte.	49105				
Johnson, Henry	Pte.	50267		31/03/18	dis.	09/11/19
Johnson, Henry K	Pte.	238104				
Johnson, James	Pte.	26002		16/06/17	dis.	02/04/18
Johnston, James H	Pte.	22326			dis.	10/09/18
Jones, Charles I	Pte.	45125				
Jones, Clarence W	Pte.	22003			k.i.a.	13/10/18
Jones, Edward	Pte.	241066				
Jones, Harry	Pte.	37486				
Jones, Harry	Pte.	32790				
Jones, Harry	Pte.	46082				
Jones, Isaac	Pte.	49152				
Jones, James A	Sgt.	204862				
Jones, John	Pte.	49137				
Jones, John	Pte.	40133				
Jones, John	Pte.	10127				
Jones, Joseph	Pte.	27089			dis.	13/10/19
Jones, Samuel	Pte.	45140				
Jones, William	Pte.	45139				

Name	Rank	No.	Coy.	Joined	Outcome	
Jones, William	Pte.	46133				
Jones, William	Pte.	19277			dis.	04/05/19
Keeble, George	Pte.	40711				
Keen, Herbert	Pte.	37461			dis.	14/12/18
Keenan, William	Pte.	1790			dis.	29/01/19
Kelly, Martin	Pte.	49239				
Kelsall, Henry	Pte.	45923				
Kelson, Albert W	Pte.	49293				
Kemp, Alfred L	Pte.	34572				
Kemp, Arthur	Pte.	22310	B	04/08/16	dis.	11/10/18
Kemp, Charles C	Pte.	22189	C	23/05/16	d.o.w.	24/06/17
Kendrick, Ellis	Pte.	46352				
Kenny, Daniel	Pte.	11519			dis.	27/03/19
Kenwright, James	Pte.	46350				
Kenyon, Herbert J	Sgt.	240179	A	28/10/18	d.	16/02/19
Kerr, Arthur E	Pte.	19620			dis.	07/01/19
Kerry, Charles S	Pte.	49117				
Kettle, William	Pte.	46326				
Kilgallon, William	Pte.	17791				
Kimble, Charles	Pte.	46134				
King, Frederick	Pte.	34540				
Kings, Enoch H	Pte.	32633		28/12/17	k.i.a.	23/03/18
Kingston, George W	Pte.	31992				
Kinsey, Edmund	Pte.	31589			dis.	10/01/19
Kinsey, Harry	Pte.	200694			dis.	15/07/19
Kinson, Harry	Pte.	46322				
Kirk, Fred R	Pte.	17460			dis.	28/01/19
Kirt, Samuel	Pte.	204875				
Kitchen, Edward Y	Pte.	34184				
Kitchingman, William	Pte.	45922				
Knight, John	Pte.	22587		09/08/18	dis.	04/03/19
Knowles, Abraham	Pte.	46575				
Knowles, Christopher T	Pte.	45308				
Knowles, Samuel	Cpl.	265495		31/07/18	dis.	29/01/19
Lacey, Lawrence R	Pte.	45128				
Lambert, Frank C	Pte.	32672				
Lancaster, John O	Pte.	34186				
Land, Frank	Pte.	36242				
Lander, Herbert F	Pte.	202953				
Lane, George A	Pte.	49019				
Lang, William	Pte.	266134				
Langley, George	Pte.	31744			dis.	05/12/18
Langley, John	Pte.	31751				
Latham, Peter	Pte.	2466	D		dis.	10/02/19
Lathbury, Leonard G	Pte.	49313		16/09/18	dis.	04/11/19
Lawrenson, John C	Pte.	46314				

Name	Rank	No.	Coy.	Joined	Outcome	
Lawton, Albert E	Pte.	43306				
Lea, Joseph	Cpl.	15827				
Leach, John	Pte.	204900				
Leah, Norman	Pte.	22347		22/08/16	k.i.a.	12/06/17
Leavesley, Joseph	Pte.	46058				
Lee, Alfred	Pte.	32655				
Leech, Harry	Pte.	203155				
Lees, Daniel G	Pte.	16847				
Leigh, James E	C.S.M.	16443	A	23/08/17	d.o.w.	04/11/18
Leigh, Samuel	Pte.	201948				
Leigh, William	Pte.	204854				
Levitt, James	Pte.	15349			dis.	29/01/19
Lewin, George W	Pte.	46538				
Lewis, John	Pte.	266253	B	29/12/17	k.i.a.	27/03/18
Lewis, Thomas G	Pte.	46122				
Lewis, William	Pte.	34492				
Liggins, John W	Pte.	18840			dis.	24/02/19
Lightfoot, Fred	Pte.	49195				
Ling, John S	Pte.	49277				
Lingard, Joshua	Pte.	203136				
Linnard, Anthony S	Cpl.	47583				
Lister, Alfred	Pte.	46161				
Littler, Harold	Pte.	22412				
Littlewood, Benjamin	Cpl.	31204				
Littlewood, Thomas	Pte.	46340				
Lock, Albert G	Pte.	49295				
Locke, John	Pte.	241199		12/02/18	dis.	10/01/19
Lofthouse, Fred	Pte.	49169			dis.	05/03/19
Longdon, Charles	Pte.	37087				
Longshaw, Peter	Pte.	201486			dis.	06/06/19
Lord, Sydney	L/Cpl.	32574			d.	19/11/18
Lovatt, James	Pte.	27306		31/07/18	dis.	13/03/19
Lowe, Harry	Pte.	46332				
Lowe, Joseph	Pte.	40252				
Lowe, William L	Pte.	46388				
Lowndes, John W	Pte.	238084			dis.	15/02/19
Lucas, Harold	Pte.	22021			dis.	04/04/19
Lucas, John	Pte.	46309				
Lyons, John	Pte.	15923			dis.	27/03/19
Lyons, Leslie	Pte.	43385				
Lyons, Nat	Sgt.	204910				
Mackarel, Ronald	Pte.	44498				
Maher, Frank	Pte.	40909				
Mahoney, Harry	Pte.	19866			dis.	10/06/19
Mainland, John J	Pte.	49119				
Makinson, Albert	Pte.	31965				

Name	Rank	No.	Coy.	Joined	Outcome	
Makinson, James	Pte.	49588				
Manifold, Harry	Pte.	202969				
Mansley, John	Pte.	46374				
Marrison, Harry	Pte.	46363				
Marsh, Alfred	Cpl.	241218		31/07/18	dis.	29/01/19
Marsh, Frederick G	Pte.	22137		24/07/16	d.	12/05/18
Marsh, Peter	Sgt.	43761				
Marshall, Frederick R	Pte.	49118				
Marshall, James S	Pte.	45790				
Martin, Henry	Pte.	19901				
Martin, Richard	Pte.	49153			d.	28/04/19
Mason, Walter K	Pte.	49120				
Massey, Frederick J	Pte.	49243				
Mather, James	Pte.	17946				
Mather, Percy	Pte.	46118				
Mathews, James	Pte.	265691				
Mattinson, Herbert	Pte.	46145				
Mayfield, Ernest R	Pte.	204901				
Mayne, Frederick	Pte.	49179				
McCarthy, Michael	L/Cpl.	22023		30/08/15	d.o.w.	28/03/18
McComas, James	Pte.	817	B	15/06/17	dis.	08/03/19
McCormack, William	Pte.	12192			dis.	19/04/19
McCompany, Henry	Sgt.	48993				
McCue, Bernard	Pte.	37470	D			
McDonald, Luke	Sgt.	11790		30/09/18	dis.	27/01/19
McDonald, William	Pte.	10268			dis.	03/12/18
McDonnell, Thomas	Pte.	240837				
McEwen, Walter	Pte.	240701				
McGrath, John	Pte.	17667				
McGrath, John	Pte.	43354				
McGrowther, James	Pte.	34323		12/05/18	dis.	30/09/19
McGurk, Hugh	Pte.	22332		06/09/16	dis.	21/06/17
McHugh, Andrew	Sgt.	49046			dis.	29/01/19
McIlwraith, Andrew	Pte.	49092			dis.	20/02/19
McKeown, James	Pte.	12995	C	02/07/17	k.i.a.	03/07/18
McKinley, John	A/Cpl.	988		05/08/17	dis.	31/03/19
McKinley, William	Pte.	49094				
McLean, Frederick W	Pte.	49242				
McLean, Ronald E	Pte.	49302			dis.	08/08/19
McMahon, John	Pte.	11739	C	24/03/18	dis.	13/01/19
McMahon, William	Pte.	43398			d.o.w.	23/04/18
McMinnis, Robert W	Pte.	40586				
McNally, William	Sgt.	16798			dis.	08/03/19
McNamee, Thomas	Pte.	40735		13/11/17	dis.	06/11/19
McNaughton, Jesse	Pte.	22271			dis.	20/05/19
Meaden, James	Pte.	240745		30/09/18	dis.	29/03/19

Name	Rank	No.	Coy.	Joined	Outcome	
Meads, Arthur A	Pte.	32634				
Mears, John	Pte.	204855			dis.	17/02/19
Medway, John	Pte.	58012			dis.	30/06/19
Meek, Arthur	Pte.	22382		06/09/16	k.i.a.	05/10/16 *
Melling, William	Pte.	46102	D			
Mellor, Albert	Pte.	203002				
Melville, Robert J	Pte.	27270			dis.	26/11/17
Messenger, Albert	Sgt.	34546			dis.	23/02/19
Metcalfe, Frederick	Pte.	46061				
Middleton, Arthur	Pte.	3539				
Middleton, Ernest	Pte.	49208				
Miles, Harry	Pte.	49282				
Miller, Arthur	Pte.	238086				
Miller, William	Pte.	49219		09/02/17	dis.	09/11/19
Millington, Charles	Pte.	31729				
Mills, Samuel	Pte.	31747				
Milsom, George	Pte.	45138				
Mitchell, Walter	Pte.	49048			dis.	24/03/19
Mitchinson, George E	Sgt.	49143			dis.	17/03/19
Mollekin, Ernest	Sgt.	204976				
Molloy, Herbert	L/Cpl.	22005	A	29/08/15	k.i.a.	14/12/16
Molyneux, John	Pte.	46308				
Monckton, Robert	Pte.	204891				
Monk, Thomas G	A/Sgt.	34533				
Montague, Samuel S	W.O. II.	203482		31/03/18	dis.	03/03/19
Mooney, John	Pte.	45794				
Moore, Edward	Pte.	26474				
Moran, John	Cpl.	14997			dis.	21/03/19
Moran, John	Pte.	22333				
Mordue, Joseph P	Pte.	37456				
Morgan, William	Pte.	31795				
Morley, Sidney H	Pte.	49265				
Moss, Albert	Pte.	49192			dis.	23/02/19
Moss, Samuel	Pte.	27724			dis.	18/08/19
Moss, Thomas	Pte.	240366				
Moston, George	Pte.	202476				
Moule, Alfred C	Pte.	49240				
Mullaney, Edward	Pte.	46395				
Munday, Arthur	Pte.	6084				
Murphy, John E	Pte.	46177				
Murrells, Frederick A	A/Cpl.	32639				
Murtough, James	Pte.	22002			dis.	14/02/19
Musgrove, Alfred	Pte.	42058				
Myers, James H	Pte.	22109				
Myers, John	Pte.	49317			dis.	26/03/19
Myers, John	Pte.	29931				

Name	Rank	No.	Coy.	Joined	Outcome	
Nash, Clarence J	Pte.	49049			dis.	02/10/16
Naylor, William	Pte.	15652			dis.	28/03/19
Naylor, William C	Pte.	46497				
Nelson, William	Pte.	22022			dis.	30/08/18
Newell, Charles	Pte.	34367			dis.	21/02/19
Newton, Harry	Pte.	10172		31/07/18	dis.	10/02/20
Newton, Robert W	Pte.	27079				
Nichols, John H	Pte.	32220				
Nicholson, Thomas	Pte.	22001			k.i.a.	21/03/18
Nicholson, Wilfred	Pte.	16031			dis.	31/03/20
Nicklen, Harold	Pte.	202363				
Noble, George	Cpl.	204892	C	13/09/18	dis.	05/02/19
Noblett, George	Pte.	46119				
Noonan, William	Pte.	26004	C	29/03/17	d.o.w.	04/06/17
Norris, George A	Pte.	22268				
Nuttall, Arthur	Cpl.	22010			dis.	11/02/19
Nuttall, Charles	Pte.	10801				
Oakley, William J	Pte.	204906				
Oddy, Richard H	Pte.	49122		13/09/18	dis.	08/02/19
O'Garra, William P	Pte.	21572		17/05/15	dis.	16/05/19
O'Grady, John	Pte.	22170	D	23/05/16	k.i.a.	09/03/17
O'Hanlon, James	Pte.	200233			dis.	23/02/19
Oldfield, Henry G	Pte.	37487				
Oldham, Frank	Pte.	10223				
Oldham, Fred	Pte.	19521				
O'Neill, Edward	Pte.	12275			dis.	02/04/19
Oram, William T	Pte.	49159				
Ord, William	Pte.	43767			dis.	28/03/19
Ormes, George	Pte.	19629				
Orton, Sydney	Pte.	49050				
Osborne, Abraham	Pte.	7942				
Osborne, John	Pte.	48705				
Osborne, Philip H	Pte.	204856			dis.	19/02/19
O'Shaugnessy, Edward	Pte.	49051				
O'Shea, Frank	Pte.	45309				
Owen, John	Pte.	46394				
Owens, Frank	Pte.	12411			dis.	04/03/19
Owens, Robert	Pte.	49121				
Paganuzzi, John	Pte.	46039				
Page, Charles B	Pte.	49267				
Palace, Alfred E	Pte.	204915				
Pareezer, Abraham	Pte.	49220				
Park, Wilfred	Pte.	49246			dis.	01/03/19
Parker, Ernest	Pte.	47621				
Parker, Herbert	Pte.	49245				
Parkey, Leonard	Pte.	42248			d.o.w.	06/11/18

Other Ranks (Posted)

Name	Rank	No.	Coy.	Joined	Outcome	
Parkin, George	Pte.	49221				
Parkinson, Benjamin	Pte.	266077	C	29/12/17	dis.	26/02/19
Parr, Harold	Pte.	31733	A			
Parr, John H	Pte.	46382				
Parr, Thomas	Pte.	241588		29/07/18	dis.	11/01/19
Parry, Francis D	Pte.	17344			dis.	08/06/19
Parry, Thomas	Pte.	46336				
Parsons, Gus	Sgt.	14495	A	14/04/17	dis.	28/01/19
Parsons, Harold	Pte.	37488				
Parsons, Tom	Pte.	49054			dis.	03/03/19
Partington, William	Cpl.	11695			dis.	17/03/19
Partington, William H	Pte.	50627			dis.	15/04/19
Paton, John	Pte.	19816				
Patterson, Edwin B	Pte.	49170				
Pattie, Percy	Pte.	34552			dis.	08/03/19
Pattrick, Albert	Pte.	31998				
Paxton, Robert	Pte.	204920				
Pearce, Alfred G	Pte.	60985				
Pearce, Alfred J	Sgt.	22516				
Pearmain, Frank	Pte.	46364				
Pearson, James H	Pte.	49244				
Pedler, William E	Pte.	32635				
Pembleton, William	A/Sgt.	48994	C	13/09/18	dis.	24/03/19
Pendlebury, John W	Sgt.	42113				
Perkins, Frank	Pte.	46204				
Perkins, Sidney	Pte.	49025				
Philbrick, Charles J	Pte.	49266				
Phillips, Alfred J	Pte.	45129	D	29/12/17	dis.	28/02/20
Phillips, Harry	Pte.	46094				
Pickett, Frederick	Pte.	49201				
Pickford, Edwin	Pte.	46370				
Pickin, George	Pte.	39021				
Pierce, Terence J	Pte.	22389			d.o.w.	26/06/17
Pilkington, Ernest	Cpl.	1495			dis.	23/01/19
Pilkington, Harold	Pte.	40529				
Pilling, William	Pte.	46339				
Platt, Thomas H	Pte.	46153				
Platt, Thomas H	Pte.	202781				
Plowright, Charles H	Pte.	49268				
Plumpton, John	Pte.	22106		30/06/16	k.i.a.	03/09/16
Plumpton, Thomas	Pte.	240190				
Pocock, Frank B	Pte.	37462				
Pointon, Frederick	Pte.	46585				
Pomfret, William	Pte.	46604				
Pool, Frederick	Pte.	22011		30/08/15	dis.	19/03/19
Portal, John	Pte.	45131				

Name	Rank	No.	Coy.	Joined	Outcome	
Porter, Edwin	Pte.	46115				
Potkins, Edward	Pte.	46055				
Potter, James	Pte.	240730			k.i.a.	22/10/18
Potter, Samuel	Pte.	240920				
Potts, John	Pte.	46165				
Povey, Ernest	Pte.	46128				
Powell, Frederick	Pte.	15500			dis.	19/03/18
Powell, Frederick	Pte.	27687				
Poxon, Edgar	Cpl.	204897				
Pratt, Bert F	Pte.	37476				
Preece, Charles	Pte.	46355				
Preece, Harold H	Pte.	49178				
Prescott, William	Pte.	203897				
Price, Arthur S	Pte.	45130			dis.	13/09/18
Price, George H	Pte.	34326			dis.	19/12/18
Price, Leonard	Pte.	28833				
Priest, Arthur	Pte.	19074			k.i.a.	13/10/18
Prime, William	Pte.	49052				
Prince, Albert E	Pte.	49202		16/09/18	dis.	14/11/19
Pritchard, Joseph	Pte.	46090				
Pritchard, William	Pte.	46345				
Probert, William	Pte.	44349				
Proctor, Fred	Pte.	49210				
Prosser, Henry J	Pte.	45141				
Pyrah, Joseph	Pte.	22416				
Quigley, Edward	Pte.	46320				
Quill, Patrick	Pte.	34228				
Radlett, Edward J	Pte.	49269				
Radmall, Richard	Pte.	49203			dis.	18/02/19
Ralphs, Victor C L	Pte.	49171				
Ranson, Austin	Pte.	40905				
Ranson, Richard	Pte.	22236				
Ratcliffe, William	Pte.	2251			dis.	11/02/19
Rathbone, Thomas	Pte.	46307				
Rawley, Alfred	Pte.	49278				
Rawson, Thomas P	Pte.	204876				
Read, Henry	Pte.	37243			dis.	31/03/19
Redhead, Thomas	Pte.	241526		31/07/18	dis.	29/01/19
Redstone, Victor H	Pte.	61090				
Reed, Arthur	Pte.	49106				
Reed, Fred	Pte.	49172				
Rees, Jenkin	Pte.	43541				
Reid, James E	Pte.	27294			k.i.a.	13/10/18
Reid, William	Pte.	63097				
Reynolds, Thomas	Pte.	46130				
Rice, William D	Cpl.	37189				

Name	Rank	No.	Coy.	Joined	Outcome	
Richards, David E	Pte.	49056				
Richards, Walter R	Pte.	49186				
Richardson, Thomas W	Pte.	49297			dis.	17/02/19
Richardson, William	Pte.	29912				
Rickers, Ernest	Pte.	36761				
Ridley, Charles E	Pte.	49138			dis.	10/10/19
Rigby, Richard	Pte.	242225		04/08/18	dis.	13/10/19
Rigby, William	Pte.	46617				
Riley, Philip	Pte.	46172				
Riley, Thomas	Pte.	30094				
Rix, Robert J	Pte.	32115				
Roaf, Charles J	Pte.	32379			dis.	23/02/19
Robbins, Edward	Pte.	29928		16/05/17	k.i.a.	21/03/18
Roberts, Howell	Pte.	14412			dis.	30/04/19
Roberts, Hugh P	Pte.	20747		01/04/15	des.	11/08/15
Roberts, John	Pte.	200586			dis.	22/02/19
Roberts, John E	Pte.	43332			d.	25/03/18
Roberts, Joseph	Pte.	37163				
Roberts, Richard	Pte.	46160				
Roberts, Robert	Pte.	18079				
Robertson, Alexander	Pte.	45132			k.i.a.	27/03/18
Robinson, Charles	Pte.	14327			dis.	28/03/19
Robinson, Sydney W	Pte.	34429				
Robson, James	Pte.	40966				
Rocke, John	Pte.	235255			k.i.a.	13/10/18
Rocke, Samuel	Pte.	40765				
Rodgers, Frank	Pte.	48996			k.i.a.	04/11/18
Rolt, Charles	Pte.	22034				
Roscoe, James V	Pte.	28815				
Roseblade, William E	Pte.	204907				
Rosser, Arthur G	Pte.	266146			dis.	26/11/19
Rossiter, Joseph	Pte.	49204				
Rothwell, William	Pte.	46533		15/07/18	k.i.a.	30/09/18
Roughley, Richard	Pte.	241018	C	30/01/18	dis.	13/02/19
Roughsedge, Henry	Pte.	22391		06/09/16	k.i.a.	14/07/17
Rowe, Walter M	Pte.	37464				
Rowlands, John	Pte.	22429				
Rowlinson, Arthur	Pte.	46164				
Rowson, William	Pte.	46092				
Royle, James	Pte.	36589				
Rumble, Stephen R	A/Cpl.	204866		02/08/18	dis.	13/03/19
Rumsey, Arthur	Pte.	49303				
Russell, Charles	Pte.	37489				
Russell, Percy A	Pte.	204914			k.i.a.	04/11/18
Russell, William H	Pte.	46166				
Ryan, Arthur S	C.S.M.	8618			dis.	19/03/19

Name	Rank	No.	Coy.	Joined	Outcome	
Rylance, Hezekiah	Pte.	46601			k.i.a.	04/11/18
Salisbury, Clifford	Pte.	46146				
Salisbury, Louis J	Pte.	19705		02/08/17	dis.	30/03/19
Sanderson, James H	Pte.	49139				
Saunders, Brinley	Pte.	14284			dis.	26/02/19
Saunders, Edward	Pte.	40701				
Saxby, Herbert G	Pte.	204927				
Scott, Edward H	Pte.	16497			dis.	21/12/18
Scott, James	Cpl.	49309				
Scott, Nathan	Pte.	46091				
Scott, William M	Pte.	22582				
Seager, Harold	Pte.	43737				
Searson, Edwin	Pte.	31390				
Seddon, James	Pte.	235427			dis.	11/04/19
Sedgwick, Orlando F	Pte.	37494				
Selby, Wilfred	Pte.	49316				
Seller, Francis W	Sgt.	238068				
Sephton, Thomas	Pte.	50648				
Shallcross, Joseph	Pte.	49059				
Sharp, Arthur C	Cpl.	49123				
Sharpe, Jesse H	Pte.	37491				
Sharples, Herbert	Pte.	43997			dis.	21/02/19
Sharratt, Alfred G	Pte.	46310				
Shaw, George	Pte.	201230				
Shaw, John W	Pte.	50647				
Shaw, Verdi	Pte.	58009				
Shawcross, Thomas	Pte.	22125				
Shipton, Arthur	Pte.	49156				
Shipton, Charles A	Pte.	49311				
Sillitoe, Henry C	Pte.	235420			d.	16/05/18
Sime, John	Pte.	37478				
Simmons, Robert	Sgt.	240374				
Simms, John T	Pte.	15211			dis.	20/01/19
Sims, Leonard A	Pte.	22397			dis.	11/07/19
Singleton, William J	Pte.	40308		13/11/17	dis.	01/03/19
Skae, Josiah S	Pte.	32658				
Skinner, Lord G	Pte.	49272			dis.	19/03/19
Slater, Albert R	Pte.	49173				
Slater, Jack	Pte.	22396	C			
Slater, Vincent	Pte.	58014				
Slater, William	Pte.	238080		12/05/18	dis.	07/02/19
Small, John	Sgt.	21879	A	24/08/15	k.i.a.	01/07/16
Smallwood, Samuel	Pte.	46182				
Smith, Albert	Pte.	36570			k.i.a.	27/03/18
Smith, Alfred G	Cpl.	43395			dis.	13/03/19
Smith, Arthur	Pte.	201822			dis.	11/03/19

Name	Rank	No.	Coy.	Joined	Outcome	
Smith, Benjamin	Pte.	49181				
Smith, Clifford J	Pte.	46157				
Smith, Edwin	Pte.	49271				
Smith, Fred	W.O. II.	240057			dis.	28/03/19
Smith, Henry	Pte.	46499				
Smith, James	Pte.	46341				
Smith, John	Pte.	22136	D			
Smith, John A	Pte.	36017			dis.	20/12/19
Smith, John H	Pte.	46361				
Smith, Samuel	Pte.	11552	A	29/07/18	dis.	27/01/19
Smith, Sydney T	Sgt.	204898				
Smith, Thomas	Pte.	15930			dis.	28/01/19
Smith, Thomas R	Pte.	49067			d.o.w.	06/11/18
Smith, William	Pte.	29886				
Smith, William	Pte.	204877				
Smith, William	Pte.	204879				
Smith, William I	Pte.	36522			d.o.w.	11/08/17
Smyth, Samuel	Pte.	202455			dis.	08/12/17
Snape, Fred	Pte.	46087				
Soden, George	Pte.	235150				
Sowden, Robert	Pte.	203121			d.	22/02/19
Spence, Albert	Pte.	17692			dis.	09/04/19
Spence, William	Pte.	49124				
Spendley, John	Pte.	34468			dis.	03/03/19
Spibey, Joseph M	Pte.	46148				
Stage, C R	Sgt.					
Stainsby, Albert	Pte.	49057				
Stainsby, Joseph	Pte.	31613				
Stanbsie, Alfred	Pte.	204878				
Stanley, Charles	Pte.	15325			dis.	11/03/19
Stephenson, Ernest	Pte.	46100				
Stewart, John	Pte.	34550				
Stewart, William	Pte.	49070			dis.	31/01/19
Stock, Maurice J	Cpl.	58005		18/09/18	dis.	02/04/19
Stockdale, John W	Pte.	49180	C	16/09/18	dis.	11/03/19
Stokes, Thomas	Pte.	22424				
Stoneman, Edward K	Pte.	49194				
Storey, Ernest	Sgt.	204896				
Storey, John B	Pte.	14073			dis.	27/02/19
Storey, Richard J	Pte.	44380				
Stovell, William A	Pte.	46158				
Street, Harry	Pte.	46112				
Stretch, George	Pte.					
Sturdy, Ernest	Pte.	22555			dis.	03/03/19
Stuttard, Herbert	Pte.	235326			dis.	17/12/19
Sumner, James	Pte.	31753				

Name	Rank	No.	Coy.	Joined	Outcome	
Sumner, John H	Pte.	34566				
Sumner, Robert	L/Cpl.	26414	D	14/04/17	d.	22/07/18
Sumner, Samuel E	Pte.	46306				
Sumner, William	Pte.	49247				
Sumner, William	Pte.	18183				
Surridge, Henry R	Pte.	49020				
Sutcliffe, Ernest	Pte.	203139		25/04/17	dis.	30/07/19
Sutton, George	Pte.	32637	B	29/12/17	dis.	25/02/19
Swallow, Jonathan	Pte.	34537				
Swarbrick, Alexander	Cpl.	34555			dis.	03/03/19
Swindells, James	Pte.	200097			k.i.a.	23/03/18
Swinford, George	Pte.	37479				
Sykes, Benjamin H	Pte.	22584			dis.	11/02/19
Sykes, Charles	Pte.	46065				
Tagell, Fred	Pte.	31785				
Talbot, Frederick W	Pte.	46193				
Taylor, Charles	Pte.	43384				
Taylor, Ernest	Pte.	202860				
Taylor, James	Pte.	40031			dis.	13/06/19
Taylor, Joel	Pte.	266156				
Taylor, Joseph	Pte.	241544				
Taylor, Robert	Pte.	65902			dis.	17/11/19
Taylor, Sidney	Pte.	266155	A	29/12/17	k.i.a.	23/03/18
Taylor, William	Pte.	46594				
Taylor, William H	Pte.	31731				
Teanby, William	Pte.	45064				
Temple, John	Pte.	49275				
Thackery, Tom	Pte.	49140				
Thomas, ...	C.S.M.		A			
Thomas, David	Pte.	203028				
Thomas, David A	Cpl.	49304				
Thomas, Garfield	Pte.	14376			dis.	03/04/19
Thomas, Godfrey	Pte.	49160				
Thomas, Harold	Pte.	58007				
Thomas, Michael	Pte.	2261			dis.	13/03/19
Thomas, Robert	Pte.	49187				
Thomas, Thomas J	Pte.	42056				
Thomas, William	Pte.	22149				
Thomason, Fred	Pte.	22399			d.o.w.	05/04/18
Thompson, Charles	Pte.	9709				
Thompson, Fred	Pte.	49196				
Thompson, James	Pte.	1730			dis.	19/03/19
Thomson, John P	Pte.	49248				
Thomson, Matthew	Pte.	49095				
Thorpe, Richard	Pte.	46358				
Tickle, Frederick G	Pte.	31740				

Name	Rank	No.	Coy.	Joined	Outcome	
Tierney, Albert	Pte.	32403				
Tillbrook, Fred R	Pte.	31298				
Tilley, Henry	Pte.	240565		28/07/18	dis.	04/03/19
Timmins, Samuel	Pte.	49175				
Timson, Nelson	Pte.	235186				
Titchard, William	Pte.	202402				
Tobin, Bernard	Pte.	22254		23/05/16	k.i.a.	16/09/18
Todd, John W	Cpl.	49099				
Tollemarche, Herbert	Pte.	49310				
Townsend, Percival W	L/Cpl.	34089		01/10/18	k.i.a.	04/11/18
Townsend, William	Pte.	46138				
Trafford, Reginald	Sgt.	31620				
Trollope, Richard G	Pte.	45134				
Troughton, Henry F	Pte.	49308				
Tuck, Harry	Pte.	49249				
Tuckey, Arthur	Pte.	37463				
Tuckwood, Leonard H	Pte.	49273				
Tunstall, John H	Pte.	202109				
Turner, David H	Pte.	31799			dis.	04/04/18
Turner, Ernest	Pte.	204924				
Turner, Frederick L	Pte.	49250				
Turner, George	Pte.	47580				
Turner, James	Pte.	46487				
Turner, Reginald R	Pte.	204205			dis.	23/11/18
Turner, Wilfred	Pte.	61221				
Turton, Frederick	Pte.	37480				
Twinning, William	Sgt.	22007			dis.	23/02/19
Tyrer, Thomas	Pte.	46599				
Unsworth, James	Pte.	26448				
Usher, William L	Pte.	49060				
Vanden, Albert	Pte.	17809			dis.	16/07/19
Varley, Thomas	Pte.	22040				
Vezey, Harry C	Pte.	50461				
Vickers, William	Pte.	204881				
Vincent, Jack	Pte.	47631				
Virrill, Charles G	Pte.	49176				
Wade, Leonard F	Pte.	49306				
Wade, William	Pte.	49072				
Wainwright, Joseph S	Pte.	22302		24/10/17	k.i.a.	09/10/18
Wainwright, William S	Pte.	40274				
Wakefield, Herbert P	Pte.	36638				
Wakefield, Joseph	Pte.	200274			dis.	01/02/19
Walker, Edwin	Pte.	48999				
Walker, Herbert	Pte.	263004				
Walker, John W	Pte.	32195				
Walker, Tom	Pte.	49108				

Name	Rank	No.	Coy.	Joined	Outcome	
Wall, Charles S	Pte.	204882				
Wallace, James W	Cpl.	49107				
Walmsley, Herbert	Pte.	49255				
Walsh, David	Pte.	42337				
Warburton, Christopher	Pte.	31743				
Wardle, Harry	Pte.	17650			dis.	18/10/17
Waring, Harold	Pte.	241245				
Waring, William S	Cpl.	29635			dis.	18/06/18
Warren, Henry T	Pte.	49021				
Warren, Leonard	Pte.	49064				
Warren, Sidney	Pte.	45135				
Waters, James	Pte.	2237			k.i.a.	08/06/17
Webb, Charles W	Pte.	19047	D	14/04/17	d.o.w.	31/05/17
Webb, Walter L	Pte.	29715				
Webber, John	Pte.	49256				
Wells, Arthur T	Pte.	49150				
Wells, Daniel H	Pte.	49162				
Welsby, William	Pte.	240127			dis.	27/03/19
Welsh, John	Pte.	49205				
Wesley, William H	Pte.	48991				
West, William J	Pte.	49022				
Western, Stanley W	Pte.	204857		03/08/18	dis.	03/02/19
Westhead, Robert	Pte.	266327				
Whalley, George	Pte.	40914				
Wheeler, Charles	Pte.	204885			dis.	28/02/19
Wheeler, James F	Pte.	204928				
Whitby, John	Pte.	22274				
Whitby, Thomas	Pte.	22284	A	15/03/16	dis.	21/03/19
White, Alfred	Pte.	31750				
White, Charles H	Pte.	49253				
White, Ernest L	Pte.	49276				
White, Harry	Pte.	45664				
White, Henry	Pte.	50664				
White, Richard	Pte.	17747				
White, Thomas	Pte.	22151				
Whitehead, Maurice	Pte.	46155				
Whitham, Leonard P	Pte.	49071				
Whiting, William H	Pte.	49127				
Whittaker, William	Pte.	200264			dis.	27/02/19
Wiggins, Frank D	Pte.	37492				
Wiggins, William H	Pte.	49252				
Wilcock, Roger	Pte.	37185				
Wilding, John W	Pte.	18443			dis.	28/03/19
Wilkins, Harry	Pte.	45986				
Wilkinson, Allen	Pte.	201658				
Wilkinson, James	Pte.	13854			dis.	20/02/19

Name	Rank	No.	Coy.	Joined	Outcome	
Wilkinson, Thomas A	Pte.	27748				
Williams, Charles	Pte.	204867				
Williams, Edward W	Pte.	43970				
Williams, Henry T	Cpl.	32131				
Williams, James	Pte.	46372				
Williams, John	Pte.	204322				
Williams, Price	Pte.	37499				
Williams, Richard	Pte.	14988			dis.	18/02/19
Williams, Thomas R	Pte.	43889				
Williams, William A	Pte.	266380				
Williams, William H	Pte.	49161				
Williams, William J	Pte.	34092			dis.	07/01/19
Williamson, Frank	A/Sgt.	1309		19/03/18	dis.	15/03/19
Williamson, Leonard	Pte.	46125				
Willian, Roland	A/Cpl.	22583				
Wills, William	Pte.	241112			k.i.a.	13/10/18
Wilshaw, Charles P	Pte.	49063				
Wilson, Frank	Pte.	50676				
Wilson, Frederick J	Pte.	26440				
Wilson, Henry	Pte.	49227				
Wilson, John	Pte.	15243			dis.	23/02/19
Wilson, Joseph A	Pte.	46095				
Wilson, Samuel	Pte.	46381				
Winrow, Thomas	Pte.	46147				
Winstanley, Robert	Pte.	42001				
Winston, Anthony	Pte.	31732				
Wood, Frederick	Pte.	49126				
Woodfield, Albert	Pte.	32638			dis.	22/01/19
Woodgate, Ernest F	Pte.	203575				
Woods, Albert A	Pte.	29974				
Woods, Alexander	Pte.	22405				
Woods, James	Pte.	29987				
Woodward, John	Pte.	39326			dis.	18/02/19
Woodward, Samuel	Pte.	240531				
Wooley, Alfred	Pte.	22619			dis.	14/08/17
Worrall, William	Pte.	46328				
Worthington, Frank	Pte.	46143				
Wrench, Frederick	Pte.	47131				
Wrench, Walter	Pte.	200492			dis.	11/02/19
Wright, David	Pte.	58006				
Wright, Horace	Pte.	49312				
Wright, Robert	Pte.	49586		05/04/17	dis.	05/11/19
Wright, Thomas H	Cpl.	15217			dis.	04/06/19
Wright, Walter V	Pte.	240176			d.	16/04/18
Wright, William	Pte.	49023				
Wyatt, Thomas	Pte.	18822			dis.	11/02/19

Name	Rank	No.	Coy.	Joined	Outcome	
Wyse, Stanley	Pte.	265956		29/12/17	dis.	11/07/19
Wyvill, Albert	Pte.	17174			dis.	28/03/19
Yates, Fred	Pte.	46181				
Yates, Herbert	Pte.	265947	A	29/12/17	dis.	25/03/20
York, William	Pte.	240156				
Youds, Isaac	Pte.	46173				
Young, Walter E	Pte.	49065				
Young, William	Pte.	37457				

Appendix 3: Statistics

The following statistics are those known at the time of writing. It is expected that they may alter in due course, as new information emerges. An unknown number of men died after the end of the war, from causes attributable to the war, but were not officially recognised as casualties. Hence it is not possible to include statistics for years after the war ended.

ORs enlisted with the Bn.   1,782

Residence			Occupation		
	Billinge	4		Clerk	41
	Haydock	14		Glass Making	302
	Prescot	32		Labourer	239
	Rainhill	10		Mining	443
	St. Helens	1,247		Other	263
	Whiston	4		Unknown	494
	Widnes	37			
	Wigan	19			
	Other	56			
	Unknown	359			

Under age on enlistment: 174
Over age on enlistment: 121

ORs transferred to the Bn.   1,297
ORs transferred from the Bn.   978
ORs deserted from the Bn.   13

Officers served with the Bn.   163

Killed in action   215
Died of wounds   116
Died of sickness   47
Total   378

		Pals	Ex Pals	Total
Deaths per year	1914	1	0	1
	1915	11	0	11
	1916	76	4	80
	1917	75	15	90
	1918	108	88	196

Appendix 4: Roll of Honour

The following includes those men who served with the 11th Bn. South Lancashire Regiment at some time and who subsequently became casualties with a different unit. The service number, rank and unit shown are those at the time of death. Where different sources show variations in the details for a soldier, those held by the Commonwealth War Graves Commission are generally taken to be the correct version and are shown here. The list is divided into sections according to the country where the cemetery or memorial is located.

Belgium

Bedford House Cemetery

Atkin, George V	17084	Pte.	11/SLR	k.i.a.	15/12/17
Champion, Eric O		2/Lt.	11/SLR	k.i.a.	10/06/17
Corbett, John E	203184	Pte.	11/SLR	k.i.a.	31/07/17
Dillon, Thomas	21086	L/Cpl.	11/SLR	k.i.a.	31/07/17
Gill, Charles	20777	Pte.	11/SLR	k.i.a.	03/12/17
Harper, George	39433	Pte.	11/SLR	k.i.a.	09/12/17
Parker, John J	20566	Sgt.	11/SLR	k.i.a.	10/06/17
Waters, James	2237	Pte.	11/SLR	k.i.a.	08/06/17
Wilkinson, Herbert	20882	Sgt.	11/SLR	d.o.w.	04/12/17
Woods, John	20376	Pte.	11/SLR	k.i.a.	02/12/17

Brandhoek Military Cemetery

Burgess, William P	21836	Pte.	11/SLR	d.o.w.	12/06/17

Brandhoek New Military Cemetery

Ashby, Edward	21176	Sgt.	11/SLR	d.o.w.	01/08/17
Edgerton, John	42333	Pte.	6/SWB	d.o.w.	17/08/17

Dickebusch New Military Cemetery Extension

Byron, Henry	21956	Pte.	11/SLR	d.o.w.	24/06/17
Sutton, Francis	20041	L/Sgt.	11/SLR	d.o.w.	05/07/17

Halle Communal Cemetery

Robinson, John J	21396 Rfn.	5/SLR	d.	18/01/19

Harlebeke New British Cemetery

Didsbury, Frank	21531 Rfn.	2/5/SLR	d.o.w.	11/01/18
Turner, Frank	49739 Pte.	2/RIF	k.i.a.	25/10/18

Helkijn (Helchin) Churchyard

Potter, James	240730 Pte.	2/SLR	k.i.a.	22/10/18

Hop Store Cemetery

Foster, Alfred	20869 L/Cpl.	11/SLR	k.i.a.	29/05/17

Ingoyghem Military Cemetery

Leyland, John	49402 L/Cpl.	2/RIF	k.i.a.	25/10/18

Kemmel Chateau Military Cemetery

Thomas, Hugh	20648 Pte.	11/SLR	k.i.a.	20/11/17

La Clytte Military Cemetery

Wade, John	21619 Cpl.	2/SLR	k.i.a.	29/04/18

Ledeghem Military Cemetery

Bray, Joseph	228860 Pte.	2/SWB	d.o.w.	15/10/18

Lijssenthoek Military Cemetery

Barlow, John E	29682 Pte.	11/SLR	d.o.w.	28/06/17
Bennett, Henry	20055 Pte.	11/SLR	d.o.w.	10/07/17
Brady, William	21907 Pte.	11/SLR	d.o.w.	25/06/17
Byrne, Martin	21625 Pte.	11/SLR	d.o.w.	26/06/17
Caddick, James	19401 Pte.	11/SLR	d.o.w.	30/07/17
Gallagher, George	21404 Pte.	11/SLR	d.o.w.	14/06/17
Heslip, James	21755 Pte.	11/SLR	d.o.w.	03/08/17
Lethbridge, Thomas	20709 L/Cpl.	11/SLR	d.o.w.	23/06/17

Lijssenthoek Military Cemetery contd.

McLoughlin, James	20883	Pte.	11/SLR	d.o.w.	29/06/17
Noonan, William	26004	Pte.	11/SLR	d.o.w.	04/06/17
Pierce, Terence J	22389	Pte.	11/SLR	d.o.w.	26/06/17
Price, John	20539	Pte.	11/SLR	d.o.w.	26/06/17
Roughsedge, Henry	22391	Pte.	11/SLR	k.i.a.	14/07/17
Webb, Charles W	19047	Pte.	11/SLR	d.o.w.	31/05/17

Locre No. 10 Cemetery

Elliott, Percival W A	34530	Pte.	11/SLR	k.i.a.	21/08/18

Menin Road South Military Cemetery

Hankinson, Thomas	20217	Pte.	11/SLR	k.i.a.	08/06/17
Leah, Norman	22347	Pte.	11/SLR	k.i.a.	12/06/17
Watkinson, Samuel	21213	Pte.	11/SLR	k.i.a.	12/06/17
Willetts, Benjamin	21741	Pte.	11/SLR	k.i.a.	12/06/17

Mons (Bergen) Communal Cemetery

Crilly, Francis	16972	L/Cpl.	2/SLR	d.o.w.	27/03/18

Oosttaverne Wood Cemetery

Haddock, William	6705	Pte.	7/SLR	k.i.a.	13/06/17

Ploegsteert Memorial

McCormick, John	67983	Pte.	23/CR	k.i.a.	02/11/18
Stott, William	30674	Pte.	11/ELR	k.i.a.	12/04/18

Pond Farm Cemetery

Melling, Richard	20963	Pte.	11/SLR	d.	22/10/17

Railway Dugouts Burial Ground (Transport Farm)

Garratt, Henry	16180	Pte.	11/SLR	k.i.a.	18/06/17
Makinson, Patrick	21154	Pte.	11/SLR	k.i.a.	27/05/17
Potter, John	20965	Pte.	11/SLR	d.o.w.	30/05/17
Woods, Samuel	21252	Pte.	11/SLR	k.i.a.	14/06/17

Reninghelst New Military Cemetery

Almond, Joseph	21318	Pte.	11/SLR	d.o.w.	24/06/17
Burrows, Charles	21170	Pte.	11/SLR	k.i.a.	29/06/17
Cooney, James	21452	Pte.	11/SLR	d.o.w.	20/06/17
Davies, Edwin	29951	Pte.	11/SLR	k.i.a.	23/06/17
Edwards, John M	20948	Pte.	11/SLR	d.o.w.	14/07/17
Foster, William	21173	Pte.	11/SLR	k.i.a.	28/06/17
Heyes, James	22279	L/Cpl.	11/SLR	k.i.a.	26/06/17
Hill, George	15381	Pte.	11/SLR	k.i.a.	28/06/17
Kelly, Thomas	20158	Pte.	11/SLR	k.i.a.	08/07/17
Kemp, Charles C	22189	Pte.	11/SLR	d.o.w.	24/06/17
Makin, Robert H	20993	Pte.	11/SLR	k.i.a.	30/06/17
Roy, George W	21145	Pte.	11/SLR	k.i.a.	02/08/17
Sanderson, George	21494	Pte.	11/SLR	k.i.a.	16/07/17
Shaw, John	20640	Cpl.	11/SLR	k.i.a.	25/06/17
Wignall, James	21880	Pte.	11/SLR	k.i.a.	16/07/17

Spa Communal Cemetery

Shacklady, Arthur	27577	Pte.	7/KLR	d.o.w.	09/12/18

Tyne Cot Memorial

Culley, John	40548	Pte.	2/LF	k.i.a.	09/10/17
Foy, Joseph	22627	Pte.	9/LF	k.i.a.	04/10/17
Jones, John	20130	Pte.	2/SLR	k.i.a.	21/08/18
Maylin, Henry	20904	Pte.	2/SLR	k.i.a.	28/04/18
Wright, Walter V	240176	Pte.	11/SLR	d.	16/04/18

Vlamertinghe Military Cemetery

Roberts, Thomas	20569	Pte.	11/SLR	d.o.w.	04/06/17

Voormezeele Enclosure No. 3

Finney, John J	20334	Sgt.	7/SLR	k.i.a.	22/07/17

Westoutre British Cemetery

Gleave, James	61437	Pte.	MGC	k.i.a.	09/08/18

Wytschaete Military Cemetery

Sowerbutts, Nathaniel	20135	Pte.	7/SLR	k.i.a.	10/06/17
Wright, Osborne G	301907	Cpl.	13/TC	k.i.a.	25/04/18

Ypres (Menin Gate) Memorial

Coombes, John	39481	Pte.	11/SLR	k.i.a.	31/07/17

Ypres Town Cemetery Extension

Davies, Bernard	20521	Pte.	11/SLR	k.i.a.	03/06/17

Ypres, The Huts Cemetery

Hall, Albert J	20828	L/Cpl.	11/SLR	d.o.w.	31/07/17

France

A.I.F. Burial Ground, Flers

Helsby, William	21441	Pte.	11/SLR	k.i.a.	21/10/16
Martin, Samuel	20345	L/Sjt.	11/SLR	k.i.a.	21/10/16

Abbeville Communal Cemetery

Houghton, Peter	20663	Pte.	11/SLR	d.o.w.	27/07/16
Parr, James	20118	Pte.	11/SLR	d.o.w.	24/07/16

Arneke British Cemetery

Flanagan, James	20984	L/Sjt.	11/SLR	d.o.w.	14/05/18
Marsh, Frederick G	22137	Pte.	11/SLR	d.	12/05/18

Arras Flying Services Memorial

Walker, George H		Lt.	RFC	k.i.a.	28/07/17

Arras Memorial

Bagnall, Sidney	16411	Pte.	2/LF	k.i.a.	03/05/17
Sparks, Josiah	74669	Pte.	7/RF	k.i.a.	24/03/18

Aulnoye Communal Cemetery

Goddard, Thomas	32629	Pte.	11/SLR	d.o.w.	09/04/18

Aveluy Communal Cemetery Extension

Plumpton, John	22106	Pte.	11/SLR	k.i.a.	03/09/16

Avesnes-Le-Comte Communal Cemetery

West, Harold	20072	Sgt.	11/SLR	d.o.w.	09/12/16

Avesnes-Sur-Helpe Communal Cemetery

McMahon, William	43398	Pte.	11/SLR	d.o.w.	23/04/18

Bailleul Communal Cemetery Extension, Nord

Ackers, John	21815	Pte.	11/SLR	d.o.w.	09/09/17
Forshaw, William	20091	Pte.	11/SLR	d.o.w.	05/07/17
Simpson, John	21825	Pte.	11/SLR	d.o.w.	21/12/17

Bailleul Road East Cemetery, St. Laurent-Blagny

Topping, Alfred	49488	Pte.	19/LF	k.i.a.	19/09/18

Bancourt British Cemetery

Hunwick, Edward N		2/Lt.	2/ELR	k.i.a.	30/08/18

Beauval Communal Cemetery

Beard, Joseph	20523	Pte.	11/SLR	d.o.w.	16/12/15

Bellacourt Military Cemetery, Riviere

Mills, Peter T	20620	L/Cpl.	11/SLR	k.i.a.	23/12/16

Berles-Au-Bois Churchyard Extension

Molloy, Herbert	22005	L/Cpl.	11/SLR	k.i.a.	14/12/16

Berneuil Communal Cemetery

Critchley, Peter	21793	Pte.	11/SLR	d.	21/12/15

Bethune Town Cemetery

Large, James	20028	L/Cpl.	11/SLR	d.o.w.	09/09/16

Beuvry Communal Cemetery Extension

Greenall, George	20853	Pte.	5/SLR	k.i.a.	10/04/18

Bois-Guillaume Communal Cemetery Extension

Brooks, George E	49317	Pte.	19/LF	d.o.w.	07/11/18
Webster, Thomas	21131	Pte.	11/SLR	d.o.w.	08/04/18

Borre British Cemetery

Clarke, Aaron	60953	Pte.	23/CR	k.i.a.	05/08/18

Bouchoir New British Cemetery

Griffiths, John B	20885	L/Cpl.	11/SLR	k.i.a.	27/03/18
Houghton, Matthew E	20359	Pte.	11/SLR	k.i.a.	28/03/18
Lewis, John	266253	Pte.	11/SLR	k.i.a.	27/03/18

Bouzincourt Ridge Cemetery, Albert

Lewis, Hugh	242879	Pte.	2/RWF	k.i.a.	22/04/18

Bray Military Cemetery

Hill, Edward	20967	Pte.	11/SLR	k.i.a.	26/06/16

Brown's Road Military Cemetery, Festubert

Cooke, Arthur	22315	Pte.	5/SLR	k.i.a.	09/04/18
Naylor, Thomas	20336	Pte.	11/SLR	k.i.a.	15/08/16

Bucquoy Road Cemetery, Ficheux

Frodsham, Richard	49327	Pte.	19/LF	d.o.w.	19/10/18
Hatton, William	49497	Sgt.	19/LF	d.o.w.	14/10/18
Sephton, William H	49542	Pte.	19/LF	d.o.w.	14/10/18

Busigny Communal Cemetery Extension

Boardman, John	16525	Pte.	11/SLR	d.o.w.	05/11/18
Leigh, James E	16443	C.S.M.	11/SLR	d.o.w.	04/11/18
Parkey, Leonard	42248	Pte.	11/SLR	d.o.w.	06/11/18

Cambrai East Military Cemetery

Gear, Henry	49469	L/Cpl.	19/LF	d.o.w.	06/11/18
Gerrard, Harold	49439	Pte.	19/LF	d.o.w.	02/11/18

Cambrai Memorial, Louverval

Byron, Edwin	241853	Pte.	5/SLR	k.i.a.	30/11/17
Culshaw, Joseph	10530	Pte.	5/SLR	k.i.a.	30/11/17

Cambrin Military Cemetery

Wilde, Harold	20978	Sgt.	5/SLR	d.o.w.	23/10/18

Caterpillar Valley Cemetery, Longueval

Baldwin, Frank	21706	Pte.	11/SLR	k.i.a.	08/10/16
Hynes, Thomas	21245	Pte.	11/SLR	k.i.a.	21/10/16

Caudry British Cemetery

Martin, Richard	49153	Pte.	11/SLR	d.	28/04/19

Cerisy-Gailly Military Cemetery

Edwards, Albert	20628	Pte.	11/SLR	k.i.a.	01/07/16
Kelly, Thomas	20629	Pte.	11/SLR	k.i.a.	01/07/16
Keogh, William	20999	Pte.	11/SLR	d.o.w.	29/06/16
Richardson, Joseph	20572	Pte.	11/SLR	k.i.a.	23/06/16
Rothwell, William	49077	Pte.	1/LNLR	k.i.a.	30/09/18
Stubbs, Arthur	20356	Pte.	11/SLR	k.i.a.	22/06/16

Chipilly Communal Cemetery

Howard, Robert	20486	Pte.	11/SLR	d.o.w.	01/03/16

Chocques Military Cemetery

Tickle, Albert	21696	Pte.	11/SLR	d.o.w.	14/08/16

Corbie Communal Cemetery

Mills, John W	20145	Pte.	11/SLR	d.o.w.	10/03/16

Corbie Communal Cemetery Extension

Dean, George	20549	Pte.	11/SLR	d.o.w.	15/06/16
Unsworth, Cyril J		2/Lt.	7/SLR	d.o.w.	07/07/16

Cross Roads Cemetery, Fontaine-Au-Bois

Greenough, Edward	241151	Pte.	11/SLR	k.i.a.	04/11/18
Rodgers, Frank	48996	Pte.	11/SLR	k.i.a.	04/11/18
Russell, Percy A	204914	L/Cpl.	11/SLR	k.i.a.	04/11/18
Rylance, Hezekiah	46601	Pte.	11/SLR	k.i.a.	04/11/18

Dainville Communal Cemetery

O'Grady, John	22170	Pte.	11/SLR	k.i.a.	09/03/17

Dantzig Alley British Cemetery, Mametz

Allender, Bertrand J	20087	L/Cpl.	11/SLR	k.i.a.	01/07/16
Beckett, Thomas	21240	Pte.	11/SLR	k.i.a.	01/07/16
Bryan, William	20057	Pte.	11/SLR	k.i.a.	01/07/16
Hodgins, James	20168	Pte.	11/SLR	k.i.a.	01/07/16
Houghton, Thomas	21378	Pte.	11/SLR	k.i.a.	01/07/16
Kay, Ralph	20200	Pte.	11/SLR	k.i.a.	10/07/16
Montgomery, Thomas	21803	Pte.	11/SLR	k.i.a.	01/07/16
Owen, George	21682	Pte.	11/SLR	d.o.w.	11/07/16
Roney, Albert E	20786	L/Cpl.	11/SLR	d.o.w.	10/07/16
Skelhorn, John	21909	Pte.	11/SLR	k.i.a.	01/07/16
Trotter, John T	20606	Pte.	11/SLR	k.i.a.	09/07/16

Daours Communal Cemetery Extension

Pike, Joseph	20985	L/Cpl.	11/SLR	d.o.w.	09/07/16
Preston, Harry	20402	Cpl.	11/SLR	d.o.w.	02/07/16

Dartmoor Cemetery, Becordel-Becourt

Creaghan, John	21633	Pte.	11/SLR	d.o.w.	05/10/16
Parr, Edgar B		2/Lt.	11/SLR	d.o.w.	21/10/16

Dive Copse British Cemetery, Sailly-Le-Sec

Stanton, William	21156	Pte.	11/SLR	d.o.w.	03/07/16

Doullens Communal Cemetery Extension No. 1

Groves, William	20995	Pte.	11/SLR	d.o.w.	24/12/15

Esquelbecq Military Cemetery

Scott, Arthur	49564	Pte.	19/LF	d.o.w.	07/06/18

Etaples Military Cemetery

Birkett, Robert	21954	Pte.	11/SLR	d.	05/08/17
Shaw, Richard J		2/Lt.	11/SLR	d.o.w.	26/06/17
Sutton, Robert A	20294	L/Sgt.	11/SLR	d.o.w.	28/10/16
Wilson, Job	20378	Sgt.	11/SLR	d.	07/09/17

Etretat Churchyard Extension

Lees, George	20930	Pte.	11/SLR	d.o.w.	04/04/18
Smith, Thomas R	49067	Pte.	11/SLR	d.o.w.	06/11/18

Favreuil British Cemetery

Forster, Robert	20696	Pte.	8/SLR	k.i.a.	22/12/17

Flesquieres Hill British Cemetery

Beesley, Edwin		Capt.	1/KLR	k.i.a.	27/09/18

Fouquieres Churchyard Extension

Cole, James	21172	L/Cpl.	5/SLR	d.o.w.	24/09/18

Gorre British and Indian Cemetery

McNichol, James	21750	Rfn.	5/SLR	k.i.a.	10/03/18

Ham British Cemetery, Muille-Villette

Atherton, William	20795	L/Cpl.	11/SLR	k.i.a.	23/03/18
Barclay, Thomas S	21097	Pte.	11/SLR	k.i.a.	23/03/18
Hughes, John	20153	Pte.	11/SLR	k.i.a.	23/03/18
Jones, John	20989	Pte.	11/SLR	d.o.w.	25/03/18
Kings, Enoch H	32633	Pte.	11/SLR	k.i.a.	23/03/18
Lidgett, John C		Lt.	11/SLR	k.i.a.	24/03/18
McKie, George	20682	Pte.	11/SLR	d.o.w.	16/04/18
Roberts, John E	43332	Pte.	11/SLR	d.	23/03/18
Swindells, James	200097	Pte.	11/SLR	k.i.a.	23/03/18

Ham British Cemetery, Muille-Villette contd.

Topping, Joseph	20511	Sgt.	11/SLR	k.i.a.	23/03/18

Haspres Coppice Cemetery, Haspres

Barbour, Andrew	49368	Pte.	19/LF	k.i.a.	13/10/18
Bate, John	49373	Pte.	19/LF	k.i.a.	13/10/18
Bigwood, Frank	49315	Pte.	19/LF	k.i.a.	13/10/18
Broadbent, Albert	49583	Pte.	19/LF	k.i.a.	13/10/18
Clark, James	49374	Pte.	19/LF	k.i.a.	13/10/18
Clarke, Harold G	49446	L/Cpl.	19/LF	k.i.a.	13/10/18
Clarke, Wilfred	49456	Pte.	19/LF	k.i.a.	13/10/18
Dring, William	49514	Pte.	19/LF	k.i.a.	13/10/18
Dunkerley, Tom	49596	Pte.	19/LF	k.i.a.	13/10/18
Hanson, Frank	49600	Pte.	19/LF	k.i.a.	13/10/18
Harvey, William	49390	Pte.	19/LF	k.i.a.	13/10/18
Hobart, John J	49522	Pte.	19/LF	k.i.a.	13/10/18
Kilroy, Henry	49550	Pte.	19/LF	k.i.a.	13/10/18
Maher, Michael	49340	Pte.	19/LF	k.i.a.	13/10/18
Newton, Thomas	49400	Pte.	19/LF	k.i.a.	13/10/18
Pilkington, George	49535	Pte.	19/LF	k.i.a.	13/10/18
Priest, Arthur	49536	Pte.	19/LF	k.i.a.	13/10/18
Reid, James E	49405	Pte.	19/LF	k.i.a.	13/10/18
Reynolds, William	49449	Pte.	19/LF	k.i.a.	13/10/18
Rocke, John	49421	Pte.	19/LF	k.i.a.	13/10/18
Roney, Daniel	49563	Pte.	19/LF	k.i.a.	13/10/18
Smart, Thomas	49566	Pte.	19/LF	k.i.a.	13/10/18
Stowell, Henry	49406	Pte.	19/LF	k.i.a.	13/10/18
Wills, William	238156	Pte.	19/LF	k.i.a.	13/10/18

Hazebrouck Communal Cemetery

Lloyd, James	20855	Pte.	11/SLR	d.o.w.	07/06/17

Heath Cemetery, Harbonnieres

Mason, John	21144	Pte.	11/SLR	k.i.a.	28/01/16

Heilly Station Cemetery, Mericourt-L'Abbe

Gibbons, William	21862	Pte.	11/SLR	d.o.w.	02/07/16

Houchin British Cemetery

Balmer, William	241515 Pte.	5/SLR	d.o.w.	27/09/18
McKeown, James	12995 Pte.	5/SLR	k.i.a.	03/07/18
Pendleton, John W	21188 Pte.	5/SLR	k.i.a.	30/05/18
Penketh, Ernest	21673 Pte.	5/SLR	k.i.a.	27/08/18
Tobin, Bernard	22254 Pte.	4/SLR	k.i.a.	16/09/18

Joncourt East British Cemetery

Ashcroft, John	2/Lt.	16/LF	k.i.a.	02/10/18

La Neuville British Cemetery, Corbie

Bowden, Frederick	21454 Pte.	11/SLR	d.o.w.	23/07/16
Brotherhood, William	6323 Pte.	11/SLR	d.	01/11/16
Cunliffe, David	21329 Pte.	11/SLR	d.o.w.	08/07/16
Mustard, William J	20531 L/Cpl.	11/SLR	d.o.w.	02/07/16

Landrecies British Cemetery

Andrews, Reginald T	49314 Pte.	11/SLR	k.i.a.	04/11/18
Townsend, Percival W	34089 L/Cpl.	11/SLR	k.i.a.	04/11/18

Le Cateau Military Cemetery

Jones, Herbert	2/Lt.	11/SLR	d.o.w.	04/11/18

Linselles Communal Cemetery

Brown, John E	20160 Pte.	2/SLR	d.o.w.	18/05/18

London Cemetery, Neuville-Vitasse

Bailey, Albert	31248 Pte.	11/SLR	k.i.a.	26/04/17
O'Reilly, Henry	20047 Pte.	11/SLR	k.i.a.	26/04/17

Longuenesse (St. Omer) Souvenir Cemetery

Collier, Frederick	20016 2/Lt.	2/8/ManR	d.o.w.	11/05/17
Reece, Frederick B	2/Lt.	R.E.	d.o.w.	20/04/18

Loos Memorial

| Bracken, William | 20551 | Rfn. | 5/SLR | k.i.a. | 20/09/18 |
| Hanley, Lawrence | 34005 | Pte. | 2/SLR | d.o.w. | 20/09/18 |

Mailly-Maillet Communal Cemetery Extension

| Lambert, Louis | 20949 | Pte. | 11/SLR | d.o.w. | 21/12/15 |
| Stanley, John | 21481 | Pte. | 11/SLR | d.o.w. | 21/12/15 |

Namps-Au-Val British Cemetery

Burgess, James	21847	Pte.	11/SLR	d.o.w.	28/03/18
Hannon, Lawrence	21679	Pte.	11/SLR	d.o.w.	28/03/18
Mather, Thomas	20909	Pte.	11/SLR	d.o.w.	28/03/18
McCarthy, Michael	22023	Pte.	11/SLR	d.o.w.	28/03/18

Outtersteene Communal Cemetery Extension, Bailleul

| McDermott, Edward | | 2/Lt. | 10/EYR | k.i.a. | 12/04/18 |

Pernes British Cemetery

| Derbyshire, Thomas | 22183 | Pte. | 5/SLR | d.o.w. | 23/05/18 |

Peronne Road Cemetery, Maricourt

Hanley, William	21526	Pte.	11/SLR	k.i.a.	11/07/16
Kelly, Patrick	21779	Pte.	11/SLR	k.i.a.	01/07/16
Kinsey, Thomas R	20121	Pte.	11/SLR	k.i.a.	01/07/16
Norbury, Charles	21037	C.S.M.	11/SLR	k.i.a.	28/07/16
Parr, George	20415	Pte.	11/SLR	k.i.a.	01/07/16

Pommereuil British Cemetery

| Hagger, Henry | 204919 | Pte. | 11/SLR | d.o.w. | 02/11/18 |

Pont-Remy British Cemetery

| Tickle, Ernest | | Lt. | 2/SLR | k.i.a. | 13/07/18 |

Pozieres Memorial

Aitken, John T	21168	Sgt.	11/SLR	k.i.a.	21/03/18
Ashman, Albert E	10213	Pte.	11/SLR	k.i.a.	23/03/18
Blake, William G	20567	L/Sjt.	11/SLR	k.i.a.	23/03/18
Boore, James E	32641	Pte.	11/SLR	k.i.a.	23/03/18
Boyer, Herbert L	240010	C.S.M.	11/SLR	k.i.a.	29/03/18
Briscoe, Robert	20971	Pte.	11/SLR	k.i.a.	21/03/18
Burrows, James	20372	Pte.	11/SLR	k.i.a.	27/03/18
Carroll, William	21334	Pte.	11/SLR	k.i.a.	23/03/18
Chamberlain, Charles	32627	Pte.	11/SLR	k.i.a.	23/03/18
Chisnall, James	20143	Pte.	11/SLR	k.i.a.	28/03/18
Clarke, William	21453	Pte.	11/SLR	k.i.a.	23/03/18
Critchley, Joseph	21205	Pte.	11/SLR	k.i.a.	23/03/18
Crook, George T	21392	Pte.	11/SLR	k.i.a.	23/03/18
Dakin, Norman L	22361	Pte.	11/SLR	k.i.a.	23/03/18
Davies, Robert	20001	Cpl.	11/SLR	k.i.a.	23/03/18
Deacle, Henry	21753	Pte.	11/SLR	k.i.a.	28/03/18
Elliott, Henry	20542	Pte.	11/SLR	k.i.a.	23/03/18
Foster, John T	21789	Pte.	11/SLR	k.i.a.	21/03/18
Frodsham, John	20089	L/Cpl.	11/SLR	k.i.a.	23/03/18
Glover, Edward	20315	Pte.	11/SLR	k.i.a.	28/03/18
Halliwell, Peter	20675	Pte.	11/SLR	k.i.a.	21/03/18
Halmshaw, James R	266342	Pte.	11/SLR	k.i.a.	23/03/18
Handforth, Thomas	28744	Pte.	11/SLR	k.i.a.	23/03/18
Hughes, David	20892	L/Cpl.	11/SLR	k.i.a.	23/03/18
Jones, Hugh	21024	Pte.	11/SLR	k.i.a.	28/03/18
Kinder, Richard	21243	Cpl.	11/SLR	k.i.a.	23/03/18
Knight, Allan		2/Lt.	11/SLR	k.i.a.	24/03/18
Lenton, Harry	21474	L/Cpl.	11/SLR	k.i.a.	21/03/18
McConnell, William	20333	Pte.	11/SLR	k.i.a.	27/03/18
Nicholson, Thomas	22001	Pte.	11/SLR	k.i.a.	21/03/18
Rigby, Edward	21472	Pte.	11/SLR	k.i.a.	28/03/18
Robbins, Edward	29928	Pte.	11/SLR	k.i.a.	21/03/18
Robertson, Alexander	45132	Pte.	11/SLR	k.i.a.	27/03/18
Smith, Albert	36570	Pte.	11/SLR	k.i.a.	27/03/18
Taylor, Sidney	266155	Pte.	11/SLR	k.i.a.	23/03/18
Whelan, Isaac	22039	Pte.	11/SLR	k.i.a.	27/03/18
Wilkinson, Joseph	20322	Pte.	11/SLR	k.i.a.	28/03/18
Wylie, Thomas	21664	Pte.	11/SLR	k.i.a.	28/03/18

Proville British Cemetery

| Leyland, Peter | 20796 | Pte. | 2/4/SLR | k.i.a. | 30/09/18 |

Quarry Cemetery, Montauban

| Kenny, William | 20381 | Pte. | 11/SLR | k.i.a. | 01/10/16 |

Roisel Communal Cemetery Extension

| Hyman, Ezra H | | 2/Lt. | 11/SLR | d.o.w. | 01/11/18 |

Rosieres Communal Cemetery Extension

| Carroll, Matthew | 21019 | C.S.M. | 11/SLR | k.i.a. | 27/03/18 |

Roye New British Cemetery

Hodges, Harold A		Capt.	11/SLR	k.i.a.	24/03/18
Jacobs, Benjamin	32671	Pte.	11/SLR	d.o.w.	24/03/18
Pye, William	20532	Pte.	11/SLR	d.o.w.	03/04/18
Ratcliffe, Joseph	21104	Pte.	11/SLR	k.i.a.	28/03/18
Sillitoe, Henry C	235420	Pte.	11/SLR	d.	16/05/18

Rue-Petillon Military Cemetery, Fleurbaix

| Stott, James | | 2/Lt. | 2/5/LF | k.i.a. | 02/10/18 |
| Wainwright, Joseph S | 22302 | Rfn. | 5/SLR | k.i.a. | 09/10/18 |

Sains-Du-Nord Communal Cemetery

| Kay, James | 20416 | Pte. | 11/SLR | d.o.w. | 11/04/18 |

Serre Road Cemetery No. 2

| Mullen, James | 21473 | Pte. | 11/SLR | k.i.a. | 01/07/16 |

St. Sever Cemetery Extension, Rouen

Batten, John	20099	L/Cpl.	11/SLR	d.o.w.	31/03/18
Beswick, Ebenezer	40842	Pte.	4/SLR	d.	30/10/18
Collins, Joseph	22357	Pte.	11/SLR	d.o.w.	28/03/18
Cooney, Michael	21892	Pte.	11/SLR	d.o.w.	29/03/18

St. Sever Cemetery Extension, Rouen contd.

Foreman, Stanley W	20147	Pte.	11/SLR	d.	20/06/16
Foster, Henry	49142	Pte.	11/SLR	d.	25/11/18
Grumley, Peter	21056	Pte.	11/SLR	d.o.w.	23/04/18
Hood, George	20958	Pte.	11/SLR	d.o.w.	14/02/16
Myers, Thomas	20210	Pte.	11/SLR	d.o.w.	20/02/16
Pendlebury, Frederick	20043	L/Sgt.	11/SLR	d.o.w.	29/03/18
Pye, John J	21630	Pte.	11/SLR	d.	29/03/18
Smith, William I	36522	Pte.	11/SLR	d.o.w.	11/08/17
Thomason, Fred	22399	Pte.	11/SLR	d.o.w.	05/04/18

Sucrerie Military Cemetery, Colincamps

Cartwright, Frederick	21325	Pte.	11/SLR	k.i.a.	20/12/15
Taylor, Henry	21005	Pte.	11/SLR	k.i.a.	19/12/15

Terlincthun British Cemetery, Wimille

Barnes, John	49440	Sgt.	19/LF	d.o.w.	12/10/18

Thiepval Memorial

Bradshaw, Robert	21725	Pte.	7/SLR	k.i.a.	18/11/16
Cotterill, William	20804	L/Cpl.	11/SLR	k.i.a.	01/07/16
Davies, William	21352	Pte.	11/SLR	k.i.a.	01/07/16
Garton, Reginald W		Lt.	11/SLR	k.i.a.	01/07/16
Jackson, Robert	21175	Pte.	11/SLR	k.i.a.	03/07/16
Jackson, Thomas	20070	Sgt.	11/SLR	k.i.a.	01/07/16
Maloney, Peter	20132	Pte.	11/SLR	k.i.a.	30/07/16
McDonald, James	21367	Pte.	11/SLR	k.i.a.	01/07/16
Mullen, Walter	21538	Pte.	11/SLR	k.i.a.	08/07/16
Oakes, William	21054	Pte.	11/SLR	k.i.a.	01/07/16
Ovens, Francis	21316	Pte.	11/SLR	k.i.a.	01/07/16
Pickles, Edward	20736	Sgt.	11/SLR	k.i.a.	02/07/16
Small, John	21879	Sgt.	11/SLR	k.i.a.	01/07/16
Tipton, Thomas	20467	L/Cpl.	11/SLR	k.i.a.	21/10/16
Webster, Charles	20189	Pte.	11/SLR	k.i.a.	10/07/16

Thistle Dump Cemetery, High Wood, Longueval

Hartley, Frank	20161	Pte.	11/SLR	k.i.a.	22/10/16
Meek, Arthur	22382	Pte.	11/SLR	k.i.a.	05/10/16

Vieille-Chapelle New Military Cemetery, Lacouture

Wilde, James	21550 Rfn.	5/SLR	k.i.a.	14/04/18

Vis-en-Artois Memorial

Bennett, Peter	21901 Pte.	2/4/SLR	k.i.a.	02/09/18
Houghton, Arthur F	49387 Pte.	19/LF	k.i.a.	13/10/18
Molyneux, William	48484 Pte.	6/MR	k.i.a.	15/08/18

Warlincourt Halte British Cemetery, Saulty

Burns, Frank	21788 Pte.	11/SLR	d.	26/01/17
Dalton, Samuel L	20290 Pte.	11/SLR	d.	22/03/17
Roughley, Henry	21491 Pte.	11/SLR	d.	19/02/17
Tierney, Walter	20159 Pte.	11/SLR	d.o.w.	19/12/16

Wimereux Communal Cemetery

Chorley, William	49320 Pte.	19/LF	k.i.a.	01/06/18
Robinson, Robert	20650 Pte.	11/SLR	d.o.w.	08/08/17

York Cemetery, Haspres, Nord

Jones, Clarence W	49394 Pte.	19/LF	k.i.a.	13/10/18

Germany

Berlin South-Western Cemetery

Cadwallader, Matthew T	235405	Pte.	11/SLR	d.o.w.	16/05/18

Cologne Southern Cemetery

Bradbury, Thomas H	20030	A/Cpl.	11/SLR	d.	29/05/18
Dally, Arthur L	32628	Pte.	11/SLR	d.	20/07/18
Garner, Joseph	20577	L/Cpl.	11/SLR	d.	10/07/18
Sumner, Robert	26414	L/Cpl.	11/SLR	d.	22/07/18

Hamburg Cemetery

Flood, Joseph	12927	Pte.	4/SLR	d.	17/07/18

Niederzwehren Cemetery

Grounds, William	21368	Pte.	11/SLR	d.	30/10/18
Horsnall, James	266346	Pte.	11/SLR	d.	28/06/18
Lord, Sydney	32574	L/Cpl.	11/SLR	d.	19/11/18
Webster, Job	20970	Pte.	11/SLR	d.o.w.	19/06/18

Greece

Doiran Memorial

Waring, Joseph	21219	Sgt.	9/SLR	k.i.a.	18/09/18

India

Madras 1914-1918 War Memorial, Chennai

Qualter, Michael	21710	Pte.	1/SLR	d.	15/10/18

Iraq

Amara War Cemetery

Atherton, James   21910   Pte.   6/SLR   d.   09/05/17

Basra Memorial

Springthorpe, William   21617   Pte.   6/SLR   k.i.a.   14/02/17
Thelwell, Frederick   21265   Pte.   6/SLR   k.i.a.   24/04/17

Basra War Cemetery

Leadbetter, Samuel   P/11164   Pte.   MFP   d.   28/03/18

United Kingdom

Ashton-in-Makerfield (St. Oswald) R.C. Churchyard

Kenyon, Herbert J   240179 Sgt.   11/SLR   d.   16/02/19

Bournemouth East Cemetery

Howarth, Albert   22006 Pte.   11/SLR   d.o.w.   26/07/16

Gravesend Cemetery

Fletcher, William G   2/Lt.   11/SLR   d.o.w.   14/10/16

Netheravon (All Saints) Churchyard

Holland, Lawrence   20338 Pte.   11/SLR   d.   10/10/15

Oldham (Greenacres) Cemetery

Elson, Daniel   17707 Pte.   11/SLR   d.   03/06/18

Oldham (Hollinwood) Cemetery

Sowden, Robert   49588 Pte.   19/LF   d.   22/02/19

Runcorn Cemetery

Holden, John   21897 Sgt.   13/SLR   d.   03/05/16

Shrewsbury General Cemetery

Douglas, Malcolm   Maj.   MGC   d.   17/11/18

Southampton, Hollybrook Memorial

Colville, John   31692 Pte.   1/G/ManR   d.   15/03/16

St. Helens Cemetery

Beesley, Thomas   20316 Pte.   11/SLR   d.   17/06/15
Carter, Cornelius   21264 Pte.   11/SLR   d.   03/02/15
Edwards, John   21187 Pte.   11/SLR   d.   27/01/15

St. Helens Cemetery contd.

Frost, Frederick J	21583	Pte.	2/SLR	d.	25/10/18
Halsall, John	20489	Pte.	D/SLR	d.	03/12/17
Hill, John	20715	Pte.	11/SLR	d.	14/03/18
Howden, James T	42321	L/Cpl.	6/SWB	d.	26/10/18
Molyneux, Joseph	20590	Pte.	11/SLR	d.o.w.	05/08/16
Sharratt, John H	20311	Sgt/	11/SLR	d.	22/02/20
Slater, Robert	20292	C.Q.M.S.	11/SLR	d.	17/07/18
Swift, William	20455	Pte.	11/SLR	d.o.w.	18/04/18

St. Helens, Eccleston (St. Thomas) Churchyard Extension

Martin, Samuel	42318	Pte.	6/SWB	d.	28/10/18
Williams, John W	20203	Sgt.	4/SLR	d.	01/11/18

St. Helens, Parr (St. Peter) Churchyard

Jervis, Abraham	20442	Pte.	11/SLR	d.	17/11/18

St. Helens, Sutton (St. Anne) R.C. Churchyard

Wilson, Thomas	21194	Pte.	11/SLR	d.	15/09/14

Tardebigge (St. Bartholomew) Churchyard

Bowen, Harold M	22554	Pte.	11/SLR	d.	30/08/16

Wigan Cemetery

Boardman, Horace	21659	Pte.	11/SLR	d.o.w.	26/04/18

Appendix 5: Gallantry Awards

Victoria Cross

Rank	No.	Name	Gazetted
Corporal	20765	J. T. Davies	21/05/18

Distinguished Service Order

Rank	No.	Name	Gazetted
Lt.-Colonel		C. C. Champion	26/07/18
Lt.-Colonel		H. F. Fenn	01/01/17

Military Cross

Rank	No.	Name	Gazetted
2/Lieutenant		J. J. Acton	26/07/18
Captain		S. E. Boulton	23/07/18
Lieutenant		A. G. Dean	01/01/18
Captain		C. J. Dixon	04/06/17
S.M.	20581	J. Harrison	01/01/17
Lieutenant		L. Henshaw	02/04/19
Lieutenant		F. L. McCreary	27/10/17
Captain		J. E. S. Pethick	26/07/18
Captain		E. R. S. Prior	20/10/16

Bar to the Military Cross

Rank	No.	Name	Gazetted
Captain		S. E. Boulton, M.C.	02/04/19
Captain		E. R. S. Prior, M.C.	25/11/16

Distinguished Conduct Medal

Rank	No.	Name	Gazetted
R.S.M.	20581	J. Harrison	30/08/18
L./Sergeant	20368	J. T. Potter	28/12/17

Distinguished Conduct Medal contd.

Rank	No.	Name	Gazetted
Private	61090	V. H. Redstone	14/02/19
C.S.M.	8618	A. S. Ryan	30/05/19
Sergeant	22007	W. Twinning	30/08/18

Military Medal

Rank	No.	Name	Gazetted
L./Corporal	21132	A. Atherton	12/06/18
L./Corporal	21456	J. Bishop	13/03/18
Private	20567	W. G. Blake	21/08/17
Private	46064	A. Dawson	22/07/19
Private	46349	J. Eglinton	22/07/19
Private	21008	J. Ellis	21/10/16
Private	20059	J. Frodsham	23/08/16
Private	204895	J. Ions	22/07/19
Private	21612	T. Jones	27/06/18
Sergeant	48993	H. McCompany	19/08/19
L./Corporal	20289	A. M. Milligan	27/06/18
Private	20842	J. Orford	21/08/17
Sergeant	20350	W. Owen	22/07/19
L./Corporal	21479	J. Percival	12/06/18
Sergeant	21157	W. Platt	13/03/18
Private	20086	W. Pounceby	03/06/16
Private	20377	J. Prescott	27/06/18
Private	20610	W. Prescott	13/03/18
Private	204866	S. Rumble	22/07/19
Sergeant	20818	H. Sandford	12/06/18
L./Corporal	21420	C. M. Saxon	14/09/17
Private	21043	W. Seaton	12/06/18
Private	21825	J. Simpson	14/08/17
Sergeant	20093	W. Smart	19/03/18
Sergeant	20813	J. Taylor	11/06/18
L./Sergeant	20203	J. W. Williams	26/10/16

Bar to the Military Medal

Rank	No.	Name	Gazetted
Private	20567	W. G. Blake	06/08/18

Meritorious Service Medal

Rank	No.	Name	Gazetted
C.Q.M.S.	20056	G. M. Boardman	03/06/19
C.S.M.	21019	M. Carroll	17/06/18
L/Sergeant	22579	W. Diggle	17/06/18
Sjt.	20408	A. Gregson	17/01/19
Sjt.	20350	W. Owen	17/06/18
C.Q.M.S.	21160	J. Roberts	03/06/19
R.Q.M.S.	20064	P. F. Routley	03/06/19

Mentioned in Despatches

Rank	No.	Name	Gazetted
R.S.M.	20313	J. Boden	15/06/16
2/Lieutenant		W. Bretherton	04/01/17
Captain		A. T. Champion	04/01/17
			08/07/19
Major		C. C. Champion	24/05/18
			28/12/18
			08/07/19
Captain		A. G. Dean	08/07/19
Captain		C. J. Dixon	04/01/17
C.S.M.	5215	E. Driscoll	08/07/19
Lt.-Colonel		H. F. Fenn	04/01/17
			24/05/18
Captain		R. Fox	21/12/17
Sergeant	20719	J. T. Halton	08/07/19
Lt.-Colonel		Sir J. L. Harrington	15/06/16
Sergeant	20219	H. Hill	18/12/17
Sergeant	20150	J. W. Hignett	08/07/19
L./Corporal	21455	H. Kettle	25/05/17
Private	20085	R. Piggott	02/01/17
Q.M.S.	20064	P. F. Routley	25/05/17
Sergeant	204898	S. T. Smith	08/07/19

Mentioned in Despatches contd.

Rank	No.	Name	Gazetted
Private	202860	E. Taylor	08/07/19
Captain		J. Taylor, M.C.	08/07/19
Sergeant	22007	W. Twinning	02/01/17
C.S.M.	20221	J. Williams	25/05/17
Lieutenant		H. J. Woolcock	25/05/17

Roumanian Medaille Barbatie si Credinta

Rank	No.	Name	Gazetted
Private	20015	J. Marsh	19/09/19

Appendix 6: Citations

Cpl. 20765 John Thomas Davies [V.C.]
Near Eppeville, France, 24th March 1918.

For most conspicuous bravery and devotion to duty under heavy rifle and machine-gun fire. When his company - outflanked on both sides - received orders to withdraw, Corporal Davies knew that the only line of withdrawal lay through a deep stream with a belt of barbed wire, and that it was imperative to hold up the enemy as long as possible. He mounted the parapet, fully exposing himself, in order to get a more effective field of fire, and kept his Lewis gun in action to the last, casing the enemy many casualties and checking their advance.

By his very great devotion to duty he enabled part of his company to get across the river, which they would otherwise have been unable to do, thus undoubtedly saving the lives of many of his comrades. When last seen this gallant N.C.O. was still firing his gun, with the enemy close on the top of him, and was in all probability killed at his gun.

[London Gazette, 21 May 1918]

T./2nd Lt. John James Acton, S. Lan. R. [M.C.]
For conspicuous gallantry and devotion to duty in leading patrols and getting in touch with troops when their position was unknown. His services were most praise worthy, and later, he set a fine example of courage to his men during a counter-attack, when he went forward in the face of heavy machine-gun and trench-mortar fire.

[London Gazette, 23 Jul 1918]

Lt. (T./Capt.) Sydney Ernest Boulton. [Bar to M.C.]
For conspicuous gallantry and devotion to duty displayed in bridging operations near Landrecies on the 4th November, 1918. His company, together with a field company of Royal Engineers, were responsible for getting the first line of infantry across the Sambre Oise Canal. For the fact that this was quickly and efficiently done under shell and heavy machine-gun fire his skill and energy were largely responsible.

[London Gazette, 9 Dec 1919]

Temp. Capt. Edward Robert Seymour Prior [M.C.]
For conspicuous gallantry during operations. For seven days his company held a point in the trenches under continuous shellfire. The trench was repeatedly blown in, but he rebuilt it each time, and also captured hostile patrols consisting of an officer and six other ranks. He set a splendid example to his company under trying circumstances.

[London Gazette, 20 Oct 1916]

Temp. Capt. Edward Robert Seymour Prior, M.C. [Bar to M.C.]
For conspicuous gallantry in action. He led the assault with great courage and initiative, gaining his objective and consolidating the position.
[London Gazette, 24 Nov 1916]

20581 R.S.M. J. Harrison, M.C., S. Lanc. R. (St. Helens). [D.C.M.]
For conspicuous gallantry and devotion to duty, when the enemy, having broken through on both flanks, he reorganised and ably fought scattered troops, throughout the whole battle, setting a fine example of high courage and coolness under fire.
[London Gazette, 30 Aug 1918]

61090 Pte. V. H. Redstone, 11th Bn., S. Lan. R. (Peterborough). [D.C.M.]
For marked gallantry and initiative on the 4th November, 1918, at Landrecies. At one period when his bridging party was held up through machine-gun fire, he went forward into several houses and secured a number of prisoners. Later he collected several of our infantry together and went forward and cleared further houses of the enemy.
[London Gazette, 9 Jan 1920]

22007 Sjt. W. Twinning, S. Lanc. R. (Manchester). [D.C.M.]
For conspicuous gallantry and devotion to duty. When acting as platoon leader he jumped on the parapet and shot one of the enemy, who had advanced within ten yards of the trench, afterwards attacking and killing several in hand-to-hand fighting. Eventually, when nearly surrounded, he withdrew his platoon with great skill and coolness.
[London Gazette, 30 Aug 1918]

Appendix 7: Sources

St. Helens Local History & Archives Library

St. Helens Newspaper & Advertiser
St. Helens Reporter

The National Archives

Officers' Service Records [WO 339 & WO 374]
25th Division A & Q War Diary [WO 95/2228]
25th Division C.R.E. War Diary [WO 95/2232]
25th Division 105 & 106 Field Coys R.E. War Diary [WO 95/2235]
30th Division A & Q War Diary [WO 95/2315]
30th Division C.R.E. War Diary [WO 95/2320]

The Lancashire Infantry Museum

11th Battalion South Lancashire Regiment War Diary
11th Battalion South Lancashire Regiment Nominal Roll of Officers
Personal diary of A. T. Champion

Internet

The Commonwealth War Graves Commission
http://www.cwgc.org/

The Long, Long Trail
http://www.1914-1918.net/

Old Front Line Battlefields of WW1
http://battlefields1418.50megs.com

Prescot Roll of Honour
http://www.prescot-rollofhonour.info/index.html

St. Helens Roll of Honour
http://www.sthelensrollsofhonour.co.uk/

Sutton Beauty & Heritage
http://www.suttonbeauty.org.uk/

Appendix 8: Further Reading

Bamber, F., *Clog Clatters in Old Sutton*, Sutton Historic Society, 1995.

Fair, R., and Fair, C., *Marjorie's War (Four Families in the Great War 1914-1918)*, Tommies Guides, 2012.

Gliddon, G., *VCs of the First World War: Spring Offensive 1918*, Sutton Publishing, 1997.

Hanson, N., *The Unknown Soldier*, Doubleday, 2005.

Hart, P., *Bloody April, Slaughter in the Skies over Arras, 1917*, Weidenfeld & Nicholson, 2005.

Kincaid-Smith, Lt.-Col. M., *The 25th Division in France and Flanders*, Naval & Military Press, 2006.

Maddocks, G., *Liverpool Pals*, Pen & Sword Books, 1991.

Maddocks, G., *Montauban*, Pen & Sword Books, 1999.

Mitchinson, K. W. and McInnes, I., *Cotton Town Comrades*, Bayonet Publications, 1993.

Mitchinson, K. W., *Pioneer Battalions in the Great War*, Pen & Sword Books, 1997.

Mullaly, Col. B. R., History of the South Lancashire Regiment, White Swan Press, 1955.

Nicholson, V., *Singled Out: How Two Million Women Survived Without Men After The First World War*, Viking, 2007.

Reed, P., *Great War Lives*, Pen & Sword Books, 2010.

Stedman, M., *Manchester Pals*, Pen & Sword Books, 2003.

Van Emden, R., *Boy Soldiers of the Great War*, Headline, 2005.

Whalley-Kelly, Captain H., *Ich Dien The Prince of Wales's Volunteers (South Lancashire) 1914-1934*, Gale & Poulden, 1935.

Wilkinson, R., *Pals on the Somme*, Pen & Sword Books, 2008.